# STUDY GUIDE

## for use with

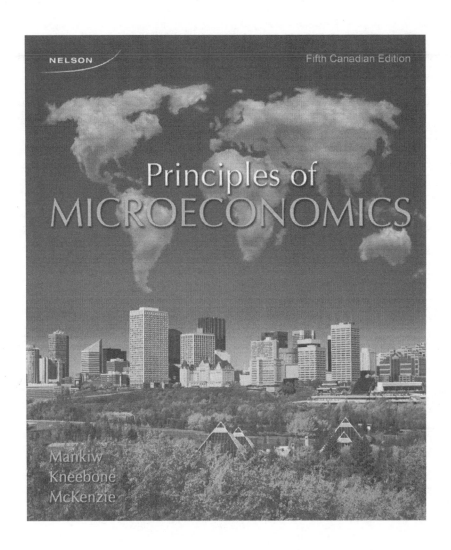

NELSON                                          Fifth Canadian Edition

Principles of
MICROECONOMICS

Mankiw
Kneebone
McKenzie

Prepared by SHAHRAM MANOUCHEHRI
and PETER FORTURA

NELSON          EDUCATION

# Study Guide
## for use with
# Principles of Microeconomics
## Fifth Canadian Edition

**N. Gregory Mankiw**
Harvard University

**Ronald D. Kneebone**
University of Calgary

**Kenneth J. McKenzie**
University of Calgary

# Shahram Manouchehri
Grant MacEwan University

## Peter Fortura
Algonquin College

NELSON / EDUCATION

# NELSON EDUCATION

ISBN-13: 978-0-17-662294-7
ISBN-10: 0-17-662294-2

*One must learn by doing the things;*
*For though you think you know it*
*You have no certainty, until you try.*

*Sophocles, c. 496–406 B.C.*
*Greek playwright*
*Trachiniae*

# PREFACE

Economics is a way of thinking. It provides a tool kit for solving problems and making decisions. You may be tempted to learn economics by simply listening to lectures or relying on common sense. Do not be fooled. Economics cannot be learned by osmosis. Learning requires active participation by the student. This means solving problems and answering questions, then looking at the reasons behind both the correct and incorrect answers.

This *Study Guide* was written to accompany the fifth Canadian edition of *Principles of Microeconomics*, by N. Gregory Mankiw, Ronald D. Kneebone, and Kenneth J. McKenzie. It was written with only one audience in mind—you, the student. It is intended to complement the material provided in the text and your instructor's lectures, thereby helping you to be successful in this course.

## Objectives of the *Study Guide*

There are three broad objectives to the *Study Guide*. First, it reinforces the text and improves your understanding of the material presented in the text. Second, it provides you with experience in using economic theories and tools to solve actual economic problems—learning by doing! Third, the questions and problems allow you to validate areas of successful learning and to highlight areas needing additional study.

## Organization of the *Study Guide*

Each chapter in the *Study Guide* corresponds to a chapter in the fifth Canadian edition of *Principles of Microeconomics* text. Each *Study Guide* chapter includes the following sections:

I.   *Chapter Overview:* This section begins with a description of the purpose of the chapter and of how the chapter fits into the overall framework of the text. The overview also includes helpful hints to guide the student's intuition in understanding the material.

II.  *Self-Testing Challenges:* This section begins with true/false questions and multiple-choice questions. These questions provide useful feedback in preparation for an exam, particularly if the student analyzes the right and wrong answers. Next, there are short-answer questions and practice problems, which provide applications and important extensions of the material in the text. The practice problems are generally multiple-step problems, while each short-answer question is generally based on a single topic in the text. The section ends with an advanced critical thinking problem, which applies the economic reasoning and tools developed in the chapter to a real-world problem.

III.   *Solutions:* This section provides answers to all of the questions and problems in the *Study Guide*. Explanations are provided for the false responses to the true/false questions.

## Use of the *Study Guide*

A study guide is not a substitute for a text. Use this *Study Guide* in conjunction with the *Principles of Microeconomics* text, not in place of it. How one best uses a study guide is largely a personal matter. Most students will prefer to read through the entire chapter in the text and then work through the *Study Guide*, identifying the areas which need further study and the areas which are already mastered.

Multiple-choice questions tend to be the most commonly used type of exam question. Yet students often encounter difficulties with this type of question because they find that many of the choices differ only slightly. Thus, students should develop and practise strategies for doing multiple-choice questions. The following are some helpful strategies: read each question and all of the choices very carefully—often, only one word is the difference between two of the choices. Eliminate any obviously wrong choices. Mark-up the page with notes, arrows, and diagrams. Remember that the correct answer may not be immediately evident—most questions will require you to analyze numerical and graphical information.

## Acknowledgments

I would like to thank Gregory Mankiw for having written such an innovative and lively text, and the Canadian authors for carefully adapting Mankiw's ideas to fit the Canadian experience. Thanks also to David Hakes who wrote the *Principles of Microeconomics Study Guide* for the U.S. market. His excellent work made producing the Canadian edition a truly enjoyable task. I also thank executive editor Craig Dyer and the development team at My Editor, for their support throughout the process. My thanks also extends to Nelson Education Limited for their invaluable guidance and assistance in bringing this work to fruition.

Finally, I thank all the students who have taken my courses over the years, for it is they who, by their questions, comments and even frustrations, have enhanced my understanding of economics. My special thanks also to Judith, who closely read the entire manuscript and provided excellent comments and suggestions. And lastly, I would particularly like to thank my sons, Eghtedar and Namdar, without whose unvarying love and support I would not have been able to persevere.

## Final Thoughts

Economics can be a tremendously exciting and enjoyable field of study. But it can also be intimidating. I hope that this *Study Guide* will improve your understanding of economics, so that you are able to enjoy the subject as much as I do.

Shahram Manouchehri

# CONTENTS

# CHAPTER 1   Ten Principles of Economics

## I. Chapter Overview

### A. Context and Purpose

Chapter 1 is the first chapter in a three-chapter section that serves as the introduction to the text. Chapter 1 introduces ten fundamental principles on which the study of economics is based. In a broad sense, the rest of the text is an elaboration on these ten principles. Chapter 2 develops how economists approach problems, while Chapter 3 explains how individuals and countries gain from trade.

The purpose of Chapter 1 is to lay out ten economic principles that will serve as building blocks for the rest of the text. The ten principles can be grouped into three categories: how people make decisions, how people interact, and how the economy works as a whole. Throughout the text, references will repeatedly be made to these ten principles.

### B. Helpful Hints

1. *Place yourself in the story.* Throughout the text, most economic situations will be composed of economic actors—buyers and sellers, borrowers and lenders, firms and workers, and so on. When you are asked to address how any economic actor would respond to economic incentives, place yourself in the story as the buyer or the seller, the borrower or the lender, the producer or the consumer. Do not think of yourself always as the buyer (a natural tendency) or always as the seller. You will find that your role playing will usually produce the right response once you learn to think like an economist—which is the topic of the next chapter.

2. *Trade is not a zero-sum game.* Some people see an exchange in terms of winners and losers. Their reaction to trade is that, after the sale, if the seller is happy, the buyer must be sad because the seller must have taken something from the buyer. That is, they view trade as a *zero-sum game* where what one gains the other must have lost. They fail to see that both parties to a voluntary transaction gain because each party is allowed to specialize in what it can produce most efficiently, and then trade for items that are produced more efficiently by others. Nobody loses, because trade is voluntary. Therefore, a government policy that limits trade reduces the potential gains from trade.

3. *An externality can be positive.* Because the classic example of an externality is pollution, it is easy to think of an externality as a cost that lands on a bystander. However, an externality can be positive in that it can be a benefit that lands on a bystander. For example, education is often cited as a product that emits a positive externality because when your neighbour educates herself, she is likely to be more reasonable, responsible, productive, and politically astute. In short, she is a better neighbour. Positive externalities, just as much as negative externalities, may be a reason for the government to intervene to promote efficiency.

## II. Self-Testing Challenges

### A. True/False Questions

_____ 1.    When the government redistributes income with taxes and welfare, the economy becomes more efficient.

_____ 2.    When economists say, "There is no such thing as a free lunch," they mean that all economic decisions involve tradeoffs.

_____ 3.    Adam Smith's "invisible hand" concept describes how corporate business reaches into the pockets of consumers like an "invisible hand."

_____ 4.    Rational people systematically and purposefully do the best they can to achieve their objectives.

_____ 5.    Canada will benefit economically if we eliminate trade with Asian countries because we will be forced to produce more of our own cars and clothes.

_____ 6.    When a jet flies overhead, the noise it generates is an externality.

_____ 7.    A tax on beer raises the price of beer and provides an incentive for consumers to drink more.

_____ 8.    An incentive is something that induces a person to act.

_____ 9.    Sue is better at cleaning and Bob is better at cooking. It will take fewer hours to eat and clean if Bob specializes in cooking and Sue specializes in cleaning than if they share the household duties evenly.

_____ 10.   High and persistent inflation is caused by moderate growth in the quantity of money in the economy.

_____ 11.   In the short run, a reduction in inflation tends to cause a reduction in unemployment.

_____ 12.   An auto manufacturer should continue to produce additional automobiles as long as the firm is profitable, even if the cost of the additional units exceeds the price received.

_____13.    An individual farmer requires property rights to benefit from a market economy.

_____14.    To a student, the opportunity cost of going to a basketball game would include the price of the ticket and the value of the time that could have been spent studying.

_____15.    Workers in Canada have a relatively high standard of living because Canada has a relatively high minimum wage.

## B.  Multiple-Choice Questions

1.  Which one of the following involve(s) a tradeoff faced by societies?
    a.  buying a new car
    b.  going to university
    c.  watching a football game on Sunday afternoon
    d.  guns and butter

2.  Which one of the following is a reason that tradeoffs are required?
    a.  because wants are unlimited and resources are efficient
    b.  because wants are unlimited and resources are economical
    c.  because wants are unlimited and resources are scarce
    d.  because wants are unlimited and resources are unlimited

3.  Which one of the following best defines what economics is the study of?
    a.  how to avoid having to make tradeoffs
    b.  how society manages its scarce resources
    c.  how to fully satisfy our unlimited wants
    d.  how to reduce our wants until we are satisfied

4.  Which one of the following describes when a rational person will act?
    a.  when the action is ethical
    b.  when the action makes money for the person
    c.  when the action produces marginal costs that exceed marginal benefits
    d.  when the action produces marginal benefits that exceed marginal costs.

5.  Which one of the following is an outcome of raising taxes and increasing welfare payments?
    a.  improved equity at the expense of efficiency
    b.  improved efficiency at the expense of equity
    c.  reduced market power

6. Suppose Candace finds $20. If she chooses to use the $20 to go to a hockey game, which one of the following is her opportunity cost of going to the game?
   a. Nothing, because Candace found the money.
   b. $20 (because Candace could have used the $20 to buy other things).
   c. $20 (because Candace could have used the $20 to buy other things) plus the value of the time spent at the game.
   d. $20 (because Candace could have used the $20 to buy other things) plus the value of the time spent at the game, plus the cost of the dinner she consumed at the game.

7. Which one of the following best describes foreign trade?
   a. makes a country more equitable
   b. increases the scarcity of resources
   c. allows a country to avoid tradeoffs
   d. allows a country to have a greater variety of products at a lower cost than if it tried to produce everything at home

8. Because people respond to incentives, which one of the following would be expected to occur if the average salary of accountants increases by 50 percent while the average salary of teachers increases by 20 percent?
   a. Fewer students will attend university.
   b. Students will shift majors from education to accounting.
   c. Students will shift majors from accounting to education.

9. Which one of the following activities is **MOST** likely to produce an externality?
   a. A student reads a novel for pleasure.
   b. A student sits at home and watches television.
   c. A student has a party in her student residence room.
   d. A student eats a hamburger in the university cafeteria.

10. Which one of the following products would be **LEAST** capable of producing an externality?
    a. food
    b. cigarettes
    c. stereo equipment
    d. inoculations against disease

11. Which one of the following situations describes the **GREATEST** *market power*?
    a. Microsoft's impact on the price of desktop operating systems
    b. a farmer's impact on the price of corn
    c. Honda's impact on the price of autos
    d. a student's impact on university tuition

12. Which one of the following statements is true about a market economy?
    a. Taxes help prices communicate costs and benefits to producers and consumers.
    b. The strength of a market system is that it tends to distribute goods and services evenly across consumers.

    c.   Market participants act as if guided by an "invisible hand" to produce outcomes that maximize social welfare.

    d.   With a large enough computer, central planners could guide production more efficiently than markets could guide production.

13.  Which one of the following is true according to Adam Smith's "invisible hand"?
    a.  Markets work even in the absence of property rights.
    b.  Many buyers and sellers acting independently and out of self-interest can promote general economic well-being without even realizing it.
    c.  Individuals who are concerned about the public good will almost invisibly promote increased social welfare.
    d.  Government plays a behind-the-scenes role in making a market economy work efficiently.

14.  Which one of the following is a reason that workers in Canada enjoy a high standard of living?
    a.  because Canada has a high minimum wage
    b.  because unions in Canada keep the wage high
    c.  because workers in Canada are highly productive
    d.  because Canada has protected its industry from foreign competition

15.  Which one of the following is a cause of high and persistent inflation?
    a.  unions increasing wages too much
    b.  OPEC raising the price of oil too much
    c.  regulations raising the cost of production too much
    d.  governments increasing the quantity of money too much

16.  Which of the following statements occurs in the short run?
    a.  An increase in inflation temporarily increases unemployment.
    b.  A decrease in inflation temporarily increases unemployment.
    c.  Inflation and unemployment are unrelated in the short run.

17.  Which one of the following could be inferred by an increase in the price of beef?
    a.  It tells consumers to buy more beef.
    b.  It tells consumers to buy less pork.
    c.  It tells producers to produce more beef.
    d.  It provides no information because prices in a market system are managed by planning boards.

18.  Which one of the following is **NOT** part of the opportunity cost of going on vacation?
    1.  the money spent on food
    2.  the money spent on airplane tickets
    3.  the money spent on a Broadway show
    4.  the money that could have been earned by staying home and working

19. Which one of the following is a way that productivity can be increased?
    a. by raising union wages
    b. by raising minimum wage
    c. by improving the education of workers
    d. by restricting trade with foreign countries

## C. Short-Answer Questions

1. Is air scarce? Is clean air scarce? _____
   _____
   _____

2. What is the opportunity cost when an employee saves some of her paycheque?
   _____
   _____

3. Why is there a tradeoff between equity and efficiency? _____
   _____
   _____

4. Water is necessary for life. Diamonds are not. Is the marginal benefit of an additional glass of water greater or less than the marginal benefit of an additional one-carat diamond? Why? _____
   _____
   _____

5. Tom's car needs to be repaired. He has already paid $800 to have the transmission fixed, but it still does not work properly. Tom can sell the car "as is" for $2000. If the car was fixed, Tom could sell it for $2500. The car can be fixed, with a guarantee, for another $300. Should Tom repair his car? Why or why not? _____
   _____
   _____

6. Why have automotive air bags reduced deaths from auto crashes less than we had hoped? _____
   _____
   _____

7. Suppose one country is better at producing agricultural products (because it has more fertile land) while another country is better at producing manufactured goods (it has a better educational system and more engineers). If each country produced its specialty and traded, would there be more or less total output than if each country produced enough of its own agricultural and manufactured goods to meet its own needs? Why?_____
   _____
   _____
   _____

8. In *The Wealth of Nations*, Adam Smith said, "It is not by the benevolence of the baker that you receive your bread." What did he mean?_____

_____

_____

9. If people save more and use it to build more physical capital, productivity will rise and people will have rising standards of living in the future. What is the opportunity cost of future growth?_____

_____

10. If the government printed twice as much money, what would happen to prices?_____

_____

_____

11. A goal for a society is to distribute resources equitably or fairly. How should resources be distributed if everyone were equally talented and worked equally hard? What if people had different talents and some people worked hard while others did not?_____

_____

_____

_____

_____

12. Why are property rights important to a market economy?_____

_____

_____

## D. Practice Problems

1. People respond to incentives. Governments can alter incentives with public policy, and hence behaviour. However, sometimes public policy generates unintended consequences by producing results that were not anticipated. Describe one unintended consequence of each of the following public policies.

   a. To help the "working poor," the government raises the minimum wage to $25 per hour._____

   _____

   _____

   b. To help the homeless, the government places rent controls on apartments that restrict rent to $100 per month._____

   _____

   _____

   c. To limit the consumption of gasoline, the government raises the tax on gasoline by $2.00 per litre. _____

   _____

   _____

    d.  To reduce the consumption of drugs, the government makes drugs illegal.

_____
_____
_____

    e.  To raise the population of wolves, the government prohibits the killing of wolves. _____

_____

2.  Opportunity cost is what is given up to get an item. Because there is no such thing as a free lunch, what would likely be given up to obtain each of the items listed below?

    a.  Susan can work full time or go to university. She chooses university._____

_____
_____
_____

    b.  Susan can work full time or go to university. She chooses work

_____
_____
_____
_____

    c.  Farmer Jones has 100 hectares of land. He can plant corn, which yields 100 tonnes per hectare, or he can plant beans, which yield 40 tonnes per hectare. He chooses to plant corn. _____

_____
_____

    d.  Farmer Jones has 100 hectares of land. He can plant corn, which yields 100 tonnes per hectare, or he can plant beans, which yield 40 tonnes per hectare. He chooses to plant beans._____

_____
_____

    e.  In (a) and (b) above, and (c) and (d) above, which is the opportunity cost of which—university for work or work for university? Corn for beans or beans for corn?_____

_____
_____

### E. Advanced Critical Thinking

Suppose the university decides to lower the cost of parking on campus by reducing the price of a parking permit from $300 per semester to $50 per semester.

1.  What would happen to the number of students desiring to park their cars on campus?_____

    _____

    _____

2.  What would happen to the amount of time it would take to find a parking place?_____

    _____

    _____

3.  Thinking in terms of opportunity cost, would the lower price of a parking sticker necessarily lower the true cost of parking? _____

    _____

    _____

4.  Would the opportunity cost of parking be the same for students with no outside employment and students with jobs earning $15 per hour?_____

    _____

    _____

## III.  Solutions

### A.  True/False Questions

1.  F; the economy becomes less efficient because it decreases the incentive to work hard.
2.  T
3.  F; the "invisible hand" refers to how markets guide self-interested people to create desirable social outcomes.
4.  T
5.  F; all countries gain from voluntary trade.
6.  T
7.  F; higher prices reduce the quantity demanded.
8.  T
9.  T
10.  F; high inflation is caused by excessive monetary growth.
11.  F; a reduction in inflation tends to raise unemployment.
12.  F; a manufacturer should produce as long as the marginal benefit exceeds the marginal cost.
13.  T
14.  T
15.  F; workers in Canada have a high standard of living because they are productive.

## B.    Multiple-Choice Questions

| | | | | |
|---|---|---|---|---|
| 1. d | 5. a | 9. c | 13. b | 17. c |
| 2. c | 6. c | 10. a | 14. c | 18. a |
| 3. b | 7. d | 11. a | 15. d | 19. c |
| 4. d | 8. b | 12. c | 16. b | |

## C.  Short-Answer Questions

1.   No, no need to give up anything to get it. Yes, it is not possible to have an unlimited amount without giving up something to get it (pollution equipment on cars, etc.).

2.   The items she could have enjoyed had she spent it (current consumption).

3.   Taxes and welfare make people more equal but reduce incentives for hard work, thus lowering total output.

4.   The marginal benefit of another glass of water is generally lower because the water supply is so large that one more glass is of little value. The opposite is true for diamonds.

5.   Yes, because the marginal benefit of fixing the car is $2500 – $2000 = $500 and the marginal cost is $300. The original repair payment is not relevant.

6.   The cost of an accident was lowered. This changed incentives, therefore people drive faster and have more accidents.

7.   There would be more total output if the countries specialize and trade because each country is doing what it does most efficiently.

8.   The baker produces the best bread possible, not out of kindness, but because it is in his best interest to do so. Self-interest can maximize social welfare.

9.   The opportunity cost of future growth is the need to give up consumption today.

10.   Prices would roughly double.

11.   Fairness would require that everyone get an equal share. Fairness would require that people not get an equal share.

12.   A farmer will not grow food if he expects his crop to be stolen. People rely on government to enforce their rights over the things they produce.

## D.  Practice Problems

1.  a.  Many would want to work at $25 per hour but few firms would want to hire low-productivity workers at this wage; therefore, it would create unemployment.

    b.  Many renters would want to rent an apartment at $100 per month, but few landlords could produce an apartment at this price; therefore, this rent control would create more homelessness.

    c.  Higher gas prices would reduce the number of kilometres driven. This would lower auto accidents, put less wear and tear on roads and cars, and reduce the demand for both cars and road repairs.

    d.  This raises the price of drugs and makes selling them more profitable. This creates more drug sellers and increases violence as they fight to protect their turf.

    e.  Restrictions on killing wolves reduce the population of animals upon which wolves may feed—e.g., rabbits, deer, etc.

2.  a.  She gives up income from work (and must pay tuition).

    b.  She gives up a university degree and the increase in income throughout life that it would have brought her (but she does not have to pay tuition).

    c.  He gives up 4000 tonnes of beans.

    d.  He gives up 10 000 tonnes of corn.

    e.  Each is the opportunity cost of the other because each decision requires giving something up.

## E.  Advanced Critical Thinking

1.  More students would wish to park on campus.

2.  It would take much longer to find a parking place.

3.  No, because the value of the time spent looking for a parking place would have to be factored in.

4.  No. Students who could be earning money working are giving up more while looking for a parking place than those with no outside employment. Therefore, their opportunity cost is higher.

# CHAPTER 2 — Thinking Like an Economist

## I. Chapter Overview

### A. Context and Purpose

Chapter 2 is the second chapter in a three-chapter section that serves as the introduction of the text. Chapter 1 introduced ten principles of economics that will be revisited throughout the text. Chapter 2 develops how economists approach problems, while Chapter 3 will explain how individuals and countries gain from trade.

The purpose of Chapter 2 is to become familiar with how economists approach economic problems. With practice, it is possible to approach similar problems in this dispassionate, systematic way. How economists employ the scientific method, the role of assumptions in model building, and the application of two specific economic models are explained. The important distinction between two roles economists can play—as scientists when they try to explain the economic world and as policymakers when they try to improve it—is clarified.

### B. Helpful Hints

1. *Opportunity costs are not usually constant along a production possibilities frontier.* Notice that the production possibilities frontier shown in the following graph is bowed outward. It shows the production tradeoffs for an economy that produces only paper and pencils.

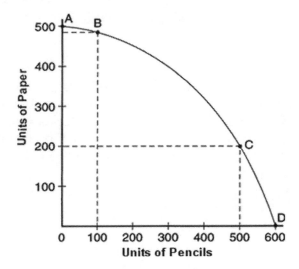

Starting at the point where the economy is using all of its resources to produce paper, the production of 100 units of pencils requires a tradeoff or an opportunity cost of only 25 units of paper (point A to point B). This is because when resources are moved from paper production to pencil production, the resources that are moved first are the ones best suited for pencil production and poorly suited for paper production. Therefore, pencil production increases with very little decrease in paper production. However, if the economy were operating at point C, the opportunity cost of an additional 100 pencils (point C to D) is 200 units of paper. This is because the resources that would now be moved toward pencil production are the ones that were extremely well suited for paper production and poorly suited for pencil production. Therefore, as more and more of any particular good is produced, the opportunity cost per unit tends to rise because resources are specialized. That is, resources are not equally well suited for producing each output.

The argument above applies when moving either direction on the production possibilities frontier. For example, by starting at point D (maximum production of pencils) a small reduction in pencil production (100 units) releases enough resources to increase production of paper by a large amount (200 units). However, moving from point B to point A increases paper production by only 25 units.

2. *A production possibilities frontier shows only the choices available—not which point of production is best.* A common mistake made by students when using production possibilities frontiers is to look at a production possibilities frontier and suggest that a point somewhere near the middle "looks best." Students make this subjective judgment because the middle point appears to provide the biggest total number of units of production of the two goods. However, ask the following question: Using the production possibilities frontier in the previous graph, what production point would be best if paper were worth $10 per sheet and pencils were worth 1 cent per dozen? The resources would be moved toward paper production. What if paper was worth 1 cent per sheet and pencils were worth $50 each? We would move our resources toward pencil production. Clearly, what we actually choose to produce depends on the price of each good. Therefore, a production possibilities frontier provides only the choices available; it alone cannot determine which choice is best.

3. *Economic disagreement is interesting but economic consensus is more important.* Economists have a reputation for disagreeing with one another because they tend to highlight their differences. While their disagreements are interesting to them, the matters on which they agree are more important to students. There are a great number of economic principles for which there is near unanimous support from the economics profession. The aim of this text is to concentrate on the areas of agreement within the profession as opposed to the areas of disagreement.

## II. Self-Testing Challenges

### A. True/False Questions

_____ 1. Economic models must mirror reality or they are of no value.

_____ 2. Assumptions make the world easier to understand because they simplify reality and focus our attention.

_____ 3. It is reasonable to assume that the world is composed of only one person when modeling international trade.

_____ 4. When people act as scientists, they must try to be objective.

_____ 5. If an economy is operating on its production possibilities frontier, it must be using its resources efficiently.

_____ 6. If an economy is operating on its production possibilities frontier, it must produce less of one good if it produces more of another.

_____ 7. Points outside the production possibilities frontier are attainable but inefficient.

_____ 8. If an economy were experiencing substantial unemployment, the economy is producing inside the production possibilities frontier.

_____ 9. The production possibilities frontier is bowed outward because the tradeoffs between the production of any two goods are constant.

_____ 10. An advance in production technology would cause the production possibilities curve to shift outward.

_____ 11. Macroeconomics is concerned with the study of how households and firms make decisions and how they interact in specific markets.

_____ 12. The statement, "An increase in inflation tends to cause unemployment to fall in the short run," is normative.

_____ 13. When economists make positive statements, they are more likely to be acting as scientists.

_____ 14. Positive statements can be refuted with evidence.

_____ 15. Most economists agree that tariffs and import quotas usually reduce economic welfare.

## B.  Multiple-Choice Questions

1.    Which one of the following is essential to the scientific method?
      a.   that the scientist be objective
      b.   that only incorrect theories are tested
      c.   that the scientist use precision equipment
      d.   that the scientist use test tubes and have a clean lab

2.    Which one of the following is **MOST** likely to produce scientific evidence about a theory?
      a.   a radio talk-show host collecting data on how financial markets respond to taxation
      b.   a lawyer employed by General Motors addressing the impact of air bags on passenger safety
      c.   a tenured economist employed at a leading university analyzing the impact of proposed bank mergers
      d.   an economist employed by the Canadian Auto Workers' union doing research on the impact of international trade

3.    Which one of the following statements regarding the circular-flow diagram is true?
      a.   The factors of production are owned by firms.
      b.   The factors of production are owned by households.
      c.   If Molson sells a case of beer, the transaction takes place in the market for factors of production.
      d.   If Susan works for Bell Canada and receives a paycheque, the transaction takes place in the market for goods and services.

4.    Which one of the following cases presents the **MOST** reasonable assumption?
      a.   To address the benefits of trade, an economist assumes that there are two people and two goods.
      b.   To estimate the speed at which a beach ball falls, a physicist assumes that it falls in a vacuum.
      c.   To address the impact of money growth on inflation, an economist assumes that money is strictly coins.
      d.   To address the impact of taxes on income distribution, an economist assumes that everyone earns the same income.

5.    Which one of the following statements is true of economic models?
      a.   built with assumptions
      b.   useless if they are simple
      c.   created to duplicate reality
      d.   usually made of wood and plastic

6.    Which one of the following is **NOT** a factor of production?
      a.   land
      b.   labour
      c.   capital
      d.   money

7.    Which one of the following refers to points on the production possibilities frontier?
   a.  efficient
   b.  inefficient
   c.  unattainable
   d.  normative

8.    Which one of the following will **NOT** shift a country's production possibilities frontier outward?
   a.  an increase in the capital stock
   b.  an advance in technology
   c.  a reduction in unemployment
   d.  an increase in the labour force

9.    Which one of the following is a depiction of economic growth?
   a.  a movement from inside the curve toward the curve
   b.  a shift in the production possibilities frontier outward
   c.  a shift in the production possibilities frontier inward
   d.  a movement along a production possibilities frontier toward capital goods

Use the following graph to answer questions 10–13.

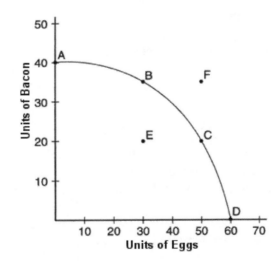

10.   If the economy is operating at point C, which one of the following is the opportunity cost of producing an additional 15 units of bacon?
   a.  10 units of eggs
   b.  20 units of eggs
   c.  30 units of eggs
   d.  40 units of eggs

11.   Which of the following is true if the economy is operating at point E?
   a.  the opportunity cost of 20 additional units of eggs is 10 units of bacon.
   b.  the opportunity cost of 20 additional units of eggs is 20 units of bacon.
   c.  the opportunity cost of 20 additional units of eggs is 30 units of bacon.
   d.  20 additional units of eggs can be produced with no impact on bacon production.

12. Which one of the following is represented by Point F?
    a. a combination of production that is inefficient because there are unemployed resources
    b. a combination of production that can be reached if we reduce the production of eggs by 20 units
    c. a combination of production that can be reached if there is a sufficient advance in technology

13. Which one of the following statements represents the results of a move from point A to point D?
    a. the economy becomes more efficient
    b. the opportunity cost of eggs in terms of bacon falls
    c. the opportunity cost of eggs in terms of bacon rises
    d. the opportunity cost of eggs in terms of bacon is constant

14. Which one of the following issues is related to microeconomics?
    a. the impact of money on inflation
    b. the impact of oil prices on auto production
    c. the impact of the government budget on saving
    d. the impact of globalization on unemployment in Canada

15. Which one of the following statements about microeconomics and macroeconomics is **NOT** true?
    a. Microeconomics is a building block for macroeconomics.
    b. Macroeconomics is concerned with economy-wide phenomena.
    c. Microeconomics and macroeconomics each has its own set of models.
    d. The study of very large industries is a topic within macroeconomics.

16. Which one of the following statements is normative?
    a. Printing too much money causes inflation.
    b. People work harder if the wage is higher.
    c. The unemployment rate should be lower.
    d. Large government deficits cause an economy to grow more slowly.

17. In which one of the following statements made by an economist is the economist acting more like a scientist?
    a. The rate of inflation should be reduced because it robs the elderly of their savings.
    b. A reduction in employment insurance benefits will reduce the unemployment rate.
    c. The unemployment rate should be reduced because unemployment robs individuals of their dignity.
    d. The government should increase subsidies to universities because the future of our country depends on education.

18. Which of the following most represents positive statements?
    a. microeconomic
    b. macroeconomic
    c. statements of description that can be tested
    d. statements of prescription that involve value judgments

19.    Suppose two economists are arguing about policies that deal with unemployment. One economist says, "The government should fight unemployment because it is the greatest social evil." The other economist responds, "Hogwash. Inflation is the greatest social evil." Which one of the following summarizes the positions of these two economists?
a.   They disagree because they have different values.
b.   They really do not disagree at all—it just looks that way.
c.   They disagree because at least one of them is incompetent.
d.   They disagree because they have different scientific judgments.

20.    Suppose two economists are arguing about policies that deal with unemployment. One economist says, "The government could lower unemployment by one percentage point if it would just increase government spending by 5 billion dollars." The other economist responds, "Hogwash. If the government spent an additional 5 billion dollars, it would reduce unemployment by only one-tenth of one percent, and that effect would only be temporary!" Which one of the following summarizes the positions of these two economists?
a.   They disagree because they have different values.
b.   They really do not disagree at all—it just looks that way.
c.   They disagree because at least one of them is incompetent.
d.   They disagree because they have different scientific judgments.

## C.  Short-Answer Questions

1.    Describe the scientific method. _____
   _____

2.    What is the role of assumptions in any science? _____
   _____

3.    Is a more realistic model always better? _____
   _____
   _____

4.    Why does a production possibilities frontier have a negative slope (slope down and to the right)? _____
   _____
   _____

5.    Why is the production possibilities frontier bowed outward? _____
   _____
   _____

6.    What are the two subfields within economics? Which is more likely to be a building block of the other? Why? _____
   _____
   _____
   _____

7.     When an economist makes a normative statement, is he or she more likely to be acting as a scientist or a policymaker? Why?_____

_____

_____

_____

8.     Which statements are testable: positive statements or normative statements? Why?_____

_____

9.     Provide two reasons why economists disagree._____

_____

_____

10.    Name two economic propositions on which more than 90 percent of economists agree. _____

_____

_____

## D. Practice Problems

1.     Identify the parts of the circular-flow diagram immediately involved in the following transactions.

a.   Mary buys a car from General Motors for $25 000._____

_____

_____

_____

b.   General Motors pays Joe $5000 per month for work on the assembly line._____

_____

_____

_____

c.   Joe gets a $15 haircut._____

_____

_____

_____

_____

d.   Mary receives $10 000 of dividends on her General Motors stock._____

_____

_____

_____

_____

2.  The following table provides information about the production possibilities frontier of Athletic Country.

| Baseball Bats | Tennis Racquets |
|---|---|
| 0 | 420 |
| 100 | 400 |
| 200 | 360 |
| 300 | 300 |
| 400 | 200 |
| 500 | 0 |

a.  Plot and connect these points to create Athletic Country's production possibilities frontier.

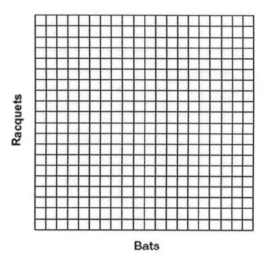

Racquets

Bats

b.  If Athletic Country currently produces 100 baseball bats and 400 tennis racquets, what is the opportunity cost of an additional 100 bats?

_____

_____

c.  If Athletic Country currently produces 300 baseball bats and 300 tennis racquets, what is the opportunity cost of an additional 100 bats?_____

_____

d.  Why does the additional production of 100 bats in part (c) cause a greater tradeoff than the additional production of 100 bats in part (b)?_____

_____

_____

_____

e.  Suppose Athletic Country is currently producing 200 baseball bats and 200 tennis racquets. How many additional bats could it produce without giving up any racquets? How many additional racquets could it produce without giving up any bats? _____

_____

_____

f.  Is the production of 200 bats and 200 racquets efficient? Explain._____

_____

_____

3.  The following production possibilities frontier shows the available tradeoffs between consumption goods and capital goods. Suppose two countries face the identical production possibilities frontier shown below.

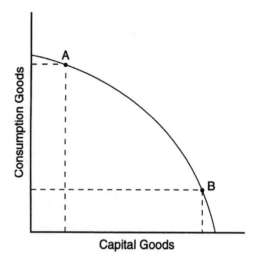

a.  Suppose Party Country chooses to produce at point A while Parsimonious Country chooses to produce at point B. Which country will experience more growth in the future? Why? _____

_____

_____

b.  In this model, what is the opportunity cost of future growth? _____

_____

c. Demonstrate the impact of economic growth on a production possibilities frontier such as the one shown above. Would the production possibilities frontier for Parsimonious Country shift more or less than that for Party Country? Why? _____

_____

d. Suppose there was an increase in technology that affected only the production of capital goods. Show the shift in the production possibilities curve.

e. Does the shift in part (d) above imply that all additional production must be in the form of capital goods? Why or why not? _____

_____

## E. Advanced Critical Thinking

Kathy is watching *The National* on CBC. On the program, there is a discussion of the pros and cons of free trade (lack of obstructions to international trade). For balance, there are two economists present—one in support of free trade and one opposed. Kathy thinks to herself, "Those economists have no idea what's going on. They cannot agree on anything. One says free trade makes us rich. The other says it will drive us into poverty. If the experts do not know, how is the average person ever going to know whether free trade is best?"

1.  Why might the economists be disagreeing on this issue?

    _____
    _____
    _____
    _____

2.  Suppose that 93 percent of economists believe that free trade is generally best (which is the greatest agreement on any single issue). Is it now possible to give a more precise answer about why economists might disagree on this issue?_____

    _____
    _____
    _____

3.  What if it was later discovered that the economist opposed to free trade worked for a labour union. Would that help explain why there appears to be a difference of opinion on this issue?_____

    _____
    _____
    _____
    _____

## III. Solutions

### A. True/False Questions

1.  F; economic models are simplifications of reality.
2.  T
3.  F; there must be at least two individuals for trade.
4.  T
5.  T
6.  T
7.  F; points outside the production possibilities frontier cannot yet be attained.
8.  T
9.  F; it is bowed outward because the tradeoffs are not constant but are increasing.
10. T
11. F; macroeconomics is the study of economy-wide phenomena.
12. F; this statement is positive.
13. T
14. T
15. T

## B. Multiple-Choice Questions

| | | | |
|---|---|---|---|
| 1. a | 6. d | 11. d | 16. c |
| 2. c | 7. a | 12. c | 17. b |
| 3. b | 8. c | 13. c | 18. c |
| 4. a | 9. b | 14. b | 19. a |
| 5. a | 10. b | 15. d | 20. d |

## C. Short-Answer Questions

1.  The dispassionate development and testing of theory by observing, testing, and observing again.

2.  To simplify reality so that we can focus our thinking on what is actually important.

3.  Not necessarily. Realistic models are more complex. They may be confusing and they may fail to focus on what is important.

4.  Because if an economy is operating efficiently, production choices have opportunity costs. If we want more of one thing, we must have less of another.

5.  Because resources are specialized and thus are not equally well suited for producing different outputs.

6.  Microeconomics and macroeconomics. Microeconomics is more of a building block of macro because macro issues (for example, unemployment) are addressed; how individuals respond to work incentives such as wages and welfare needs to be considered.

7.  As a policymaker, because normative statements are prescriptions about what ought to be and are somewhat based on value judgments.

8.  Positive statements are statements of fact and are refutable by examining evidence.

9.  Economists may have different scientific judgments. Economists may have different values.

10. A ceiling on rents reduces the quantity and quality of housing available. Tariffs and import quotas usually reduce general economic welfare.

### D.  Practice Problems

1.  a.  $25 000 of spending from households to market for goods and services. Car moves from market for goods and services to households. $25 000 of revenue from market for goods and services to firms, while car moves from firms to market for goods and services.

    b.  $5000 of wages from firms to market for factors of production. Inputs move from market for factors of production to firms. Labour moves from households to market for factors of production, while $5000 income moves from market for factors of production to households.

    c.  $15 of spending from households to market for goods and services. Service moves from market for goods and services to households. Service moves from firms to market for goods and services in return for $15 revenue.

    d.  $10 000 of profit from firms to market for factors of production. Capital moves from market for factors of production to firms. Capital moves from households to market for factors of production in return for $10 000 income.

2.  a.

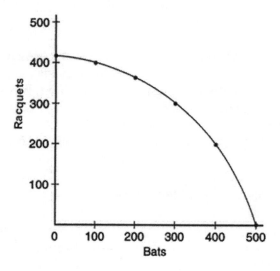

    b.  40 tennis racquets.

    c.  100 tennis racquets.

    d.  Because as more baseball bats are produced, the resources best suited for making bats are already being used. Therefore, it takes even more resources to produce 100 bats and greater reductions in racquet production.
    e.  200 baseball bats. 160 tennis racquets.

    f.  No. Resources were not used efficiently if production can be increased with no opportunity cost.

3. a.    Parsimonious Country. Capital (plant and equipment) is a factor of production and producing more of it now will increase future production.

   b.  Fewer consumption goods are produced now.

   c.

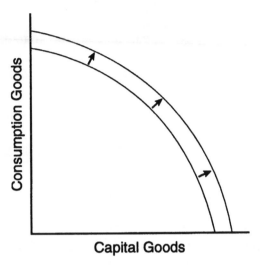

   The production possibilities curve will shift more for Parsimonious Country because it has experienced a greater increase in factors of production (capital).

   d.

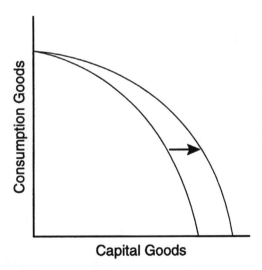

   e.  No, the outward shift improves choices available for both consumption and capital goods.

### E. Advanced Critical Thinking

1.  Economists may have different scientific judgments. Economists may have different values.

2.  Those opposed to free trade are likely to have different values. There is not much disagreement on this issue within the mainstream economics profession.

3.  Yes. It suggests that impediments to international trade may benefit some groups (unionized labour) but these impediments are unlikely to benefit the public in general. Those opposed to free trade are promoting their own interests.

---

## IV. APPENDIX: Graphing: A Brief Review

### A. True/False Questions

_____ 1.    When graphing in the coordinate system, the $x$-coordinate tells us the horizontal location of the point while the $y$-coordinate tells us the vertical location of the point.

_____ 2.    When a line slopes upward in the coordinate system, the two variables measured on each axis are positively related.

_____ 3.    Price and quantity demanded for **MOST** goods are positively related.

_____ 4.    If three variables are related, one of them must be held constant when graphing the other two in the coordinate system.

_____ 5.    If three variables are related, a change in the variable not represented on the coordinate system will cause a movement along the curve drawn in the coordinate system.

_____ 6.    The slope of a line is equal to the change in $y$ divided by the change in $x$ along the line.

_____ 7.    When a line has negative slope, the two variables measured on each axis are positively related.

_____ 8.    There is a positive correlation between lying down and death. If the conclusion from this evidence is that it is unsafe to lie down, then there is an omitted variable problem because critically ill people tend to lie down.

_____ 9.    Reverse causality means that while people think A causes B, B may actually cause A.

_____ 10.   Because people carry umbrellas to work in the morning and it rains later in the afternoon, carrying umbrellas must cause rain.

## B. Practice Problems

1. The following ordered pairs of price and quantity demanded describe Joe's demand for cups of gourmet coffee:

2.

| Price per cup of coffee | Quantity demanded of coffee |
|---|---|
| $5 | 2 cups |
| $4 | 4 cups |
| $3 | 6 cups |
| $2 | 8 cups |
| $1 | 10 cups |

a. Plot and connect the ordered pairs on the graph provided below.

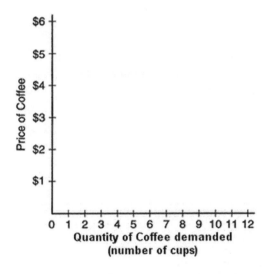

b. What is the slope of Joe's demand curve for coffee in the price range of $5 and $4? _____

c. What is the slope of Joe's demand curve for coffee in the price range of $2 and $1? _____

d. Are the price of coffee and Joe's quantity demanded of coffee positively related or negatively related? How can you tell?_____

e. If the price of coffee moves from $2 per cup to $4 per cup, what happens to the quantity demanded? Is this a movement along a curve or a shift in the curve?_____

f. Suppose Joe's income doubles from $20 000 per year to $40 000 per year. Now the following ordered pairs describe Joe's demand for gourmet coffee. Plot these ordered pairs on the graph provided in part (a) above.

| Price per cup of coffee | Quantity demanded of coffee |
|---|---|
| $5 | 4 cups |
| $4 | 6 cups |
| $3 | 8 cups |
| $2 | 10 cups |
| $1 | 12 cups |

g. Did the doubling of Joe's income cause a movement along his demand curve or a shift in his demand curve? Why?_____

_____

_____

3. An alien lands on earth and observes the following: On mornings when people carry umbrellas, it tends to rain later in the day. The alien concludes that umbrellas cause rain.

a. What error has the alien committed? _____

b. What role did *expectations* play in the alien's error? _____

_____

_____

c. If rain is truly caused by humidity, temperature, wind currents, and so on, what additional type of error has the alien committed when it decided that umbrellas cause rain? _____

_____

_____

## V. Solutions for Appendix

### A. True/False Questions

1. T
2. T
3. F; they are negatively related.
4. T
5. F; a change in a variable not represented on the graph will cause a shift in the curve.
6. T
7. F; negative slope implies a negative relation.
8. T
9. T
10. F; this is an example of reverse causation.

## B.  Practice Problems

1.  a.

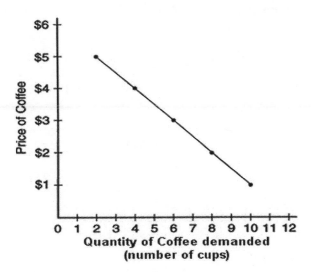

b.  −0.5

c.  −0.5

d.  Negatively related. Because an increase in price is associated with a decrease in quantity demanded. That is, the demand curve slopes downward.

e.  Decrease by 4 cups. Movement along curve.

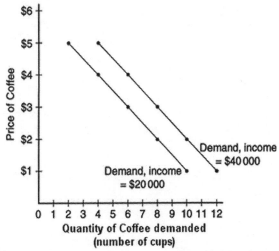

f.  Shift in his demand curve because a variable changed (income) that is not measured on either axis.

2.   a.   Reverse causality.

     b.   Because rain can be predicted, people's expectation of rain causes them to carry umbrellas before it rains, making it appear as if umbrellas cause rain.

     c.   Omitted variables.

# CHAPTER 3 Interdependence and the Gains from Trade

## I. Chapter Overview

### A. Context and Purpose

Chapter 3 is the third chapter in the three-chapter section that serves as the introduction of the text. The first chapter introduced ten fundamental principles of economics. The second chapter developed how economists approach problems. This chapter shows how people and countries gain from trade (which is one of the ten principles discussed in Chapter 1).

The purpose of Chapter 3 is to demonstrate how everyone can gain from trade. Trade allows people to specialize in the production of things for which they have a comparative advantage and then exchange them for things that other people produce. Because of specialization, total output rises and through trade people are all able to share in the bounty. This is as true for countries as it is for individuals. Because everyone can gain from trade, restrictions on trade tend to reduce welfare.

### B. Helpful Hints

1.  *A step-by-step example of comparative advantage.* What follows is an example that will demonstrate most of the concepts discussed in Chapter 3. It will provide a pattern to follow when answering questions at the end of the chapter in the text and for the problems that follow in this Study Guide.

Suppose the following information about the productivity of industry in Japan and Korea is true.

### Output

|       | Steel (units/h) | Televisions (no./h) |
|-------|-----------------|---------------------|
| Japan | 6               | 3                   |
| Korea | 8               | 2                   |

A Japanese worker can produce 6 units of steel or 3 units of televisions per hour. A Korean worker can produce 8 units of steel or 2 units of televisions per hour.

The production possibilities frontier for each country can be plotted, assuming each country has only one worker and the worker works only one hour. To plot the frontier, plot the end points and connect them with a line. For example, Japan can produce 6 units of steel with its worker or 3 units of televisions. It can also allocate one half hour to the production of each and get 3 units of steel and 1.5 televisions.

Any other proportion of the hour can be allocated to the two productive activities. The production possibilities frontier is linear in these cases because the labour resource can be moved from the production of one good to the other at a constant rate. The same can be done for Korea. Without trade, the production possibilities frontier is the consumption possibilities frontier, too.

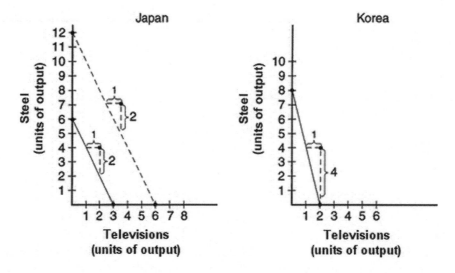

*Comparative advantage* determines specialization and trade. The opportunity cost of a television in Japan is 2 units of steel, which is shown by the slope of the production possibilities frontier in the previous graph. Alternatively, the opportunity cost of 1 unit of steel in Japan is one-half of a television. In Korea, the opportunity cost of a television is 4 units of steel and the cost of 1 unit of steel is one-quarter of a television. Because the opportunity cost of a television is lower in Japan, Japan has a comparative advantage in television production and should specialize in televisions. Because the opportunity cost of steel is lower in Korea, Korea has a comparative advantage in steel production and should specialize in steel.

What is the range of prices at which each country would be willing to exchange? If Japan specializes in television production and produces 3 televisions, it would be willing to trade televisions for steel as long as the price of steel is below one-half a television per unit of steel because that was the Japanese price for 1 unit of steel prior to trade. Korea would be willing to specialize in steel production and trade for televisions as long as the price of a television is less than 4 units of steel because that was the Korean price of a television prior to trade. In short, the final price must be between the original tradeoffs each faced in the absence of trade. One television will cost between 2 and 4 of units of steel. One unit of steel will cost between one-half and one-quarter of a television.

2.  *Trade allows countries to consume outside their original production possibilities frontier.* Suppose that Japan and Korea settle on a trading price of 3 units of steel for 1 television (or one-third of a television for 1 unit of steel). (This price is provided. There is nothing in the problem that would permit the final trading price to be calculated. It is possible to calculate only the range in which it must lie.) This price is halfway between the two prices that each faces in the absence of trade. The range for the trading price is 4 units of steel for 1 television to 2 units of steel for 1 television.

If Japan specializes in television production, produces 3 televisions, and exports 1 television for 3 units of steel, Japan will be able to consume 2 televisions and 3 units of steel. When this point (2 televisions and 3 units of steel) is plotted on Japan's graph, it lies outside its production possibilities frontier. If Korea specializes, produces 8 units of steel, and exports 3 units for one television, Korea will be able to consume 5 units of steel and 1 television. When this point (5 units of steel and one television) is plotted on Korea's graph, it also lies outside its production possibilities frontier.

This is the gain from trade. Trade allows countries (and people) to specialize. Specialization increases world output. After trading, countries consume outside their individual production possibilities frontiers. In this way, trade is like an improvement in technology. It allows countries to move beyond their current production possibilities frontiers.

3. *Only comparative advantage matters—absolute advantage is irrelevant.* In the previous example, Japan had an absolute advantage in the production of televisions because it could produce 3 per hour while Korea could produce only 2. Korea had an absolute advantage in the production of steel because it could produce 8 units per hour compared to 6 for Japan.

To demonstrate that comparative advantage, not absolute advantage, determines specialization and trade, the previous example is altered such that Japan has an absolute advantage in the production of both goods. To this end, suppose Japan becomes twice as productive as in the previous table. That is, a worker can now produce 12 units of steel or 6 televisions per hour.

## Output

|        | Steel (units/h) | Televisions (no./h) |
|--------|-----------------|---------------------|
| Japan  | 12              | 6                   |
| Korea  | 8               | 2                   |

Now Japan has an absolute advantage in the production of both goods. Japan's new production possibilities frontier is the dashed line in the previous graph. Will this change the analysis? Not at all. The opportunity cost of each good within Japan is the same—2 units of steel per television or one-half of a television per unit of steel (and Korea is unaffected). For this reason, Japan still has the identical comparative advantage as before and it will specialize in television production while Korea will specialize in steel. However, because productivity has doubled in Japan, its entire set of choices has improved and, thus, its material welfare has improved.

## II. Self-Testing Challenges

### A. True/False Questions

_____ 1.  If Japan has an absolute advantage in the production of an item, it must also have a comparative advantage in the production of that item.

_____ 2.  Comparative advantage, not absolute advantage, determines the decision to specialize in production.

_____ 3.  Absolute advantage is a comparison based on productivity.

_____ 4.  Self-sufficiency is the best way to increase one's material welfare.

_____ 5.  Comparative advantage is a comparison based on opportunity cost.

_____ 6.  If a producer is self-sufficient, the production possibilities frontier is also the consumption possibilities frontier.

_____ 7.  If a country's workers can produce five hamburgers per hour or ten bags of French fries per hour, absent trade, the price of one bag of fries is two hamburgers.

_____ 8.  If producers have different opportunity costs of production, trade will allow them to consume outside their production possibilities frontiers.

_____ 9.  If trade benefits one country, its trading partner must be worse off due to trade.

_____ 10.  Talented people who are the best at everything have a comparative advantage in the production of everything.

_____ 11.  The gains from trade can be measured by the increase in total production and consumption that comes from specialization.

_____ 12.  When a country removes a specific import restriction, it always benefits every worker in that country.

_____ 13.  If Germany's productivity doubles for everything it produces, this will not alter its prior pattern of specialization because it has not altered its comparative advantage.

_____ 14.  If an advanced country has an absolute advantage in the production of everything, it will benefit if it eliminates trade with less developed countries and becomes completely self-sufficient.

_____ 15.  If gains from trade are based solely on comparative advantage, and if all countries have the same opportunity costs of production, then there are no gains from trade

## B.  Multiple Choice Questions

1.   Which one of the following situations is most likely for a nation that has an **absolute** advantage in the production of a good?
     a.   It can benefit by restricting imports of that good.
     b.   It will specialize in the production of that good and export it.
     c.   It can produce that good using fewer resources than its trading partner.
     d.   It can produce that good at a lower opportunity cost than its trading partner.

2.   Which one of the following situations is most likely for a nation has a **comparative** advantage in the production of a good?
     a.   It can benefit by restricting imports of that good.
     b.   It must be the only country with the ability to produce that good.
     c.   It can produce that good at a lower opportunity cost than its trading partner.
     d.   It can produce that good using fewer resources than its trading partner.

3.   Which one of the following statements about trade is true?
     a.   People who are skilled at all activities cannot benefit from trade.
     b.   Unrestricted international trade benefits every person in a country equally.
     c.   Trade can benefit everyone in society because it allows people to specialize in activities in which they have an absolute advantage.
     d.   Trade can benefit everyone in society because it allows people to specialize in activities in which they have a comparative advantage.

4.   Which one of the following does the principle of comparative advantage state?
     a.   Countries with a comparative advantage in the production of every good need not specialize.
     b.   Countries should specialize in the production of goods that they enjoy consuming more than other countries enjoy consuming them.
     c.   Countries should specialize in the production of goods for which they use fewer resources in production than do their trading partners.
     d.   Countries should specialize in the production of goods for which they have a lower opportunity cost of production than do their trading partners.

5.   Which one of the following statements is true?
     a.   Self-sufficiency is the road to prosperity for most countries.
     b.   A self-sufficient country consumes outside its production possibilities frontier.
     c.   A self-sufficient country can, at best, consume on its production possibilities frontier.
     d.   Only countries with an absolute advantage in the production of every good should strive to be self-sufficient.

6.  Suppose a country's workers can produce 4 watches per hour or 12 rings per hour. Which one of the following is the domestic price of 1 ring if there is no trade?
    a.  The domestic price of 1 ring is one-third of a watch.
    b.  The domestic price of 1 ring is 3 watches.
    c.  The domestic price of 1 ring is 4 watches.
    d.  The domestic price of 1 ring is one-quarter of a watch.

7.  Suppose a country's workers can produce 4 watches per hour or 12 rings per hour. Which one of the following is the opportunity cost of 1 watch if there is no trade?
    a.  The opportunity cost of 1 watch is 3 rings.
    b.  The opportunity cost of 1 watch is one-third of a ring.
    c.  The opportunity cost of 1 watch is 4 rings.
    d.  The opportunity cost of 1 watch is one-quarter of a ring.

The following table shows production data for Australia and Korea. Use this table for questions 8–15.

## Output

|           | Food (no. units/worker/month) | Electronics (no. units/worker/month) |
|-----------|:-----------------------------:|:------------------------------------:|
| Australia | 20                            | 5                                    |
| Korea     | 8                             | 4                                    |

8.  From the production data, which one of the following statements can be made about absolute advantage??
    a.  Korea has an absolute advantage in the production of both food and electronics.
    b.  Australia has an absolute advantage in the production of both food and electronics.
    c.  Australia has an absolute advantage in the production of food while Korea has an absolute advantage in the production of electronics.
    d.  Korea has an absolute advantage in the production of food while Australia has an absolute advantage in the production of electronics.

9.  Which one of the following is the opportunity cost of 1 unit of electronics in Australia?
    a.  5 units of food
    b.  one-fifth of a unit of food
    c.  4 units of food
    d.  one-quarter of a unit of food

10. Which one of the following is the opportunity cost of 1 unit of electronics in Korea?
    a.  2 units of food
    b.  one-half of a unit of food
    c.  4 units of food
    d.  one-quarter of a unit of food

11.    Which one of the following is the opportunity cost of 1 unit of food in Australia?
   a.   5 units of electronics
   b.   one-fifth of a unit of electronics
   c.   4 units of electronics
   d.   one-quarter of a unit of electronics

12.    Which one of the following is the opportunity cost of 1 unit of food in Korea?
   a.   2 units of electronics
   b.   one-half of a unit of electronics
   c.   4 units of electronics
   d.   one-quarter of a unit of electronics

13.    Which one of the following statements can be made about comparative advantage?
   a.   Australia has a comparative advantage in the production of food while Korea has a comparative advantage in the production of electronics.
   b.   Korea has a comparative advantage in the production of food while Australia has a comparative advantage in the production of electronics.
   c.   Australia has a comparative advantage in the production of both food and electronics.
   d.   Korea has a comparative advantage in the production of both food and electronics.

14.    Which recommendation below would be the best for Korea?
   a.   specialize in food production, export food, and import electronics
   b.   specialize in electronics production, export electronics, and import food
   c.   produce both goods because neither country has a comparative advantage
   d.   produce neither good because it has an absolute disadvantage in the production of both goods

15.    Prices of electronics can be stated in terms of units of food. Which one of the following is the range of prices of electronics for which both countries could gain from trade?
   a.   The price must be greater than 4 units of food but less than 5 units of food.
   b.   The price must be greater than 2 units of food but less than 4 units of food.
   c.   The price must be greater than one-quarter of a unit of food but less than one-half of a unit of food.
   d.   The price must be greater than one-fifth of a unit of food but less than one-quarter of a unit of food.

16.    Suppose the world consists of two countries—the United States and Canada. Further, suppose there are only two goods—food and clothing. Which one of the following statements best represents the situation?
   a.    If the United States has an absolute advantage in the production of food, then Canada must have an absolute advantage in the production of clothing.
   b.    If the United States has a comparative advantage in the production of food, Canada might also have a comparative advantage in the production of food.
   c.    If the United States has a comparative advantage in the production of food, it must also have a comparative advantage in the production of clothing.
   d.    If the United States has a comparative advantage in the production of food, then Canada must have a comparative advantage in the production of clothing.

Use the following production possibilities frontiers to answer questions 17–19. Assume each country has 20 workers and that each axis is measured in tonnes per month.

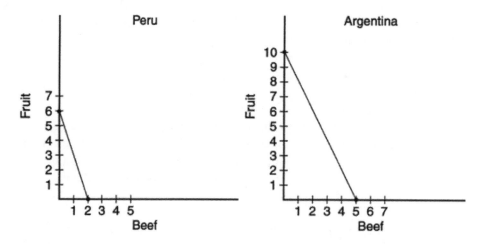

17. For which one of the following does Argentina have a comparative advantage in production?
   a.    fruit
   b.    beef
   c.    both fruit and beef
   d.    neither fruit nor beef

18. Which one of the following will Peru export?
   a.    beef
   b.    fruit
   c.    both fruit and beef
   d.    neither fruit nor beef

19. Which one of the following is the opportunity cost of producing a tonne of beef in Peru?
    a. one-third of a tonne of fruit
    b. 1 tonne of fruit
    c. 2 tonnes of fruit
    d. 3 tonnes of fruit

20. Joe is a tax accountant. He receives $100 per hour for preparing tax returns. He can type 5000 characters per hour into spreadsheets. He can hire an assistant who types 2500 characters per hour into spreadsheets. Which one of the following statements is the best recommendation?
    a. Joe should not hire an assistant because the assistant cannot type as fast as he can.
    b. Joe should hire the assistant as long as he pays the assistant less than $100 per hour.
    c. Joe should hire the assistant as long as he pays the assistant less than $50 per hour.

## C.  Short-Answer Questions

1. Why do people choose to become interdependent as opposed to self-sufficient?

2. Why is comparative advantage instead of absolute advantage important in determining trade?

3. What are the gains from trade?

4. Why is a restriction of trade likely to reduce economic welfare?

5. Suppose that a lawyer earning $200 per hour can also type at 200 words per minute. Should the lawyer hire a secretary who can type only 50 words per minute? Why or why not?

6. Evaluate this statement: A technologically advanced country, which is better than its neighbour at producing everything, would be better off if it closed its borders to trade because the less productive country is a burden to the advanced country.

### D.  Practice Problems

1. Angela is a college student. She takes a full load of classes and has only 5 hours per week for her hobby. Angela is artistic and can make 2 clay pots per hour or 4 coffee mugs per hour.

    a. Draw Angela's production possibilities frontier for pots and mugs based on the amount produced per week.

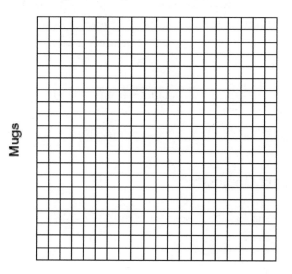

Pots

    b. What is Angela's opportunity cost of 1 pot? 10 pots? _____
    _____

    c. What is Angela's opportunity cost of 1 mug? 10 mugs?_____
    _____

    d. Why is her production possibilities frontier a straight line instead of bowed out like those presented in Chapter 2? _____
    _____

2. Suppose a worker in Germany can produce 15 computers or 5 tonnes of grain per month. Suppose a worker in Poland can produce 4 computers or 4 tonnes of grain per month. For simplicity, assume that each country has only one worker.

    a.    Fill out the following table:

Output

| | Computers (no./worker/month) | Grain (tonnes/worker/month) |
|---|---|---|
| Germany | | |
| Poland | | |

b.   Graph the production possibilities frontier for each country.

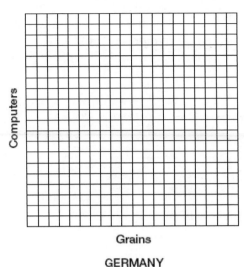

GERMANY

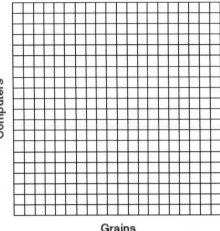

POLAND

c.   What is the opportunity cost of 1 computer in Germany? What is the opportunity cost of 1 tonne of grain in Germany?_____

_____

d.   What is the opportunity cost of 1 computer in Poland? What is the opportunity cost of 1 tonne of grain in Poland?_____

_____

e.   Which country has the absolute advantage in producing computers? Grain?_____

_____

f.   Which country has the comparative advantage in producing computers? Grain?_____

_____

_____

_____

g.   Each country should tend toward specialization in the production of which good? Why?_____

_____

_____

_____

h.   What are the range of prices for computers and grain for which both countries would benefit?_____

_____

_____

i.   Suppose Germany and Poland settle on a price of 2 computers for 1 tonne of grain or 0.5 tonnes of grain for a computer. Suppose each country specializes completely in production and they trade four computers for 2 tonnes of grain. Plot the final consumption points on the graphs made in part (b) above. Are these countries consuming inside or outside of their production possibilities frontier?_____

_____

_____

_____

j.   Suppose the productivity of a worker in Poland doubles so that a worker can produce 8 computers or 8 tonnes of grain per month. Which country has the absolute advantage in producing computers? Grain?_____

_____

_____

_____

k.   After the doubling of productivity in Poland, which country has a comparative advantage in producing computers? Grain? Has the comparative advantage changed? Has the economic welfare of either country changed?_____

_____

_____

_____

_____

l.   How would the analysis change if it was assumed, more realistically, that each country had 10 million workers?_____

_____

_____

_____

3.   Suppose a worker in Canada can produce 4 cars or 20 computers per month while a worker in Russia can produce 1 car or 5 computers per month. Again, for simplicity, assume each country has only one worker.

a.   Fill out the following table:

|  | Output | |
|---|---|---|
|  | Cars | Computers |
|  | (no./worker/month) | (no./worker/month) |
| Canada |  |  |
| Russia |  |  |

b.   Which country has the absolute advantage in the production of cars? Computers?_____

_____

_____

c.  Which country has the comparative advantage in the production of cars? Computers?

_____

_____

_____

d.  Are there any gains to be made from trade? Why or why not?_____

_____

_____

e.  Does the answer in (d) above help pinpoint a source for gains from trade?_____

_____

_____

f.  What might make two countries have different opportunity costs of production? (Use your imagination. This was not directly discussed in Chapter 3.)_____

_____

_____

_____

## E.  Advanced Critical Thinking

In an election debate a candidate says, "We need to stop the flow of foreign automobiles into our country. If we limit the importation of automobiles, our domestic auto production will rise and Canada will be better off."

1.  Is it likely that Canada will be better off if it limits auto imports? Explain._____

_____

_____

2.  Will anyone in Canada be better off if it limits auto imports? Explain._____

_____

_____

_____

3.  In the real world, does every person in the country gain when restrictions on imports are reduced? Explain._____

_____

_____

_____

### III. Solutions

#### A. True/False Questions

1.    F; absolute advantage compares the quantities of inputs used in production while comparative advantage compares the opportunity costs.
2.  T
3.  T
4.  F; restricting trade eliminates gains from trade.
5.  T
6.  T
7.  F; the price of 1 bag of fries is one-half of a hamburger.
8.  T
9.  F; voluntary trade benefits both traders.
10. F; a low opportunity cost of producing one good implies a high opportunity cost of producing the other good.
11. T
12. F; it may harm those involved in that industry.
13. T
14. F; voluntary trade benefits all traders.
15. T

#### B. Multiple-Choice Questions

| | | | |
|---|---|---|---|
| 1. c | 6. a | 11. d | 16. d |
| 2. c | 7. a | 12. b | 17. b |
| 3. d | 8. b | 13. a | 18. b |
| 4. d | 9. c | 14. b | 19. d |
| 5. c | 10. a | 15. b | 20. c |

#### C. Short-Answer Questions

1. Because a consumer gets a greater variety of goods at a much lower cost than he or she could produce by himself or herself. That is, there are gains from trade.

2. What is important in trade is how a country's costs without trade differ from another country's costs. This is determined by the relative opportunity costs across countries.

3. The additional output and consumption that comes from countries with different opportunity costs of production specializing in the production of the item for which they have the lower domestic opportunity cost.

4. Because it forces people to produce at a higher cost than they would pay when they trade.

5. Yes, as long as the secretary earns less than $50 per hour, the lawyer is ahead.

6.  This is not true. All countries can gain from trade if their opportunity costs of production differ. Even the least productive country will have a comparative advantage at producing something, and it can trade this good to the advanced country for less than the advanced country's opportunity cost.

## D. Practice Problems

1.  a.

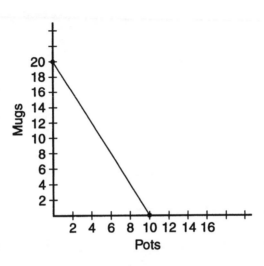

b.  2 mugs. 20 mugs.

c.  One-half of a pot. 5 pots.

d.  Because her resources can be moved from the production of one good to another at a constant rate.

2.  a.

|  | Output | |
|---|---|---|
|  | Computers (no./worker/month) | Grain (no./worker/month) |
| Germany | 15 | 5 |
| Poland | 4 | 4 |

b.

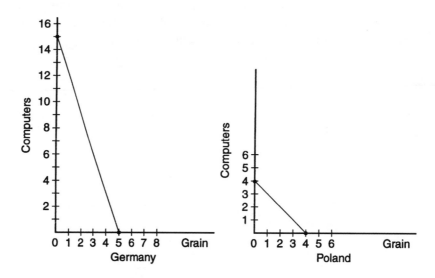

c.   One-third of a tonne of grain. 3 computers.

d.   1 tonne of grain. 1 computer.

e.   Germany because 1 worker can produce 15 compared to 4. Germany because 1 worker can produce 5 compared to 4.

f.   Germany because a computer has the opportunity cost of only one-third of a tonne of grain compared to 1 tonne of grain in Poland. Poland because 1 tonne of grain has the opportunity cost of only 1 computer compared to 3 computers in Germany.

g.   Germany should produce computers while Poland should produce grain because the opportunity cost of computers is lower in Germany and the opportunity cost of grain is lower in Poland. That is, each has a comparative advantage in those goods.

h.   Grain must cost less than 3 computers to Germany. Computers must cost less than 1 tonne of grain to Poland.

i.

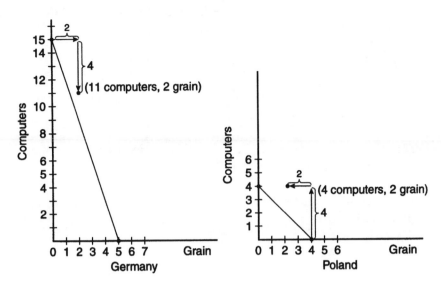

They are consuming outside their production possibilities frontier.

j.  Germany because one worker can produce 15 compared to 8. Poland because one worker can produce 8 compared to 5.

k.  Germany has comparative advantage in computers. Poland has comparative advantage in grain. No change in comparative advantage. Poland is better off, however, because it now has a larger set of choices.

l.  It would not change absolute advantage or comparative advantage. It would change the scale in the previous two graphs by a factor of 10 million.

3.  a.

### Output

|  | Cars (no./worker/month) | Computers (no./worker/month) |
| --- | --- | --- |
| Canada | 4 | 20 |
| Russia | 1 | 5 |

b.  Canada because 1 worker can produce 4 compared to 1. Canada because 1 worker can produce 20 compared to 5.

c.  In both, the opportunity cost of 1 car is 5 computers. In both, the opportunity cost of 1 computer is one-fifth of a car. Therefore, neither has a comparative advantage in either good.

d.  No. Each can get the same tradeoff between goods domestically.

e.  Yes. There needs to be differences in opportunity costs of producing goods across countries for there to be gains from trade.

f.  Resources or technology might be different across countries. That is, workers could be differently educated, land could be of different quality, or the available technology might be different.

## E.  Advanced Critical Thinking

1.  No. If Canada imports autos, it is because the opportunity cost of producing them elsewhere is lower than in Canada.

2.  Yes. Those associated with the domestic auto industry—shareholders (owners) of domestic auto producers and autoworkers.

3.  No. When we reduce restrictions on imports, the country gains from the increased trade but individuals in the affected domestic industry may lose.

# 4 The Market Forces of Supply and Demand

## I. Chapter Overview

### A. Context and Purpose

Earlier chapters provided an overview of the "economic way of thinking" in order to explain the operation of a market economy such as that of Canada. One of the cornerstones of a market economy is the interaction of supply and demand. Unfortunately, these terms are not well understood: A parrot can be taught to squawk "supply and demand" without any knowledge of the concepts. In reading the newspapers on any given day, examples of the misuse of supply and demand can be found. The terms take on a very specific meaning in economics that differs from their everyday use. This chapter explains what an economist means by supply and demand and shows how they interact to determine prices and quantities of goods and services. It also shows how various factors that change either supply or demand ultimately lead to changes in market prices and quantities.

### B. Helpful Hints

1. *Supply means willingness to sell.* In everyday usage, supply often refers to physical stocks of a product or resource in the form of inventories available for sale. In economics, however, **supply** means ***willingness to sell***. For example, the newspapers often report changes in global petroleum supplies, when really they mean inventories or petroleum reserves. The supply of petroleum is the willingness to sell those reserves, not the stock of petroleum itself.

2. *Demand means willingness to buy.* Demand is not simply consumer wants. Demand represents wants backed up by dollars and willingness to spend them.

3. *A market is a collection of buyers and sellers.* Markets are not physical locations; rather, they are the interaction of buyers and sellers. Such interaction *can* occur at a physical location: for example, an auction may represent a separate market. However, buyers and sellers can interact on a national or even global level, particularly as electronic communications grow. Money markets, for example, involve buyers and sellers around the world.

4. *"Demand" is the entire schedule or curve.* Demand refers to the whole demand schedule or demand curve, not just a point on the curve. It represents all of the price–quantity combinations that are acceptable to consumers. Because of this, increased sales that occur due to a price cut are not referred to as an increase in *demand*. There is, of course, an increase in the *quantity demanded*, but this is not an increase (or shift to the right) in demand itself.

5. *"Quantity demanded" is a point on the demand curve.* When there is a change in price, quantity demanded changes, but demand itself does not change.

6. *"Supply" is the entire schedule or curve.* Supply refers to the whole supply schedule or supply curve, not just a point on the curve. For supply to shift, the underlying factors that are held constant in plotting a supply curve must change. Changing the price simply means that we move to a new point on the existing supply curve, which represents a new quantity. Of course an increase in price encourages suppliers to sell more; however, this response to higher price is called an increase in *quantity supplied*, rather than an increase (or shift) in *supply*.

7. *"Quantity supplied" is a point on the supply curve.* When there is a change in price, the quantity supplied changes, even though the supply curve itself does not shift. The quantity supplied at a particular price is the amount that sellers are willing to sell at that price.

## II. Self-Testing Challenges

### A. True/False Questions

_____1. A decrease in the price of soft drinks will increase their demand (shift the curve to the right).

_____2. The supply of petroleum is fixed because there is only a finite amount in the ground.

_____3. At the equilibrium price, the amount that sellers are willing to sell is just equal to the amount that buyers are willing to buy.

_____4. An improvement in technology tends to reduce the supply (shift it to the left).

_____5. An increase in raw materials prices tends to reduce the supply (shift it to the left).

_____6. If sellers expect prices to rise in the future, this could cause prices to rise today by encouraging sellers to reduce their current supply in anticipation of a price hike.

_____7. A market refers to a physical location in which buyers and sellers interact.

_____8. A price that is below equilibrium results in excess supply.

_____9. Excess demand tends to drive price up until the market reaches equilibrium price and quantity.

_____10. An increase in supply tends to increase equilibrium price and quantity.

_____11. An equal increase in both supply and demand tends to increase equilibrium price and quantity.

_____12.   An increase in supply accompanied by an equal decrease in demand tends to decrease equilibrium price while leaving equilibrium quantity unchanged.

_____13.   The market supply curve is the vertical summation of all the individual supply curves.

_____14.   Assuming that pizza and beer are complements, a decrease in the price of pizza would increase the demand for beer.

_____15.   If pizza and hamburgers are substitutes for each other, a decrease in the price of pizza would increase the demand for hamburgers.

## B.  Multiple-Choice Questions

1.  Which one of the following would decrease the demand (shift the curve to the left) for beer?
    a.   The price of a substitute, wine, falls.
    b.   The price of beer increases to $5.00 per bottle.
    c.   Bars begin giving away spicy snacks to their customers.
    d.   A new Health Canada study concludes that beer helps to reduce heart disease.

2.  If buyers believe that the price of gasoline will rise soon, which one of the following is the **MOST** likely immediate result?
    a.   an increase in the quantity demanded, due to the change in supply
    b.   a decrease (shift to the left) in the demand for gasoline, due to a shift to substitutes
    c.   a decrease (shift to the left) in the demand for gasoline, due to a change in tastes
    d.   an increase (shift to the right) in the demand for gasoline, due to a change in expectations

3.  A new technological breakthrough in genetic engineering makes it possible to grow twice as much corn per hectare as had been possible in the past. Which one of the following is the **MOST** likely outcome of this development?
    a.   an increase in the demand for corn, due to the greatly reduced price
    b.   an increase in quantity supplied, due to the increased willingness to sell corn
    c.   an increase (shift to the right) in the supply of corn, due to the reduced cost of production
    d.   a decrease (shift to the left) in the supply of corn, due to the increased costs associated with the new technology

4. A university student made the following statement to a friend at a university sporting event: "This football stadium is a good example of how unrealistic economics is: my economics professor claims that, according to a so-called 'Law of Supply,' supply varies directly with price, yet anybody can look around and see that the supply is fixed at 10 000 seats, no matter what the price is!" Which one of the following explains what is wrong with the student's statement?
   a. Supply is not fixed at 10 000 seats; it is quantity supplied that is fixed.
   b. This is simply an exception to the Law of Supply; it does not mean that it is not relevant for most cases.
   c. Supply is not the same thing as the physical stock of a good or service that is available; rather, supply is willingness to sell.

Use the following graph to answer questions 5–8:

The Market for Personal Sized Pizzas

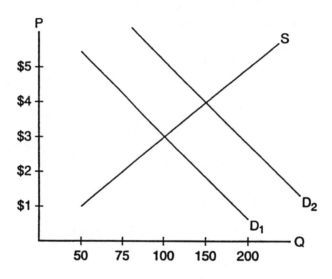

5. Referring to the graph above, which one of the following describes the initial equilibrium price and quantity?
   a. P = $2.00; Q = 75.
   b. P = $2.00; Q = 150.
   c. P = $3.00; Q = 100.
   d. P = $4.00; Q = 75.

6. Which one of the following would cause the demand for pizzas among university students to shift to the right?
   a. an increase in financial aid to university students
   b. half-price pizzas for anybody with a university ID
   c. an increase in the price of a complement, i.e., beer
   d. a decrease in the price of a substitute, i.e., hamburgers

7.  After an increase in demand, which one of the following describes the new equilibrium price and quantity?
    a.  P = $2.00; Q = 75.
    b.  P = $2.00; Q = 150.
    c.  P = $3.00; Q = 100.
    d.  P = $4.00; Q = 150.

8.  Which one of the following describes the effect of increase in demand on supply?
    a.  It would first increase, then decrease over time.
    b.  It would neither rise nor fall, although quantity supplied would increase.
    c.  It would decrease (shift to the left).
    d.  It would increase (shift to the right).

Use the following graph to answer questions 9–12:

The Market for Hand-Held Calculators

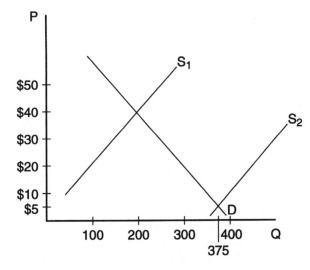

9.  Referring to the graph above, which one of the following describes the initial equilibrium price and quantity?
    a.  P = $5; Q = 375.
    b.  P = $10; Q = 350.
    c.  P = $20; Q = 100.
    d.  P = $40; Q = 200.

10. Which one of the following is a factor that would cause an increase (shift to the right) in supply?
    a.  improved technology
    b.  higher labour costs
    c.  lower number of sellers
    d.  increased demand

11. Which choice below would be the new equilibrium price and quantity as a result of the increase in supply?
    a. P = $5; Q = 375.
    b. P = $10; Q = 350.
    c. P = $20; Q = 100.
    d. P = $30; Q = 250.

12. Suppose that the demand for calculators rose even more than the supply had increased. Which one of the following describes the changes in equilibrium price and quantity that would be the net effect of the two increases?
    a. an increase in price but a decrease in quantity
    b. an increase in quantity but a slight decrease in price
    c. decreases in both quantity and price
    d. increases in both quantity and price

13. Which one of the following describes what supply curves represent?
    a. inventories
    b. physical stocks
    c. total production
    d. willingness to sell

14. Which one of the following does a supply curve for a good or service show?
    a. the seller's target price.
    b. the seller's minimum acceptable price.
    c. the seller's maximum acceptable price.
    d. the seller's average acceptable price.

15. If equilibrium quantity rises but equilibrium price remains unchanged, which one of the following is the cause?
    a. an increase in both supply and demand
    b. a decrease in both demand and supply
    c. a decrease in demand and an increase in supply
    d. an increase in demand and a decrease in supply

16. If equilibrium price rises but equilibrium quantity remains unchanged, which one of the following is the cause?
    a. a decrease in demand and an increase in supply
    b. an increase in demand and a decrease in supply
    c. an increase in both supply and demand
    d. a decrease in both demand and supply

17. If equilibrium quantity and price rise, which one of the following is the cause?
    a. a decrease in both demand and supply.
    b. an increase in demand and decrease in supply.
    c. a decrease in demand and increase in supply.
    d. an increase in demand without a change in supply.

18. A freeze that destroys half of the coffee crop in South America would likely raise the price of coffee. Which one of the following would happen in turn?
    a. reduced demand for both coffee and tea
    b. reduced quantity demanded for both coffee and tea
    c. reduced demand for coffee and increased demand for tea
    d. reduced quantity demanded for coffee and increased demand for tea.

19. Which one of the following describes an inferior good?
    a. one for which demand rises as income rises
    b. one for which demand falls as income rises
    c. one for which demand is unrelated to income
    d. one for which demand is low because of the low quality of the good

20. Suppose that there is a shortage of parking spaces in downtown Toronto during weekdays. Which one of the following explains how the shortage can be eliminated?
    a. by lowering the price
    b. by decreasing the supply
    c. by allowing the price to rise
    d. by increasing the quantity demanded

## C. Short-Answer Questions

1. What would happen to the demand for apples if consumers' incomes rose, and apples are a normal good? What if apples are an inferior good?

    _____
    _____
    _____
    _____

2. Explain why the price of a complement or a substitute can alter the demand for a good, even though the price of the good itself does not shift the demand.

    _____
    _____
    _____
    _____

## D.  Practice Problems

The supply and demand schedules below show hypothetical prices and quantities in the market for corn. The initial quantity supplied is shown by $Q_s$, and the quantity demanded is $Q_d$.

### The Market for Corn
#### (in thousands of tonnes)

| Price | $Q_d$ | $Q_s$ | $Q_{s'}$ |
|-------|-------|-------|----------|
| $6.00 | 220 | 400 | ____ |
| $5.50 | 240 | 360 | ____ |
| $5.00 | 260 | 320 | ____ |
| $4.50 | 280 | 280 | ____ |
| $4.00 | 300 | 240 | ____ |
| $3.50 | 320 | 200 | ____ |
| $3.00 | 340 | 160 | ____ |

1.  Plot the supply and demand curves for the initial supply and demand, $Q_s$ and $Q_d$, on the graph that follows the questions.

    a.  The equilibrium price of corn is $_____.

    b.  The equilibrium quantity of corn is _____ thousand tonnes.

    c.  At a price of $3.00 per tonne, there would be a (shortage, surplus) _____ of _____ thousand tonnes, and the price would tend to (fall, rise) _____.

    d.  At a price of $5.00 per tonne, there would be a (shortage, surplus) _____ of _____ thousand tonnes, and the price would tend to (fall, rise) _____.

2.  Suppose that the supply of corn increased by 60 thousand tonnes at every price. Show the new supply schedule as $Q_{s'}$ on the previous table.

    a.  The new equilibrium price of corn is $_____.

    b.  The new equilibrium quantity of corn is _____ thousand tonnes.

    c.  Has the demand for corn changed as a result of this change in supply? Explain briefly._____
    _____
    _____

3.  Give an example of a factor that could have caused such an increase in the supply of corn, and explain briefly._____
    _____
    _____

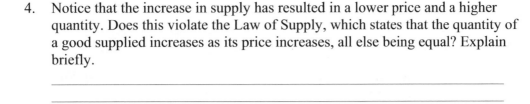

4. Notice that the increase in supply has resulted in a lower price and a higher quantity. Does this violate the Law of Supply, which states that the quantity of a good supplied increases as its price increases, all else being equal? Explain briefly.

_____

_____

_____

**The Market for Corn**

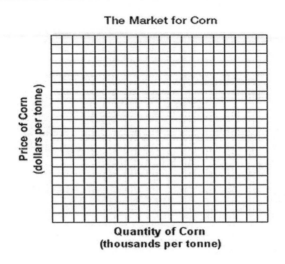

**Quantity of Corn**
**(thousands per tonne)**

## E. Advanced Critical Thinking

Consider the following editorial that appeared in a leading U.S. business publication following a freeze that destroyed much of the coffee crop in the late 1970s:

*Coffee prices, it seems, are coming down again, after hitting a record high of $4.42 last year. An Agriculture Department economist, who had predicted $5-a-pound coffee this year, says he "underestimated the power of the U.S. consumer movement." Perhaps, or maybe, as with so many economists these days, he simply forgot his freshman economics, which has nothing to do with "movements." The coffee market is behaving the way the basic textbooks say a market behaves: Prices go up, demand falls, and prices come down.*

— The Wall Street Journal, *November 30, 1977*

1. Suppose that coffee had started out at an equilibrium price of $1.00 per pound prior to the freeze.

    a. Show graphically the initial equilibrium, labelling supply and demand as $S_1$ and $D_1$, respectively. Use $Q_1$ to identify the original equilibrium quantity.

    b. Show graphically the effect of a freeze that destroys much of the coffee crop, labelling the new supply as $S_2$ and the new equilibrium quantity as $Q_2$. (The new equilibrium price is $4.42.)

c.  Does the answer to part (b) show a change in demand? Why or why not?

_____

_____

d.  Based on your analysis in parts (a–c), critique the *Wall Street Journal* editorial. What's wrong with its analysis? _____

_____

_____

_____

## III.  Solutions

### A.  True/False Questions

1.  F; quantity demanded, not demand, will increase.
2.  F; the physical stock of petroleum in the ground is fixed, but the supply is willingness to sell, which is not fixed.
3.  T
4.  F; technology tends to *increase* the supply (shift it to the right) by increasing productivity; that is, increasing output per unit of input.
5.  T
6.  T
7.  F; a market need not be in a specific physical location; buyers and sellers can interact without being in the same location.
8.  F; price below equilibrium results in excess demand, as buyers try to buy more than sellers are willing to sell at the low price.
9.  T
10. F; increased supply moves the equilibrium to the right along the demand curve, resulting in a higher quantity and lower price.
11. F; an increase in both supply and demand will increase equilibrium quantity, but the effect on price depends on which curve shifts more; if they shift equally, price remains unchanged.
12. T
13. F; market supply is the horizontal summation of the individual supply curves; for each price, it represents the sum of all of the individual quantities supplied.
14. T
15. F; a decrease in the price of a good tends to decrease the demand for its substitutes.

### B.  Multiple-Choice Questions

| | | | |
|---|---|---|---|
| 1.  a | 6.  a | 11. a | 16. b |
| 2.  d | 7.  d | 12. d | 17. d |
| 3.  c | 8.  b | 13. d | 18. d |
| 4.  c | 9.  d | 14. b | 19. b |
| 5.  c | 10. a | 15. a | 20. c |

## C. Short-Answer Questions

1. An increase in consumer income increases the demand for normal goods and decreases the demand for inferior goods.

2. Prices of other goods are held constant in deriving a demand curve, even though they can affect consumption. When they change, the demand also changes (shifts right or left). The price of the good itself does not shift the demand, however, because price is already built into our definition of demand. Demand for a good includes all of the quantities that consumers are willing to buy at various prices of the good, thus holding other factors constant.

## D. Practice Problems

1. a. $4.50

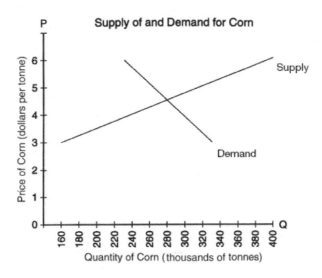

b. 280

c. Shortage, 180, rise

d. Surplus, 60, fall

2. a. $4.00

b. 300

c. Demand has not changed. Supply increased, thus moving the equilibrium along the existing demand curve to a higher quantity and lower price.

3. Any of the factors that lower cost of production could shift the supply to the right, indicating increased willingness to sell at each price. For example, improvements in technology that increase productivity would lower cost and increase the supply.

4.  No, this does not violate the Law of Supply. The Law of Supply holds other factors, such as technology, constant. The increase in supply represents a new supply curve, with an increased *willingness to sell*. Both the old and new supply curves follow the Law of Supply: as long as those other factors are constant, sellers will tend to be willing to sell more, but only at a higher price.

## E.  Advanced Critical Thinking

1.  a   The original equilibrium should be at a price of $1.00, with the quantity simply labelled $Q_1$.

    b.  The new equilibrium should be at a price of $4.42 and a quantity of $Q_2$, after a leftward shift in supply and a movement along the (unchanged) demand curve. Equilibrium price is higher and quantity is lower.

    c.  Demand did not change; only the quantity demanded changed as the supply shifted left, thus moving along the existing demand curve. There were no changes in the factors that are held constant in deriving a demand curve.

    d.  The newspaper's analysis was flawed. They confused (shifts in) demand with simple changes in quantity demanded in response to a price change. For the price to fall, one of the factors (other than price) affecting either supply or demand must have changed.

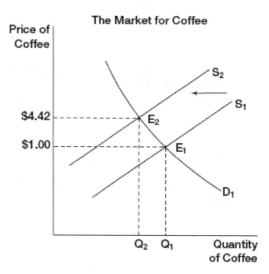

# 5 Elasticity and Its Application

## I. Chapter Overview

### A. Context and Purpose

This chapter extends the discussion of supply and demand, which was introduced in the previous chapter, to the exploration of consumer and producer responsiveness to changes in market conditions such as price. To measure this responsiveness, economists use the term *elasticity*. Consumers' (or producers') relative responsiveness to changes in any one of the determinants of demand (or supply) is known as elasticity of demand (or supply). Price elasticity of demand (or supply) measures the degree of response of quantity demanded (or quantity supplied) to any change in price. When consumers (or producers) are relatively more responsive to changes in price, their demand (or supply) is considered to be more elastic, just as a rubber band that is very elastic is highly responsive or stretchy. Knowledge of consumers' and producers' elasticity is useful to sellers, who need to know how price changes will affect sales and total revenues, as well as to government officials, who need to know how changes in taxes or other public policies will affect behaviour.

### B. Helpful Hints

1. *Elasticity means responsiveness.* In its most general sense, elasticity is responsiveness, whether we are talking about rubber bands or people. In economics, we use various types of elasticity to measure people's responsiveness to changes in economic factors such as price or income. The price elasticity of demand is particularly important because it provides immediate information about the effect of a change in price upon total consumer spending on the product. To the seller, this spending represents revenue. If consumer demand is highly elastic, or responsive to price, sellers can raise total revenue by cutting price. Even though price falls, the increased quantity demanded (and sold) more than makes up for the drop in price as the dollar value of consumer spending (and revenue for the seller) rises. On the other hand, if demand is inelastic, cutting price will not generate enough additional sales to compensate, and total revenue will fall.

2. *Elasticity is not the same thing as slope.* Slope is constant along a straight-line demand curve, but price elasticity of demand varies with the point on the curve. This should be apparent if you keep in mind that slope is the steepness of the curve, which does not change along a straight-line demand curve; but the elasticity is the ratio of the relative changes in quantity and price, which depends on the starting point. Clearly a $1 change in price is a

bigger percentage change when the initial price is $1 than if the initial price is $1000!

## II. Self-Testing Challenges

### A. True/False Questions

_____1.    The demand for Chevrolets is more elastic than the demand for automobiles in general.

_____2.    The longer the time period, the more elastic the demand for a good or service, all else equal.

_____3.    A normal good is one for which the income elasticity is greater than one.

_____4.    A good perceived by the consumer to be a necessity will tend to have an elastic demand.

_____5.    For a good with a price elasticity of demand of 0.8, an increase in price will cause total consumer spending on that good to rise.

_____6.    The major problem facing agriculture in Canada today is the slow pace in implementing necessary technological changes in the production and distribution of food.

_____7.    If Dennis allocates $24 as his monthly expenditure on beer, and he spends no more and no less, regardless of price, then his demand for beer is unit elastic.

_____8.    Generally speaking, goods that are considered necessities tend to have inelastic demands.

_____9.    The supply of land overlooking the Niagara River is highly price elastic.

_____10.   If price elasticity of demand is zero, then any price change will also have a zero effect on total revenue.

### B.  Multiple-Choice Questions

1.    All else equal, which of the following indicates when the price elasticity of
demand tends to be higher?
    a.   when the time period involved is shorter
    b.   when the market is more broadly defined
    c.   when there are more substitutes for the good or service
    d.   when consumers perceive the good to be more of a necessity.

2.    If a seller wants to increase total revenue, which one of the following
describes what he should do?
    a.   lower price if demand is inelastic
    b.   raise price only if demand is elastic
    c.   raise price only if demand is inelastic
    d.   lower price if demand has unitary elasticity

3.    Suppose the Minister of Health wants to reduce cigarette smoking by
increasing tobacco taxes. Which one of the following describes why it will
probably take a fairly large tobacco tax to make much of a difference?
    a.   because price is irrelevant for consumers
    b.   because supply of tobacco is relatively inelastic
    c.   because demand for cigarettes is totally inelastic
    d.   because demand for cigarettes is relatively inelastic

4.    As income rises during economic upturns, consumption of potatoes
declines, yet as income falls during economic downturns, consumption of
potatoes rises. Which one of the following is the likely explanation for the
changes in potato consumption?
    a.   high income elasticity of demand
    b.   very high price elasticity of supply
    c.   very low price elasticity of demand
    d.   negative income elasticity of demand

5.    Which one of the following statements is true?
    a.   When the price of meat rises, the supply of hamburgers falls.
    b.   When the price of pencils falls, the quantity supplied of pencils rises.
    c.   When the weather gets hotter, the quantity demanded for ice cream
rises.
    d.   A negative cross-price elasticity for two goods—Good A and Good
B—would arise if A and B were complements.

6.    Which one of the following is likely to have a high income elasticity of
demand?
    a.   fancy restaurant meals
    b.   lunches at fast-food restaurants
    c.   brown bag lunches from home

7.   Which of the following is the income elasticity of demand for housing if people always spend 25% of their incomes on housing?
   a.  0.25
   b.  1.00
   c.  2.50
   d.  25.00

Use the following information to answer questions 8 and 9.
The city is considering a fare hike for its city bus service. At the current fare of $2.00, daily ridership is 2400 people. The city estimates that if it raises fares to $2.50, ridership will decline to 2100.

8.   Using the midpoint method of calculating elasticity, which of the following is the price elasticity of demand?
   a.  0.0
   b.  0.6
   c.  1.0
   d.  6.0

9.   Which of the following is recommended if the city wants to raise more revenue from its bus system?
   a.  raise the price to $2.50
   b.  keep the price at $2.00 and wait for demand to increase
   c.  first lower the price to attract riders, then gradually increase price
   d.  first raise price to get revenues, then lower price after the buses are paid off

10.  Which one of the following is the likely outcome of the prevailing laws aimed at reducing the supply of illegal drugs?
   a.  It reduces drug consumption but increases drug-related income and crime
   b.  It reduces both drug consumption and drug-related income and crime
   c.  It increases both drug consumption and drug-related income and crime
   d.  It increases drug consumption but reduces drug-related income and crime

11.  If the price elasticity of demand is 0.5, then which of the following will a 20% price hike lead to?
   a.  5% drop in quantity demanded
   b.  10% drop in quantity demanded
   c.  20% drop in quantity demanded
   d.  40% drop in quantity demanded

12.  If a 20% decline in price leads to a 30% decrease in quantity supplied, then which statement below is correct?
  a.  price elasticity of demand is 1.5
  b.  price elasticity of supply is 1.5
  c.  price elasticity of demand is 3.0
  d.  price elasticity of supply is 3.0

13.  Which one of the following is the **MAIN** reason that OPEC has been unable to keep oil prices high?
  a.  Government regulations have prevented it.
  b.  Supply tends to be more inelastic in the long run.
  c.  Demand tends to become more elastic in the long run.
  d.  Massive new petroleum discoveries have increased the supply.

14.  If price elasticity of supply tends to be higher, which one of the following will be the outcome?
  a.  The time period will be longer.
  b.  It will be easier for more new firms to enter the industry.
  c.  The firms can be more adaptable to changing market conditions.
  d.  The demand will also be higher.

15.  Suppose Bill buys one six-pack of beer each week, regardless of price, and he drinks it on Saturday night. Which one of the following statements is correct?
  a.  price elasticity of demand is 0
  b.  price elasticity of demand is 1
  c.  price elasticity of demand is 6
  d.  price elasticity of supply is greater than 1

16.  For a given increase in demand, which of the following indicates when price increases the **MOST**?
  a.  supply is elastic
  b.  supply is inelastic
  c.  supply is unit elastic
  d.  supply is perfectly elastic

17.  Which one of the following describes the elasticity of a straight-line (constant-slope) demand curve?
  a.  elasticity remains constant along its length.
  b.  elasticity increases as quantity demanded increases along its length.
  c.  elasticity decreases as quantity demanded increases along its length.
  d.  elasticity first increases and then decreases as quantity demanded increases.

18. Which one of the following is the cross-price elasticity of demand for orange golf balls with respect to any change in the price of white golf balls?
    a. positive and probably high
    b. negative and probably high
    c. positive and probably low
    d. negative and probably low

19. Which of the following is the cross elasticity of demand for bindings if, all else is equal, the demand for ski bindings falls by 40% when the price of skis increases by 20%?
    a. 0.5
    b. −0.5
    c. 2.0
    d. −2.0

20. Which one of the following describes a circumstance in which an increase in demand will not have any effect on price?
    a. where supply is unit elastic
    b. where supply is perfectly elastic
    c. where supply is perfectly inelastic
    d. where supply is a straight line through the origin

## C. Short-Answer Questions

1. How could a good such as a new mid-priced car be both an inferior good and a normal good? _____
   _____
   _____
   _____

2. A 2004 study determined the following elasticities.

   |                                      | Short run | Long run |
   | ------------------------------------ | --------- | -------- |
   | Price elasticity of demand for fuel  | 0.25      | 0.64     |
   | Income elasticity of demand for fuel | 0.40      | 1.00     |

   Based on this information, assess whether the following statements are true or false. Explain your answers.

   a. If the price of fuel rises by 10% and stays at that level, the reduction in the volume of fuel consumed in the short run is more than that in the long run.

      _____
      _____
      _____

b.  If the consumer's income goes up by 10%, the amount of fuel consumed will increase by 4% within a year and by 10% in the long run. These changes suggest that fuel is considered to be an inferior good. _____

_____

_____

_____

## D.  Practice Problems

1.  The City Zoo is losing money. City Council is unwilling to contribute any tax dollars to support the zoo, asserting that the administration should simply raise prices in order to balance its budget. The price of admission is currently $4 per person, with average daily attendance of 600 people. City Council argues that the zoo needs to raise only one additional dollar per visitor to break even (the zoo is currently losing about $600 per day). The zoo management has hired a consultant to estimate the demand for admissions to the zoo and recommend a pricing policy.
The demand schedule that the consultant estimated is shown below:

### Demand for Zoo Admissions

| Price | Quantity of tickets demanded/day | Total revenue | % change in price | % change in quantity | Elasticity |
|-------|----------------------------------|---------------|-------------------|----------------------|------------|
| $0    | 1200                             | $____         | ____%             | ____%                | ____       |
| $1    | 1050                             | $____         | ____%             | ____%                | ____       |
| $2    | 900                              | $____         | ____%             | ____%                | ____       |
| $3    | 750                              | $____         | ____%             | ____%                | ____       |
| $4    | 600                              | $____         | ____%             | ____%                | ____       |
| $5    | 450                              | $____         | ____%             | ____%                | ____       |
| $6    | 300                              | $____         | ____%             | ____%                | ____       |
| $7    | 150                              | $____         | ____%             | ____%                | ____       |
| $8    | 0                                | $____         |                   |                      |            |

a.  Fill in the blanks in the preceding table. (Use the midpoint method to calculate the percentage changes and elasticity.)

b.  What should be the consultant's recommendation regarding pricing, given the zoo's budget crisis? Should they change the price from the current $4? Justify the position, based upon the estimate of the elasticity of demand. _____

_____

_____

_____

2.  Consider the demand curve for sofas shown below. Use the midpoint method to calculate elasticity in the questions that follow.

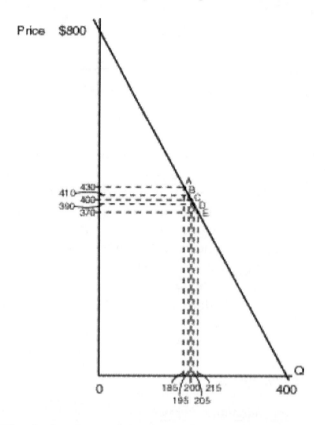

a.  What is the slope of the demand curve for sofas? _____

b.  What is the elasticity between points A and B? _____

c.  What is the elasticity between points B and D? _____

d.  What is the elasticity between points D and E? _____

e.  In general, what happens to elasticity as quantity increases along a straight-line demand curve? Which part of the demand curve is elastic? Which part is inelastic? Explain. _____

    _____

    _____

    _____

### E.  Advanced Critical Thinking

BizExpress Airlines of Alberta must decide on a pricing policy for flights between Calgary and Edmonton. It has two types of travellers—business and leisure passengers—whose demand curves are $D_B$ and $D_L$, respectively.

| | Business travellers | | Leisure travellers |
| --- | --- | --- | --- |
| Price | $D_B$ quantity demanded | Price | $D_L$ quantity demanded |
| $400 | 200 | $400 | 0 |
| $300 | 300 | $300 | 100 |
| $200 | 400 | $200 | 300 |
| $100 | 500 | $100 | 500 |

1.  If BizExpress Airlines' goal is to maximize total revenue, and it has enough seats to satisfy all of the demand, what price should it charge business travellers? What about leisure travellers? Explain. Do airlines actually behave this way? How can an airline charge two different prices for essentially the same product (how do they separate the two markets)?

\
\
\
\
\

2.  Provide some other examples of real-world price discrimination—charging different prices to different people for the same product—based on differences in the price elasticity of demand between two (or more) groups of consumers.

\
\
\
\

## III.    Solutions

### A.  True/False Questions

1.    T
2.    T
3.    F; a normal good has an income elasticity greater than zero.
4.    F; necessities tend to have inelastic demand curves.
5.    T

6.    F; the major problem is inelastic demand, so that increased supply lowers total revenues.

7.    T

8.    T

9.    F; the supply of land overlooking the Niagara River is highly inelastic because it is almost impossible to produce more of it.

10.    F; if elasticity is less than one (including zero), then total revenue will move in the same direction as price. If elasticity is zero, then quantity does not change, and total revenue will change in proportion to the change in price.

## B.  Multiple-Choice Questions

| | | | | |
|---|---|---|---|---|
| 1. c | 5. d | 9. a | 13. c | 17. c |
| 2. c | 6. a | 10. a | 14. a | 18. a |
| 3. d | 7. b | 11. b | 15. a | 19. d |
| 4. d | 8. b | 12. b | 16. b | 20. b |

## C.  Short-Answer Questions

1.  Goods are not likely to have constant income elasticity's over all income ranges. Many products are normal goods initially, but as income rises, they often become inferior goods as people switch to more upscale products. For example, a mid-priced automobile tends to have fairly high income elasticity for most people, but above a certain income level, the income elasticity actually becomes negative, as people substitute more expensive automobiles for the mid-priced models. Even a luxury model could be an inferior good for some very high-income consumers.

2.  a.    False. A 10% increase in the price of fuel reduces the volume of fuel consumed by 2.5% (= 0.25 × 10%) in the short run and 6.4% (= 0.64 × 10%) in the long run.

    b.    The first part of the statement is correct. The income elasticity's suggest that an increase in the consumer's income increases the demand for fuel by 4% (= 0.4 × 10%) in the short run and by 10% (= 1.0 × 10%) in the long run. The second part, however, is false. Fuel is a normal good because income elasticity's are positive.

## D.  Practice Problems

1.  a.

| Price | Quantity of tickets demanded/day | Total revenue | % change in price | % change in quantity | Elasticity |
|-------|--------------|---------------|-------------------|----------------------|------------|
| $0 | 1200 | $0 | 200% | 13% | 0.07 |
| $1 | 1050 | $1050 | 67% | 15% | 0.22 |
| $2 | 900 | $1800 | 40% | 18% | 0.45 |
| $3 | 750 | $2250 | 29% | 22% | 0.76 |
| $4 | 600 | $2400 | 22% | 29% | 1.32 |
| $5 | 450 | $2250 | 18% | 40% | 2.22 |
| $6 | 300 | $1800 | 15% | 67% | 4.47 |
| $7 | 150 | $1050 | 13% | 200% | 15.38 |
| $8 | 0 | $0 | | | |

b.  The zoo should leave the price as it is. The demand is price elastic upwards, so if the zoo increased price, quantity demanded would fall more than enough to compensate for the increase, and total revenue would actually fall. The zoo is already gathering as much total revenue as it can, given its attractiveness to consumers; if it is to pay for itself, either costs must be cut, its attractiveness must be increased, or both.

2.  a.  The slope of the demand curve for sofas is –2.0. Remember: Slope = rise/run = $\Delta$price/$\Delta$quantity, for any two points on this straight-line or constant slope demand curve. Even the end points will work: 800/400 = 2.

b.  The elasticity between points A and B is 1.1. $\Delta$quantity/quantity ÷ $\Delta$price/price = 10/190 ÷ 20/420.

c.  The elasticity between points B and D is 1.0. $\Delta$quantity/quantity ÷ $\Delta$price/price = 10/200 ÷ 20/400.

d.  The elasticity between points D and E is 0.9. $\Delta$quantity/quantity ÷ $\Delta$price/price = 10/210 ÷ 20/380.

e.  Elasticity falls as quantity increases along the straight-line demand curve. The upper part of the demand curve is always elastic, and the lower part is always inelastic. To see how this happens, consider points A, B, C, and D along the demand curve in the previous figure. Even though price and quantity change by constant amounts, the percentage changes also depend on the *levels* of price and quantity, which vary as we move along the demand curve. All straight-line demand curves behave this way: as price declines and quantity increases (down the demand curve), the elasticity declines, and as price increases and quantity declines (up the demand curve), elasticity increases.

## E.  Advanced Critical Thinking

1.  BizExpress Airlines should sell 300 business tickets at $300 each, for total revenues of $90 000. It should sell 300 leisure tickets at $200 each, for total revenues of $60 000 from leisure travellers. This will maximize revenues from both groups. Of course the airline should make sure that it has enough seats first, so that it does not sell seats for $200 that it could have sold for $300 to business travellers. Airlines separate the leisure and business markets through restrictions such as advance purchase and Saturday-night layover requirements that business travellers are generally unwilling to meet. Leisure travellers, whose demand tends to be relatively elastic, are generally more willing than business travellers to accept such restrictions in order to get a low fare.

2.  Any example of a product that is sold for different prices to different groups of people would work here, as long as the price differentials are not due to differences in cost of production. For example, senior citizen or student discounts for movie tickets or restaurants are used to lower the price for those people with higher elasticity of demand without cutting the price for everyone. Another example is "early bird" specials that restaurants use to cut the price for those who are willing to eat at a less popular time.

# CHAPTER 6  Supply, Demand, and Government Policies

## I. Chapter Overview

### A. Context and Purpose

To provide a transition from the basics of supply and demand into the extended supply-and-demand discussion, this chapter broadens the analysis of supply and demand to include the role of government in a mixed market economy. In exploring the role of government, Chapter 6 considers the effects of price controls such as minimum-wage and rent-control laws. It also deals with questions of tax incidence; that is, who actually pays various taxes.

### A. Helpful Hints

1. *Price ceilings and floors matter only if they are binding.* Remember that not all price ceilings and floors cause disturbances in markets. A price ceiling causes shortages only if it is *below* the equilibrium price (and is enforced). A ceiling, or maximum price, that is above the equilibrium price cannot prevent the market from reaching equilibrium. Similarly, a price floor causes surpluses only if it is *above* the equilibrium price and it is enforced. A price floor set below the equilibrium price will not prevent the market from reaching equilibrium.

2. *Taxes cause vertical shifts.* Even though economists normally look at supply-and-demand shifts in terms of left and right, it is useful in the case of tax incidence to look at the vertical shifts. A tax on buyers causes a vertical shift down in the demand curve that is just equal to the tax. For quantity demanded to stay the same, price must fall by the full amount of the tax that the buyer must pay. A tax on sellers causes a vertical shift up the price axis in the supply curve just equal to the tax. For quantity supplied to stay the same, price must increase by the full amount of the tax that the seller must pay.

3. *Taxes on buyers and taxes on sellers are equivalent.* Consider the case of a tax imposed in a market in which neither supply nor demand is totally elastic or totally inelastic. Although a tax on buyers shifts the demand curve, and a tax on sellers shifts the supply curve, the end result of either tax is reduced quantity sold, a higher price paid by buyers, and a lower price received by sellers. The difference between the prices paid and received is the tax, which introduces a wedge between buyers and sellers. Politically, it sometimes makes sense to switch a tax from buyers to sellers, or vice versa, but economically, it makes no sense: the result is the same.

For example Employment Insurance taxes by law are split 42–58% between workers and employers, but the tax incidence is determined by the market, after supply and demand shift and wages adjust.

## II.  Self-Testing Challenges

### A.  True/False Questions

_____1.    A price ceiling above equilibrium tends to cause shortages.

_____2.    A price floor above equilibrium tends to cause surpluses.

_____3.    A tax levied on buyers of a good or service shifts the demand curve up.

_____4.    A tax levied on sellers of a good or service shifts the supply curve up.

_____5.    A $1 per unit tax on sellers generally will raise price by $1.

_____6.    A $5 per unit tax on buyers generally will lower the equilibrium price by less than $5.

_____7.    A binding price ceiling on a competitive market causes a shortage in the market, and sellers must ration the scarce good among a large number of potential buyers.

_____8.    A $1 per unit tax on sellers is economically equivalent to a $1 per unit tax on buyers, except that the tax on sellers is more equitable for low-income buyers.

_____9.    Rent controls are least likely to cause large shortages of housing if the supply of housing is inelastic.

_____10.   The burden of a tax always falls on the side of the market with the smaller price elasticity.

### B.  Multiple-Choice Questions

1.   Which of the following describes the shift caused by a $500-per-automobile pollution tax on the manufacturers?
    a.   demand curve down by $500.
    b.   demand curve up by $500.
    c.   supply curve up by $500.
    d.   supply curve down by $500.

2. Which one of the following describes when a tax is **MOST** likely to be paid by the seller?
   a. when supply and demand are elastic
   b. when supply and demand are inelastic
   c. when demand is elastic and supply is inelastic
   d. when demand is inelastic and supply is elastic

3. Which one of the following is caused by a binding price ceiling?
   a. shortages
   b. excess supply
   c. quantity supplied greater than quantity demanded
   d. competition among buyers, driving price up to equilibrium

4. Which one of the following would **NOT** be predicted to result if the government impose a ceiling on the price of rental accommodation that is lower than the market equilibrium price??
   a. A shortage of rental units would develop.
   b. The existing stock of rental units would deteriorate.
   c. Those who obtain rental units at the controlled price would benefit.
   d. Construction of new rental accommodation would be encouraged.

5. Which one of the following describes when a tax would be split equally between buyers and sellers?
   a. when supply and demand are equal
   b. when supply and demand have equal elasticities
   c. when supply has a zero elasticity and demand has an infinite elasticity
   d. when supply has an infinite elasticity and demand has a zero elasticity.

6. Which one of the following will occur if the Government of Alberta imposes a $4 recycling fee on the buyer whenever a new tire is sold?
   a. It will move the demand curve down by $4.
   b. It will move the demand curve up by $ 4.
   c. It will move the supply curve up by $ 4.
   d. It will move the supply curve down by $ 4.

7. Which one of the following describes who will bear the burden of a sales tax imposed on a commodity with perfectly inelastic supply?
   a. It will be borne mostly by sellers.
   b. It will be borne completely by sellers.
   c. It will be borne mostly by buyers.
   d. It will be borne completely by buyers.

8. Which one of the following describes what economists mean when they say that a tax introduces a wedge in a market?
   a. It wedges money away from buyers.
   b. It wedges money away from sellers.
   c. It creates a wedge between the new and old equilibrium prices.
   d. It introduces a wedge between the price paid by the buyer and that received by the seller.

9. All else equal, which one of the following describes conditions under which a binding price ceiling will cause greater shortages?
   a. if both supply and demand are inelastic
   b. if both supply and demand are elastic
   c. if supply is elastic, but demand is inelastic
   d. if supply is inelastic, but demand is elastic

10. Which one of the following is a good way to distinguish shortage from scarcity?
    a. A shortage can be eliminated by raising price, but scarcity cannot be eliminated.
    b. Shortages result from price controls, but scarcity results from sellers holding back output.
    c. A shortage means that people cannot have all that they want at a zero price; scarcity means that people cannot have all they want at any price.
    d. At a high enough price, there is no scarcity, but shortages continue to exist even at high prices.

11. If the price of a commodity does not change after the government levies a sales tax on it, which one of the following is true?
    a. Supply of the commodity is more elastic than its demand.
    b. Demand for the commodity is more elastic than its supply.
    c. Supply of the commodity is perfectly elastic.
    d. Demand for the commodity is perfectly elastic.

12. All else equal, which one of the following describes when a binding price floor will cause **LESS** of a surplus?
    a. if both supply and demand are inelastic.
    b. if both supply and demand are elastic.
    c. if supply is elastic, but demand is inelastic.
    d. if supply is inelastic, but demand is elastic.

13. Which of the following statements about minimum-wage legislation is correct?
    a.  effective only if the minimum wage is set below the market equilibrium wage
    b.  has no effect on the quantity of labour hired
    c.  is a price floor that creates unemployment
    d.  is a price ceiling that creates a shortage of workers

14. Which one of the following will, in effect, occur with an increase in the demand in a market with a binding price ceiling?
    a.  an increase the quantities bought and sold
    b.  a decrease the quantities bought and sold
    c.  no alteration of the quantities bought and sold
    d.  an increase the amount of shortage

### C. Short-Answer Questions

1.    The Employment Insurance (EI) contribution may be viewed as a tax on labour. In 2006, the EI rate was approximately 5% of gross income (subject to a contribution ceiling of $39 000), comprised of 2.1% (or 42% of the tax) contributed by employees and 2.9% (or 58% of the tax) contributed by employers. In other words, employers pay 1.4 times the employee rate. Suppose that conflicting pieces of legislation before Parliament would change the statutory or legal burden of the tax for a variety of alleged efficiency and equity reasons. One group would like to place the entire tax on employees, in order to provide an incentive for employers to create more jobs. An opposing group would like to place the entire tax on employers, in order to help workers who are facing a reduced standard of living.

Employment Insurance Taxes

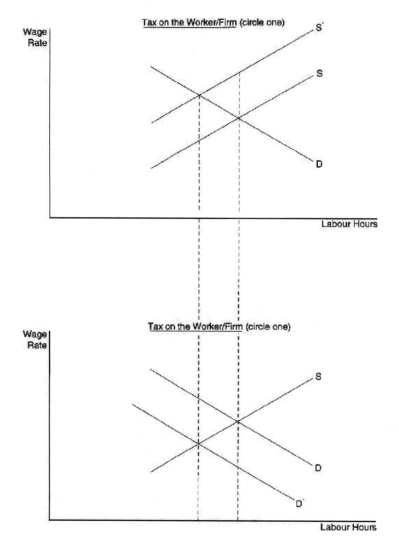

a. Show graphically the effects of the two proposals. Identify which curve shifts in each case (labour supply or demand for labour) by circling the appropriate response (worker or firm) in the subtitle above each diagram. On both diagrams, label the original wage as $W_e$ and the equilibrium quantity of labour hired as $L_e$. Label the wage actually received by the workers (after the tax) as $W_w$. Label the wage actually paid (after a tax) by the firms as $W_f$. Label the resulting tax wedge between supply and demand. Show the effect on employment (number of hours of labour hired) as $L_1$.

b. What will happen to wages if the tax is levied against the employers? What if the tax is levied against the employees? What about employment (compare the results of the two proposals in terms of the effect on equilibrium hours worked)?

_____

_____

_____

c. Who are the winners and who are the losers (if any) if either of these proposals is enacted? Explain. _____

_____

_____

_____

2. Suppose that crude oil prices skyrocket because of a simultaneous failure in the Alberta oil patch and increased tension in the Middle East. As a result, gasoline prices rise by 50%. Parliament caves in to political pressure and places a 6-month price ceiling on gasoline at the previous year's level.

a. What will be the effect on quantity demanded of rolling back gasoline prices? Explain how this could happen. _____

_____

_____

_____

b. What will be the effect on quantity supplied of rolling back gasoline prices? Explain.

_____

_____

_____

c. What will be the overall effect of this price ceiling?

_____

_____

_____

_____

3.    Minimum-wage laws dictate the lowest wage that employers must pay their employees. Such laws are enacted when policymakers believe that the market wage rate is unfair to workers, and their introduction is viewed as one way to raise the income of the working poor. How can the benefits received and the costs incurred of a minimum-wage law be measured? Should policymakers use minimum-wage laws as a tool to raise the income of the working poor and increase society's overall level of welfare?

_____

_____

_____

_____

## D.  Practice Problems

Use the table to answer the questions below. Note that $Q_D$ is the initial quantity demanded and $Q_S$ is the initial quantity supplied.

### The Market for Widgets

| Price | $Q_D$ | $Q_S$ | $Q_{S'}$ | $Q_{D'}$ |
|---|---|---|---|---|
| $1.00 | 1000 | 0 | 0 | 800 |
| $1.50 | 900 | 100 | 0 | 700 |
| $2.00 | 800 | 200 | 0 | 600 |
| $2.50 | 700 | 300 | 100 | 500 |
| $3.00 | 600 | 400 | 200 | 400 |
| $3.50 | 500 | 500 | 300 | 300 |
| $4.00 | 400 | 600 | 400 | 200 |
| $4.50 | 300 | 700 | 500 | 100 |
| $5.00 | 200 | 800 | 600 | 0 |

1.  What are the initial equilibrium price and quantity?    $P_1 = \$$ ____ ; $Q_{1=}$ _____

2.  Suppose that the provincial government imposes a new $1 per unit tax on the sellers of widgets. The tax shifts the supply schedule from the original $Q_S$ to the new $Q_{S'}$.

    a.  The new equilibrium price and quantity are:    $P_2 = \$$ ____ ; $Q_{2=}$ _____

    b.  How much of the $1 tax is borne by the seller? _____

    c.  How much of the tax is borne by the buyer? _____

d.  Show graphically the old and new equilibria, labelling the original supply as S and the new supply as S₁. Label clearly the vertical shift in supply and the change in price and quantity as a result of the tax.

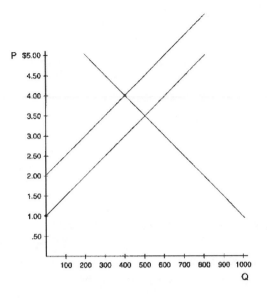

3.  Suppose Ms. Malak, a provincial MLA in whose riding several widget factories are located, has proposed a new piece of legislation that would change the widget tax. Her bill would switch the tax from the seller to the buyer, under the rationale that the widget makers are losing money and cannot afford to pay the tax. If the bill passes the legislature, quantities supplied will change back from $Q_{S'}$ to $Q_S$, and quantities demanded will change from $Q_D$ to $Q_{D'}$.

a.  The new equilibrium price and quantity are:    $P_3 = \$\_\_\_\_$ ; $Q_3 = \_\_\_\_$

b.  How much of the $1 tax is borne by the seller?_____

c.  How much of the tax is borne by the buyer?_____

d.  Did the new legislation help the sellers? Why or why not?

_____

_____

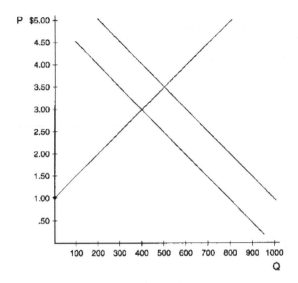

e.  Show graphically the original (pre-tax) equilibrium and the new equilibrium, labelling the original demand as D and the new demand as D₁. Label clearly the vertical shift in demand and the change in price and quantity as a result of the tax.

4.  Suppose the legislature has voted to abolish the widget tax; therefore price and quantity have returned to the original equilibrium. To help the widget makers in her province, Ms. Malak has proposed legislation that would enact a price floor of $4 in the market for widgets.

   a.  As a result of her legislation:
       (i) The price will be $ _____.
       (ii) Quantity supplied will be $Q_S = $_____.
       (iii) Quantity demanded will be $Q_D = $_____.
       (iv) And there will be (choose one)
               a) a shortage
               b) a surplus
               c) neither of the above
           _____ of _____.
       (v) The actual quantity sold will be_____.

   b.  Who is helped and who is hurt by the price floors?

       _____
       _____
       _____
       _____

c.  If the price floor had been enacted while the $1 tax on sellers was already in effect, what would have happened to price and quantity? Would there have been a shortage or surplus? _____

_____

_____

_____

5.  Suppose that pressure from consumer groups leads to a reduction in the price floor from $4 to $3.

a.  With the new price floor (and no tax), the price will be $ _____, quantity supplied will be $Q_S =$ _____, and the quantity demanded will be $Q_D =$ _____.

b.  What is the effect of the new price floor at $3? Explain. _____

_____

_____

_____

c.  Show graphically the effects of a price floor of $4 and $3, labelling clearly the equilibrium price and quantity, and any shortages or surpluses that result in each case. Label the $4 price floor as $P_{F1}$ and the $3 price floor as $P_{F2}$.

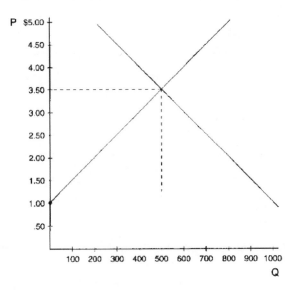

6.  If the government had enacted a $3 price ceiling rather than a price floor, the result would have been: _____

_____

_____

_____

### E.  Advanced Critical Thinking

"Granny stunned by $400 rent hike," screamed the headlines of the *Edmonton Journal* on April 27, 2007. "Antonina Bielancska, 86, simply threw up her arms and said, 'Too much!'" Mrs. Bielancska had recently received a notice advising her that the monthly rent on her modest apartment would increase by $400 or 62%. The Letters to the Editor pages of Edmonton's newspapers were flooded with letters from outraged citizens. They suggested that it was simply landlords' greed and not the flawed logic of economics and the concept of scarcity that prevented everyone from having affordable housing. The outraged citizens provided statistics showing that the number of dwellings and number of families were roughly equal, which they felt provided proof that there was not a scarcity of housing. Consequently, the citizens argued for rent controls as a solution to the housing crisis in Edmonton. What's wrong with this thinking? Is it valid to argue that scarcity does not exist just by counting the number of dwellings? Are dwellings freely available at zero price? Suppose that rent controls forced the rent on a $1,050 apartment down to $650 per month. What would happen to new construction? To maintenance on existing apartments? What would happen to the quantity demanded? Write an economist's response to these critics of mainstream economics.

_____

_____

_____

_____

_____

_____

## III.  Solutions

### A.  True/False Questions

1. F; a ceiling (maximum price) above equilibrium has no effect, because the market will reach equilibrium before it reaches the legal maximum price.
2. T
3. F; a tax on buyers reduces their willingness to buy (the quantity demanded) at each price; which means that demand falls (shifts down).
4. T
5. F; normally demand has some nonzero elasticity that prevents sellers from passing the entire tax along to the buyer; price will normally go up, but by less than $1.
6. T
7. T
8. F; the two taxes are equivalent, even in terms of equity.
9. T
10. T

## B.  Multiple-Choice Questions

| | | | |
|---|---|---|---|
| 1. c | 5. b | 9. b | 13. c |
| 2. c | 6. a | 10. a | 14. c |
| 3. a | 7. d | 11. d | |
| 4. d | 8. d | 12. a | |

## C.  Short-Answer Questions

1.     a.     and b. (See the following graph.)

### Employment Insurance Contribution (Taxes)

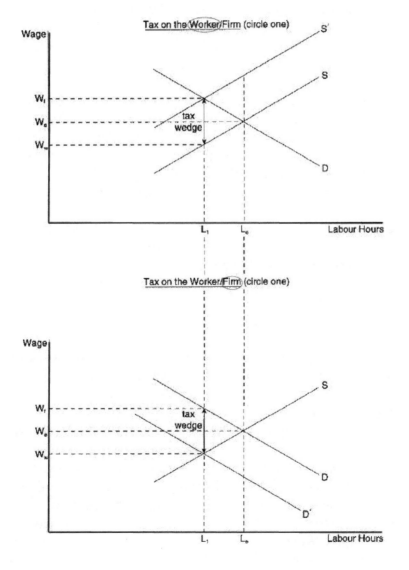

c.  Neither the employers nor the employees gain or lose as a result of a change in the legal burden of the Employment Insurance contribution. The actual tax incidence depends on the relative elasticities of the supply of and demand for labour. A payroll tax like Employment Insurance contribution is a tax on the labour market. How the tax burden is actually allocated between workers and employers is determined by the market rather than by government. Of course, there may be political winners or losers. Politicians who supported one of these proposals would gain or lose, depending upon the popularity of the proposal.

2.    a.  When government rolls back gasoline prices, one result is an increase in quantity demanded. Buyers who would have carpooled or cut back on leisure driving, or taken mass transit will not make the effort when the price of gasoline is reduced. People respond to economic incentives.

b.  Sellers will respond to the lower gasoline prices by cutting back on the production of gasoline. To some extent, they will switch from gasoline production to other petroleum products. They will also cut back on petroleum production until the price goes back up by capping existing wells. If they expect the lower prices to continue, they will even cut back on exploration for new oil reserves.

d.  The result would be a shortage of gasoline, evidenced by long lines at gasoline stations. Buyers would try to get around the controls by offering bribes under the table to sellers. Because price will no longer work to ration scarce gasoline, the government may enact a rationing system to deal with the shortage. Otherwise, long waits may serve as the rationing device for gasoline.

3.    It is difficult to measure the benefits and costs associated with the enactment of minimum-wage laws. Advocates of such laws point out that workers who earn the minimum wage can afford only a meager standard of living. One objective, therefore, is to help reduce the level of poverty among the working poor. However, opponents of such measures point to the fact that using minimum wage to fight poverty results in unemployment, encourages teenagers to drop out of school, and prevents some unskilled workers from getting the on-the-job training they need. The greatest impact of such laws is on the market for teenage labour, because teenagers are among the least skilled and least experienced members of the labour force. Relatively few of them are heads of households trying to help their families escape poverty. Minimum-wage laws, therefore, may raise the income of some workers, but they also cause other workers to be unemployed. It is not possible to make some workers better off without making others worse off. Policymakers should perhaps look for alternatives

to the minimum-wage laws. Wage subsidies, for example, raise the living standards of the working poor, without discouraging firms from hiring them.

## D. Practice Problems

1. $P_1 = \$3.50$; $Q_1 = 500$

2. a. $P_2 = \$4$; $Q_2 = 400$

   b. $0.50

   c. $0.50

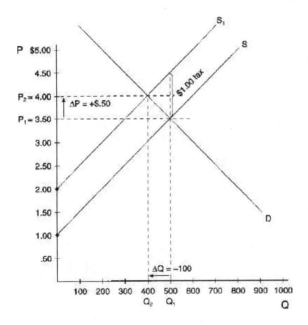

3. a. $P_3 = \$3$; $Q_3 = 400$.

   b. $0.50

   c. $0.50

d.  No. The change in the legal burden did not help either the buyers or the sellers. The actual tax incidence after the market adjusts is identical. With either version of the tax, the quantity is 400 and buyers end up paying a total of $4 per widget, with sellers receiving only $3. The $1 gap is the tax that goes to the government. The only thing that changes is who actually writes the cheque to the government.

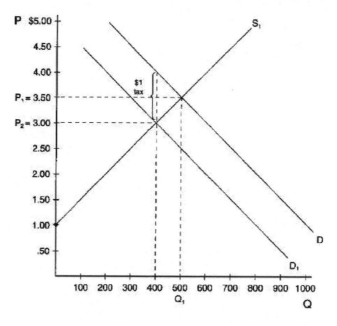

4.  a.    As a result of her legislation:

(i) The price will be P = $4.

(ii) Quantity supplied will be Q_S = 600.

(iii) Quantity demanded will be Q_D = 400.

(iv) And there will be a (surplus) of 200.

(v) The actual quantity sold will be 400.

b.  Consumers are hurt by the price floor because they must pay an additional $0.50 per widget. Some sellers benefit by receiving higher prices for their product, but others are made worse off because they cannot find a market for all that they produce at $4.

c.  With a $1 tax on sellers, the price already would have been at $4, so the floor would have had no effect on either price or quantity. It simply would have mandated a price that already existed. The price would stay at $4 and the quantity at 400. The market would clear, so there would be neither a shortage nor a surplus.

5.  a.  With the new price floor, the price will be $3.50, quantity supplied will be $Q_{S} = 500$, and the quantity demanded will be $Q_D = 500$.

    b.  The new price floor is below the equilibrium price; therefore, it will have no effect on either price or quantity.

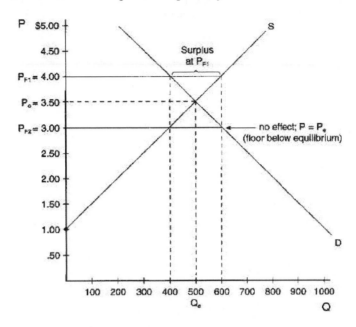

6.  A shortage, or excess demand, of 200 units, because quantity demanded at $3 is 600, which is greater than the quantity supplied of 400.

## E.  Advanced Critical Thinking

Scarcity means that people cannot have everything they want at a zero price. People respond to economic incentives. If rent controls reduce the price of housing below the equilibrium level, quantity demanded will rise as people respond. Some buyers will choose to move into more spacious or luxurious housing; others may choose to move out of the family home and live on their own. All else equal, more people will also want to move into the area if housing is cheaper. On the supply side, however, nothing has happened to make more housing available to meet the demand. On the contrary, the seller (landlord) has an incentive to supply less housing. It may be tempting to think of the supply of housing as fixed; however, this view is not correct. Consider the extreme case: is it realistic to think that at a zero price, housing would still be available? Of course not! Particularly in the long run, the market will respond to below-equilibrium rents by building fewer housing units and allowing existing housing to deteriorate without repair or replacement. The stock of housing will shrink as quantity supplied responds to the lower price. It will benefit those buyers who are lucky enough to get housing at a reduced price. However, it will hurt those buyers who cannot get housing, even though they were willing to pay a higher price. It will also hurt sellers in general. The old saying is true: there really are no free lunches (or apartments).

# 7 Consumers, Producers, and the Efficiency of Markets

## I. Chapter Overview

### A. Context and Purpose

Earlier chapters provided an overview of supply and demand as a way to set prices and determine how much to produce. This chapter looks at the question of whether or not supply and demand produce an outcome that is desirable from the standpoint of society. That is, does the market give people the maximum possible social well-being? The following two chapters will apply these results to policy questions regarding taxation and trade with other countries. In an economic sense, do people really know what's good for them? This section of three chapters will help to find the answers.

### A. Helpful Hints

1. *Consumer surplus is the amount that a buyer is willing to pay for a good minus the amount actually paid.* That is, consumer surplus is the additional amount that the buyer would have willingly paid beyond the market price that he or she actually paid to get the product. Because the demand curve measures willingness to pay, the area under the demand curve but above the market price represents consumer surplus. As an example, suppose that Parminder is looking for cheap transportation; he will pay up to $3000 for a reliable used car that gets decent mileage. Luckily for Parminder, reliable, if not beautiful, cars are available for $2000. If Parminder buys at the market price of $2000, he will gain a consumer surplus of $1000 ($3000–$2000).

2. *Producer surplus, the mirror image of consumer surplus, is the amount a seller is paid, minus the cost of production.* That is, producer surplus is the excess that the seller receives beyond his or her opportunity cost of providing the good or service. As an example, suppose that Gladys is interested in selling her old car in order to buy a newer one. She is willing to unload it for $500, but luckily for her, the market values the car at $2000. If Gladys sells it, she will earn a producer surplus of $1500 ($2000–$500). The market price of $2000 was determined by the interaction of the marginal buyer (i.e., the buyer who would leave the market first if the price were any higher) and the marginal seller (i.e., the seller who would leave the market first if the price were any lower), each of whom valued the car at $2000.

3. *Efficiency is the property of a resource allocation that maximizes the total surplus received by all members of society.* In the used-car example above, the total surplus is $2500 ($1000 + $1500).

4. *Equity refers to the fairness of the distribution of well-being among the members of society, that is, the various buyers and sellers.* It requires normative judgments that go beyond positive economics.

5. *Market failure refers to inefficient allocation of resources* and may occur where market power (the ability of a single buyer or seller, or a small group of them, to influence the price) or externalities (costs and benefits borne by those who are not participants in the market) are present.

6. *A change in price alone simply reallocates the total surplus between consumers and producers.* It is very tempting to argue that price is directly responsible for differences in social welfare. For example, when sellers take advantage of inelastic demand to raise price, this directly lowers social welfare. Only if the quantity sold changes does the total surplus change. The used car example demonstrates that the total surplus can remain the same even when consumer surplus is either maximized or eliminated, as long as there is an offsetting change in producer surplus. People may feel that a certain outcome is unfair, but that is a separate question from the efficiency resulting from maximizing total welfare.

7. *Remember that exchanges are voluntary.* Market exchanges make both the buyer and the seller better off because nobody is forced to trade if they do not want to. The more voluntary exchanges that occur, the more gains from trade there are.

## II. Self-Testing Challenges

### A. True/False Questions

_____1. Consumer surplus measures the benefit that buyers receive from a good as the buyers themselves perceive it.

_____2. Producer surplus refers to unsold inventories, due to a market price above equilibrium.

_____3. When free markets work effectively, they maximize the sum of consumer and producer surplus.

_____4. An efficient allocation of resources is one that maximizes the fairness of the outcome.

____5.     Equity and efficiency are two economic goals that typically go together—usually an efficient outcome is an equitable outcome.

____6.     Policymakers always want to respect the preferences of buyers in order to promote the economic well-being of society.

____7.     The major advantage of using supply and demand to allocate resources is the inherent fairness of the outcome.

____8.     Efficiency is an objective goal that can be judged on strictly positive grounds, but equity involves normative judgments that go beyond economics and delve into the realm of political philosophy.

____9.     Competitive markets are efficient in that they allocate the demand for goods to the sellers who can produce them at the least cost, and they allocate the supply of goods to the buyers who value them most highly.

____10.    From the standpoint of society, the willingness of drug addicts to pay a high price for heroin is a good measure of the buyers' benefit, and their consumer surplus is a good measure of economic well-being

## B.  Multiple-Choice Questions

1.     Which one of the following is maximized for economic efficiency?
    a.  total economic well-being
    b.  consumer surplus
    c.  producer surplus
    d.  total equity

2.     Which one of the following is producer surplus?
    a.  total cost to the sellers of participating in the market
    b.  difference between what the consumer offered and the actual price paid
    c.  inventories that could not be sold at the market price

3.     Which one of the following is the total economic well-being to society?
    a.  consumer surplus less the producer surplus
    b.  sum of consumer surplus plus producer surplus
    c.  ratio of consumer surplus to producer surplus

4.  Which one of the following is consumer surplus?
    a.  unused products that may be sold at auction
    b.  the quantity of a good the consumer gets but did not have to pay for
    c.  the amount that the consumer would have paid in excess of the actual price
    d.  the total value of a good to a consumer

5.  Which one of the following defines the term 'market failure'?
    a.  income distribution is not equitable
    b.  externalities are present in the economy
    c.  the best attainable outcome has not been achieved
    d.  the economy is not in equilibrium

6.  Which choice below would be the most likely if less than the market's equilibrium quantity of diet colas was produced?
    a.  resources must have had a higher valued alternative use producing something else
    b.  consumer surplus will be higher than otherwise would be the case
    c.  producer surplus will be higher than otherwise would be the case

7.  Suppose that a technological breakthrough occurs in the production of cell phones. All else equal, the equilibrium price of cell phones will _____, the equilibrium quantity of cell phones sold will _____, consumer surplus will _____, and producer surplus will _____.
    a.  increase, decrease, increase, decrease
    b.  decrease, decrease, decrease, increase
    c.  decrease, decrease, increase, increase
    d.  decrease, increase, increase, increase

Use the following information to answer questions 8–10. Suppose that Cameron owns a classic Fender guitar. He has lost interest in it, and so it is worth only $50 to him. His friend, Juan, loves the guitar and would be willing to pay as much as $950 for it.

8.  Which one of the following describes what would happen to social welfare if Cameron sells his guitar for $100?
    a.  Social welfare decreases by $400.
    b.  Social welfare remains unchanged.
    c.  Social welfare rises by $50.
    d.  It turns out that Juan is not the only friend who is interested in the guitar.

9. Ben also likes it and would pay $500, Sanam would pay $1200, and Bill would actually pay $2000! Which one of the following describes what Cameron should do in order to maximize this small society's well-being?
   a. He should sell the guitar to Juan, because Juan was the first to offer to buy it, but only if Juan matches Bill's offer.
   b. He should sell the guitar to Juan, even if Juan does not match Bill's offer.
   c. He should sell the guitar to Bill, but only if Bill pays $2000.
   d. He should sell the guitar to Bill, even if Bill pays no more than the others.

10. Judith is willing to sell her homemade brownies for $15 per box. She sells them and realizes a producer surplus of $12 per box. Which of the following indicates, in order, Judith's cost per box, and her sale price per box?
    a. $15, $12
    b. $12, $15
    c. $12, $27
    d. $15, $27

11. Medical care is vital to society's survival. From society's standpoint, under which one of the following conditions should people increase their spending on health care?
    a. as long as anyone is sick
    b. as long as total benefit increases when people increase their spending
    c. as long total cost is less than total benefit
    d. as long as an extra dollar of health-care spending generates at least a dollar in added benefits

12. Is an auction socially inefficient, efficient, equitable, or inequitable?
    a. inefficient, because goods go to those with the most money, rather than to those who want them the most
    b. efficient, because it allocates the units of the product to the buyers who value them the most, as evidenced by their willingness to pay
    c. equitable, because it is only fair for goods to go to those who are willing to pay for them
    d. inequitable, because not everyone can afford to keep up with the bidding

13. The price of a new car is $25 000. Consumers will continue to buy additional cars until the consumer surplus from the last car purchased is at which one of the following points?
    a. zero
    b. $25 000
    c. maximized
    d. minimized

14. In the previous question, **auto producers** will continue to supply additional cars until the producer surplus from the last car produced is at which one of the following points?
    a. zero
    b. $20 000
    c. maximized
    d. minimized

15. As a matter of public policy, people are not allowed to sell their organs. Which one of the following is a reason some economists believe that there would be large benefits to allowing a free market in organs?
    a. The shortage of organs for transplant would disappear.
    b. Sellers of organs would be worst off with less cash in their pockets.
    c. Buyers of organs would be better off having the quantity of organs available.
    d. Such a market would lead to a non-efficient outcome.

16. Which one of the following arguments would economists generally make about restricting ticket scalping?
    a. It increases the audience for events.
    b. It deprives the government of tax revenue and wastes police time.
    c. It increases the efficiency of ticket distribution.
    d. It eliminates the unfair price discrepancies.

17. Which of the following statements best represents externalities?
    a. they cause wealth in a market to depend on more than just the value to the buyers and the cost to the sellers
    b. they are side effects of production or consumption passed on to a party other than the sellers and buyers in the market
    c. they are examples of market success

## C. Short-Answer Questions

1. Contrast the efficiency and equity goals in economic policymaking. How do they differ? _____

_____

_____

_____

2. Economists tend to see ticket scalping as an example of how markets reach efficient outcomes. Why? _____

_____

_____

_____

_____

_____

## D. Practice Problems

1.  There are five consumers looking for a particular used car in Farmville, Saskatchewan. Shayan is willing to pay $6000, Kathy would pay $5000, Fred would pay $4000, Gwen would pay $3000, and Camille would pay $2000. There are also five local dealers with cars that would satisfy the consumers: Bill's Beautiful Bargains has a car that cost Bill $6000, Al's Autos has one for which his opportunity cost was $5000, Cal's Classic Cars has one that cost $4000, Tim's Transportation has one that cost $3000, and Buy-A-Bomb has one that it is willing to sell for $2000. (Assume that all of the used cars are identical, except for the price charged.)

    a.  Plot the supply and demand diagrams for the used cars in the space below.

    b.  If the market moves to a single equilibrium price, how many autos will be sold, and at what price? Will this maximize efficiency? Explain.____

        _____

        _____

        _____

        _____

    c.  Label the consumer and producer surplus on your diagram. What is the dollar value of the consumer surplus? The producer surplus? The total surplus? Explain how the calculations were made.

        _____

        _____

        _____

        _____

    d.  It appears that each consumer could find a seller that would sell at a price that would coincide with the consumer's willingness to pay, if each buyer negotiated separately with a seller that matched his or her willingness to buy. For example, Bill is not very competitive, with a minimum price of $6000, but there is one buyer—Shayan—who would pay that much. Of course, for this to work, buyers and sellers would have to be unaware of the better options available elsewhere; otherwise, Shayan, for example, could do better buying from a lower-cost seller. Would it be more or less efficient for the buyers and sellers to be matched according to their willingness to buy and sell? (Hint: What would happen to total surplus, compared to the competitive solution?) _____

        _____

        _____

        _____

2.    a. Explain how the free market maximizes total surplus. What assumptions are required for this result to occur?

_____

_____

_____

   b. What happens to total surplus if production goes beyond the equilibrium? Explain. _____

_____

_____

   c. What happens to total surplus if production stops short of equilibrium? Explain._____

_____

_____

_____

3.    a. Will a price ceiling always make consumers better off? How?_____

_____

_____

_____

   b. Will a price floor always make producers better off? How? _____

_____

_____

_____

## E.  Advanced Critical Thinking

Some groups argue for legalization of currently illegal drugs—perhaps even cocaine and heroin. They argue that free markets are inherently more efficient than government edicts in allocating resources, and that there is also the issue of freedom involved. Evaluate their arguments. What is the case for legalizing at least some currently illegal, controlled substances? What are the arguments against legalization? Do markets operate efficiently in the case of such controlled substances? _____

_____

_____

_____

## III. Solutions

### A. True/False Questions

1. T
2. F; producer surplus refers to the difference between market price and sellers' costs of production.
3. T
4. F; an efficient allocation of resources is one that maximizes total surplus.
5. F; equity and efficiency often conflict, because there is no reason for the mechanism that maximizes total surplus to also distribute it fairly.
6. F; in most markets, but not always. In some cases, policymakers might choose not to respect the preferences of buyers. For instance, a cocaine addict is willing to pay a high price for cocaine, but from society's point of view the willingness to pay, and hence consumer surplus, is not a good measure of economic well-being.
7. F; the major advantage of using supply and demand to allocate resources is the *efficiency* of the outcome, although it may be considered unfair.
8. T
9. T
10. F; because society believes that addicts do not look after their own best interests, neither their willingness to pay nor their consumer surplus are considered good measures.

### B. Multiple-Choice Questions

| | | | | |
|---|---|---|---|---|
| 1. a | 5. c | 9. d | 13. a | 17. b |
| 2. c | 6. c | 10. d | 14. a | |
| 3. b | 7. d | 11. d | 15. a | |
| 4. c | 8. d | 12. b | 16. b | |

### C. Short-Answer Questions

1. Efficiency means maximizing the total combined producer and consumer surplus from the market. It does not, however, guarantee any particular distribution of the resulting outcome. Efficiency is objectively measured as what is, but equity requires normative or value judgements about what ought to be.

2. If an economy is to allocate its scarce resources efficiently, goods must get to those consumers who value them most highly. Scalpers buy tickets to arts, entertainment, and sports events, and then resell them at a price above what they paid originally. By charging the highest prices the market will bear, scalpers help consumers with the greatest willingness to pay for the tickets to actually get them and, therefore, to increase the efficiency of ticket distribution.

## D.  Practice Problems

1. a.  Supply-and-demand diagrams for the used cars are plotted below.

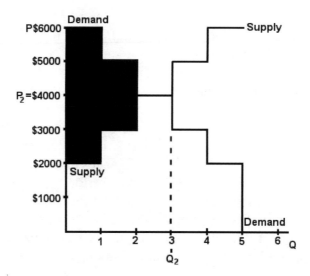

   b.  Market equilibrium would result in three cars sold at a price of $4000 each. It would leave out two buyers with low willingness to pay and two high-cost sellers, but it would maximize efficiency by maximizing total surplus (consumer surplus + producer surplus), as shown on the diagram.

   c.  The dollar value of consumer surplus is $3000 (Shayan gains $2000 at a price of $4000, and Kathy gains $1000 at that price). The producer surplus is also $3000 (Tim's gains $1000 at a price of $4000, and Buy-A-Bomb gains $2000). The total surplus is, therefore, $6000.

   d.  If the highest-cost seller sold to the highest-marginal-value consumer, and the lowest-cost seller sold to the consumer with the lowest marginal value, and so on, each auto would be sold and each consumer would have a car. However, it would be less efficient: there would be no consumer or producer surplus, because each buyer and seller would have broken even. Compared to the competitive solution, society would lose a $6000 total surplus.

2. a.  Free markets encourage the production of every good that adds more to benefits than it adds to cost. If decision makers take into account all of the social benefits and social costs of their actions when they choose, then their decisions will also maximize society's total surplus. This assumes that there is no market failure, due to, for example, externalities or concentration of market power.

b.  If production occurs beyond equilibrium, then the additional units will have marginal costs greater than the marginal benefits from their production, resulting in a net loss of social well-being, because total surplus is reduced from its level at equilibrium.

c.  Stopping short of equilibrium means that society is failing to produce some units of a good or service that have marginal benefits greater than the marginal cost. In this range, willingness to buy is higher than sellers cost of production, so society would gain from the additional output; that is, total surplus would rise.

3.  a.  Price ceilings will not always make consumers better off. If the supply curve is completely inelastic, a price ceiling will increase consumer surplus. If the demand is inelastic, price ceiling may result in a net loss of consumer surplus.

b.  Price floors will not always make producers better off. If the demand curve is perfectly inelastic, a price floor will increase producer surplus. If the supply is inelastic, a price floor may result in a net loss of producer surplus.

## E.  Advanced Critical Thinking

It is true that free markets tend to be efficient in maximizing economic efficiency, by ensuring, at least under competition, that the market will provide every unit of output that adds more to society's benefits than it adds to its costs. One can also make the case that people should have the freedom to decide for themselves what is good for them. However, the counterargument is that there are external costs involved with the production and use of illegal drugs. The buyers and sellers of illegal drugs do not bear all of the costs of their actions. Increased crime rates, declining neighbourhoods, health costs, and other social costs are ignored by those in the market. (Of course, some of the external costs are a result of the illegality of the drugs, rather than the drugs themselves.) Such externalities result in market failure, leading to overproduction of those goods that have external costs.

# 8 | Application: The Costs of Taxation

## I. Chapter Overview

### A. Context and Purpose

The previous chapter provided a foundation for welfare economics by looking at the net social gain from production at the competitive equilibrium. That chapter explained that maximizing society's total surplus requires production up to but not beyond the point at which the marginal benefit of another unit of output equals its marginal cost. This chapter applies that analysis to policy questions about the efficiency effects of taxation. Specifically, how does taxation distort behaviour and cause a deadweight loss to society in excess of the actual taxes paid?

### A. Helpful Hints

1.  *Deadweight loss of taxation arises because taxes introduce a wedge between the price paid by buyers and the price received by sellers.* The tax wedge decreases the quantity sold below the socially optimal level that would have resulted under the pre-tax competitive market. As a result, the tax costs the buyers and sellers more than the actual tax paid; it also costs them a loss of total surplus because of the distortion of behaviour that results in underproduction relative to the outcome of the pre-tax competitive market.

2.  *The size of deadweight loss depends on the elasticities of demand and supply.* As elasticity increases, the responsiveness to the incentive effect of taxation increases and, as a result, the deadweight loss will be greater. On a supply-and-demand diagram, the triangle of welfare loss is greater when the curves are more elastic.

3.  *Deadweight loss and tax revenues vary as tax rates change.* Deadweight loss actually changes more than proportionately when the tax rates change. Further, as tax rates rise, tax revenues first rise, then eventually fall as the tax reduces the quantity sold so much that even higher rates cannot raise additional revenues.

4.  *Taxes do more than raise revenue; they also influence people's behaviour.* Sometimes that is desirable, for example, when cigarette taxes are used to discourage smoking. Other times, however, the distortion caused by taxation is undesirable and represents the loss of well-being to society.

5.  *If taxes did not alter behaviour, there would be no net loss of well-being to society.* Even though taxpayers would be worse off in terms of the amount of the taxes paid, the recipients of those revenues would be better off, and the net effect would be zero, because the gains and losses would cancel each other out.

## II. Self-Testing Challenges

### A. True/False Questions

___1.    Higher tax rates always lead to higher tax revenues, although the outcome may be inefficient.

___2.    A tax that raises no tax revenue cannot have a deadweight loss.

___3.    If labour supply is fairly inelastic, then the deadweight loss associated with a labour tax will be small and not very distorting.

___4.    Taxes cause deadweight losses because they prevent buyers and sellers from realizing some of the gains from trade.

___5.    A subsidy (negative tax) tends to cause deadweight loss by encouraging overproduction of a good, beyond the point at which the marginal benefit equals the marginal cost to society.

___6.    If policymakers desire to minimize deadweight loss from taxation, they should tax goods and services that have relatively close substitutes.

___7.    The less elastic the supply and demand in a market, the less taxes will distort behaviour in that market, and the more likely it is that a tax hike will raise tax revenue.

___8.    Most economists agree that Canada would raise more revenue under the individual income tax if tax rates were lowered.

___9.    The greater the elasticities of demand and supply, the greater the deadweight loss of a tax.

___10.   A tax on producers tends to distort output decisions and result in higher deadweight losses than a tax on buyers.

## B. Multiple-Choice Questions

1.    Which one of the following is a reason that taxes cause deadweight losses?
   a.  because they reduce taxpayers' incomes
   b.  because they are used to support government programs, which are less valuable than private spending to society
   c.  because they prevent buyers and sellers from realizing some of the gains from trade
   d.  because they redistribute income from productive to unproductive members of society

Use the following information to answer questions 2 and 3.

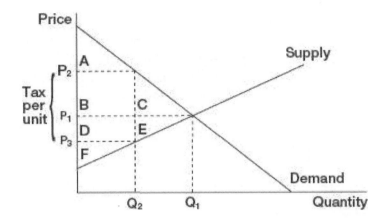

2.    If a tax is levied on *buyers* of the good, which one of the following is the price the sellers receive after tax and the deadweight loss to society?
   a.  $P_1$; A + B + D + F
   b.  $P_2$; C + E
   c.  $P_3$; B + D + C + E
   d.  $P_3$; C + E

3.    If a tax is levied on *sellers* of the good, which one of the following is the price buyers pay after tax and the deadweight loss to society?
   a.  $P_1$; A + B + D + F
   b.  $P_2$; C + E
   c.  $P_2$; B + D + C + E
   d.  $P_3$; C + E

4.    Which one of the following describes when deadweight loss from taxation is likely to be the **GREATEST?**
   a.  if supply is elastic and demand is inelastic
   b.  if both supply and demand are elastic
   c.  if supply is inelastic and demand is elastic
   d.  if both supply and demand are inelastic

5.  Which one of the following is **MORE** likely to increase the deadweight loss of income taxes on labour?
    a.  if workers have no control over their hours of work, because the work week is standardized
    b.  if retirement age is mandated by law or custom
    c.  if the underground economy becomes more widespread
    d.  if parliament shifts the legal burden of the income tax to the employer

6.  Suppose cigarette taxes are cut in order to reduce smuggling. Cigarette manufacturers argue that the tax revenue losses would be small because more cigarettes would be legally purchased. Anti-smoking groups argue that the revenue losses would be larger. Based on this information, which one of the following can be presumed?
    a.  anti-smoking groups believe that the demand for legally purchased cigarettes is less elastic than the manufacturers believe
    b.  anti-smoking groups believe that the demand for legally purchased cigarettes is more elastic than the manufacturers believe
    c.  anti-smoking groups believe that the supply of smuggled cigarettes is equal to what the manufacturers believe
    d.  anti-smoking groups believe that the supply of smuggled cigarettes is more elastic than the manufacturers believe

7.  Which one of the following taxes would be **LEAST** likely to result in a deadweight loss?
    a.  a tax on labour
    b.  a tax on housing
    c.  a tax on automobiles
    d.  a tax on the unimproved value of land

8.  Which one of the following **BEST** describes the implication of the Laffer Curve?
    a.  Policymakers should consider the relevant market elasticities.
    b.  Policymakers should consider whether a reduction in the tax rate would increase or decrease tax revenues.
    c.  Policymakers should consider whether raising taxes would discourage foreign investment.
    d.  Policymakers should consider whether lowering taxes would encourage immigration.

9.  Suppose that beer is taxed at a very low rate. Which one of the following describes what will happen to tax revenues if the government gradually increases the tax rate on beer?
    a.  revenues fall
    b.  revenues rise
    c.  revenues rise initially, then eventually fall
    d.  revenues fall initially, then eventually rise

10.  Which one of the following describes the effect of raising tax rates on deadweight loss?
  a.  Deadweight loss increases more than proportionately.
  b.  Deadweight loss increases less than proportionately.
  c.  Deadweight loss decreases less than proportionately.
  d.  Deadweight loss decreases more than proportionately.

11.  Imposing a sales tax on a product will _____ consumer surplus and _____ producer surplus.
  a.  decrease, increase
  b.  increase, decrease
  c.  decrease, decrease
  d.  increase, increase

Questions 12–15 refer to the graph below, which shows a market both before and after a tax.

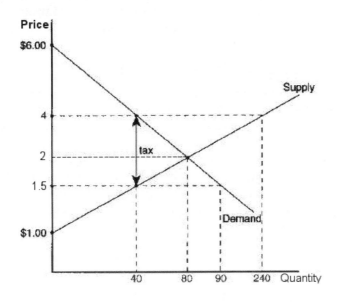

12.  Which one of the following describes the effect the tax will have on output?
  a.  Output will increase from 40 to 80.
  b.  Output will increase from 80 to 90.
  c.  Output will decrease from 80 to 40.
  d.  Output will decrease from 90 to 40.

13.  Which one of the following will be the deadweight loss from the tax?
  a.  $50
  b.  $80
  c.  $100
  d.  $150

14. Which one of the following describes the output if the tax is increased to $5?
    a. Output will drop to zero, as will tax revenues.
    b. Output will decrease, but tax revenues will rise.
    c. Output will decrease (but not to zero), along with tax revenues.
    d. Output will increase, but tax revenues will fall.

15. With the $5 tax, which one of the following will be the deadweight loss?
    a. zero
    b. $50
    c. $100
    d. $200

## C. Short-Answer Questions

1. Often taxes that promote economic efficiency have negative effects on equity, especially if equity is perceived to require progressive taxes (taxes with a higher average tax rate on those with higher incomes). Why would this goal conflict with efficiency?_____

    _____

    _____

    _____

    _____

2. An old and long-standing debate over the appropriate size of government hinges on the relative size of the deadweight loss of taxation and the cost of any government program. How big should the government be? Evaluate this question considering the tax on labour—the most important tax in Canada. _____

    _____

    _____

    _____

3. Sales taxes cause markets to allocate resources inefficiently because they distort incentives. How?_____

    _____

    _____

    _____

## D.  Practice Problems

1.   The following graph shows the market for gasoline both before and after the imposition of a gasoline tax.

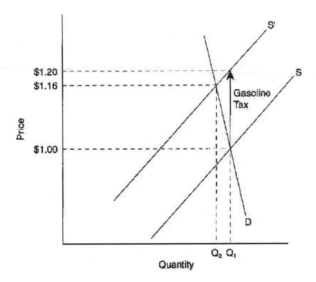

a.   How much is the gasoline tax, and by how much does the price of gasoline rise in response to the tax? Explain. By law, is this a tax on the buyer or the seller? How can you tell? _____

_____

_____

_____

b.   Label the area of deadweight loss on the diagram and explain. What would happen to the total deadweight loss if demand were more elastic? Why?_____

_____

_____

_____

c.   What would happen to the market for gasoline if the tax were switched to the other side of the market, but at the same tax rate? Does it matter whether the buyer or the seller is responsible for the tax? Would the equilibrium quantity change if the tax is switched? Would there be any change in the deadweight loss? Explain. _____

_____

_____

_____

_____

d.  Who really pays the tax? The consumer? The seller? Both? How is it possible to tell? What caused this result?_____

_____

_____

_____

_____

## E.  Advanced Critical Thinking

In recent years, proposals to increase the cigarette tax drastically have gained strength. Critics of the proposed tax argue that such an increase would be undesirable, because it would cause tremendous deadweight loss to society. They also argue that it would be unproductive in reducing smoking, because the demand for cigarettes is inelastic. Is this argument consistent? If the demand is inelastic, will the tax have a large impact on total surplus? Is the notion of deadweight loss even appropriate when the goal is to distort behaviour away from smoking? Discuss. _____

_____

_____

_____

_____

_____

## III.  Solutions

### A.    True/False Questions

1.   F; higher tax rates tend to lead to higher tax revenues initially, but after a point, revenue falls.
2.   F; a tax that raises no tax revenue can have a large deadweight loss, if it destroys the market for a product.
3.   T
4.   T
5.   T
6.   F; if policymakers tax goods and services that have relatively close substitutes, deadweight loss is likely to be greater, because people are more likely to change their behaviour in response to the tax.
7.   T
8.   F; most economists would agree that Canadian tax rates are not so high that they would reduce revenue, if rates were lowered.
9.   T
10.  F; taxes on producers (supply) have the same effects as taxes on the buyers (demand); the market adjusts price and output to compensate.

## B.   Multiple-Choice Questions

| | | | |
|---|---|---|---|
| 1. c | 5. c | 9. c | 13. a |
| 2. d | 6. a | 10. a | 14. a |
| 3. b | 7. d | 11. c | 15. d |
| 4. b | 8. b | 12. c | |

## C.   Short-Answer Questions

1.   There is no reason for equity and efficiency to go together. One (efficiency) is objective and the other (equity) depends on our values—our sense of what is fair. In fact, taxes that do not alter behaviour are most likely to be efficient, yet they are more likely to be lump-sum taxes or taxes on necessities that tend to be more burdensome to the poor.

2.   If taxation entails small deadweight losses, then government programs financed by these taxes are less costly and there would be a strong argument for a larger government. However, taxation accompanied by large deadweight losses would be an argument for a smaller government.

   Advocates of a leaner government argue that deadweight losses of labour tax are large because labour supply is rather elastic—the quantity of labour supplied responds to the wage. The decisions of these workers, therefore, are distorted when their earnings are taxed.

   Those who argue that labour taxes are not very distorting believe that labour supply is rather inelastic and a tax results in a small deadweight loss.

3.   A sales tax raises the price to buyers and lowers the price to sellers, thereby giving buyers an incentive to consume less and sellers an incentive to produce less than they otherwise would.

## D.   Practice Problems

1.   The graph on the next page shows the market for gasoline before and after the imposition of a gasoline tax. Use the graph to answer the following questions.

   a.   The gasoline tax rate is $0.20, as shown by the $0.20 vertical shift in supply. This shows that willingness to sell has shifted, requiring an additional $0.20 for any given quantity to be supplied. The equilibrium price rises by $0.16, from $1.00 to $1.16, indicating that the buyer is paying most of the tax. The legal burden is on the seller, as shown by the shift in supply, rather than demand.

b. The deadweight loss is the shaded triangle shown, which is the area between the supply (willingness to sell) and demand (willingness to buy), and between the new equilibrium output ($Q_2$) and the old output before the tax ($Q_1$). It represents the lost total surplus due to the loss of output. If demand were more elastic, then the tax would cause a greater loss of output, as quantity demanded falls more dramatically, resulting in a greater deadweight loss (a larger triangle of lost surplus).

c. The effect would be the same if the tax were switched to the buyer instead of the seller. Output would still drop to $Q_2$, and the consumer would still be stuck with $0.16 of the $0.20 tax. However, the graph would look different, because demand would shift by $0.20, rather than supply. The drop in demand would lower the price to $0.96, plus the $0.20 tax, for a total cost to the consumer of $1.16, which is the same as before. The deadweight loss would be the same.

d. Eighty percent of the tax ($0.16 of the $0.20) is borne by the consumer; the rest of the tax is borne by the seller, as shown by the effect on market price. When demand is less elastic than supply, the consumer is less adaptable and will be stuck with a larger share of the tax. If demand is relatively more elastic, then the seller will bear more of the burden of the tax.

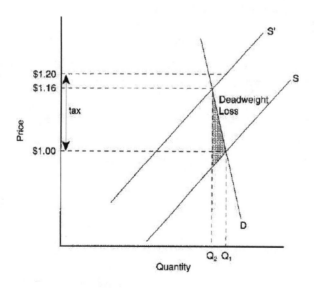

## E.   Advanced Critical Thinking

The usual notion of deadweight loss is not appropriate for evaluating the cigarette tax. Normally, distortion of behaviour is an undesirable effect of taxation. However, in the case of cigarettes, a major reason for the tax is to discourage consumption, because the free-market equilibrium is not considered to be efficient. There are externalities involved that smokers do not take into account (the health costs of second-hand smoke, for example), and to the extent that cigarettes may be addictive, it is not clear that truly voluntary exchange results from the free market. As a result, the deadweight loss from reducing production and consumption of cigarettes may actually be a social gain. Ironically, the inelastic demand means that even if the distortion of behaviour is positive, it is also relatively slight, unless the tax rate is quite high.

# 9  Application: International Trade

## I.  Chapter Overview

### A.  Context and Purpose

The previous chapter provided an application of welfare economics to the efficiency effects of taxation. This chapter adds another application of welfare economics, but in this case to international trade. The chapter identifies the winners and losers from free trade, as well as the welfare effects of protectionism.

### A.  Helpful Hints

1. *The determinants of trade involve world price.* When the price of a good within a country differs from the world price, then there is an incentive for that country to enter the international market for the good. If the world price is higher than the domestic price, then domestic producers will have an incentive to export the good. If the world price is lower than the domestic price, then domestic consumers will have an incentive to import the good from abroad.

2. *Exporting a good causes the domestic price to rise, which hurts domestic consumers but helps domestic producers.* However, the gains of the sellers are greater than the losses of the buyers, and total surplus rises. Similarly, importing a good causes the domestic price to fall, hurting domestic producers but helping domestic consumers. The gains for the consumers are greater than the losses by the producers, causing total surplus to rise. As a result, both imports and exports cause a net gain in total surplus, and the country's economic well-being rises.

3. *Countries do not trade, people do.* When someone in Canada buys from someone in Mexico, both parties benefit, just as surely as if both the buyer and seller had been in Canada.

4. *There are winners and losers from international trade.* It is this fact that accounts for much of the resistance to free trade. The losers tend to be more vocal than the winners, who are more diffused and less visible.

## II.  Self-Testing Challenges

### A.  True/False Questions

_____ 1.   The main problem with the argument that tariffs are needed to protect domestic jobs is that such trade restrictions never really save jobs.

_____ 2.   Free international trade raises the economic well-being of all trading nations in the sense that the gains of the winners exceed the losses of the losers.

_____ 3.   International trade creates jobs.

_____ 4.   When a country allows trade and becomes an exporter of a good, domestic consumers of a good are better off and domestic producers of the good are worse off.

_____ 5.   Free trade makes the nation better off, even though it may not make everyone in the country better off.

_____ 6.   A country whose price of steel is less than the world price must be subsidizing its steel industry.

_____ 7.   If a government imposes a tariff on an imported good, it increases the country's gain from trade.

_____ 8.   According to the infant-industry argument, new small industries may need temporary trade restrictions to help them get started.

_____ 9.   An increased variety of goods, lower costs through economies of scale, increased competition, and enhanced flow of ideas are all benefits that make the case for free international trade.

_____ 10.   The difference between a tariff and an import quota is that while the former raises revenue for the government, the latter creates surplus for those who get the licences to import.

### B.  Multiple-Choice Questions

1.   Which one of the following describes the outcomes when a country allows trade and becomes an importer of a good?
   a.   Domestic consumers of the good are better off, and domestic producers of the good are worse off.
   b.   Domestic consumers of the good are worse off, and domestic producers of the good are better off.

c.  Both domestic consumers and domestic producers are better off.

d.  Both domestic consumers and domestic producers are worse off.

2.  Which one of the following describes the outcomes when a country allows trade and becomes an importer of a good?

a.  Both the price paid by domestic consumers and the price received by domestic producers of the good rise.

b.  The price paid by domestic consumers rises, but the price received by domestic producers falls.

c.  The price paid by domestic consumers falls, but the price received by domestic producers rises.

d.  Both the price paid by domestic consumers and the price received by domestic producers fall.

3.  Which one of the following occurs when a country allows trade and becomes an importer of a good?

a.  The economic well-being of everyone in the country rises.

b.  The economic well-being of everyone in the country falls.

c.  The gains of the producers exceed the losses of the consumers.

d.  The gains of the consumers exceed the losses of the producers.

4.  Which one of the following would occur if a tariff was placed on imported steel in Canada?

a.  It would raise the total surplus in the Canadian market for steel.

b.  It would lower the total surplus in the Canadian market for steel.

c.  It would raise the total surplus of foreign exporters and consumers of steel.

d.  It would raise the Canadian standard of living at the expense of the exporting country.

The graph below shows the market for good Y in a small country, along with the world price for Y. Use the information provided to answer questions 5–7.

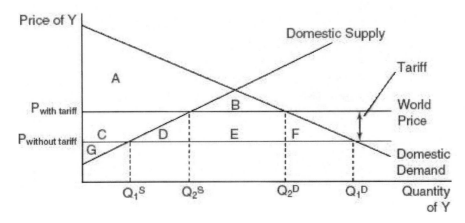

5.    Which one of the following is represented by Area E?
   a.  government revenues as a result of tariff
   b.  gain in welfare of domestic consumers as a result of tariff
   c.  deadweight loss from underconsumption as a result of tariff
   d.  gain in welfare of domestic producers as a result of the tariff

6.    Which one of the following is represented by Area D?
   a.  government revenues as a result of tariff
   b.  gain in welfare of domestic consumers as a result of tariff
   c.  deadweight loss from overproduction as a result of tariff
   d.  gain in welfare of domestic producers as a result of tariff

7.    Which one of the following is represented by Area F?
   a.  government revenues as a result of tariff
   b.  gain in welfare of domestic consumers as a result of tariff
   c.  deadweight loss from underconsumption as a result of tariff
   d.  gain in welfare of domestic producers as a result of tariff

8.    Which one of the following is the main difference between a tariff and a quota?
   a.  A tariff generates added revenue for the government, but revenue generated from a quota is received by the industry.
   b.  A quota harms consumers, but a tariff harms producers.

   c.  A quota increases the volume of imports, but a tariff decreases volume of imports.

The graph below shows the market for good Z in the small country of Alphaland. Use the information to answer questions 9–11.

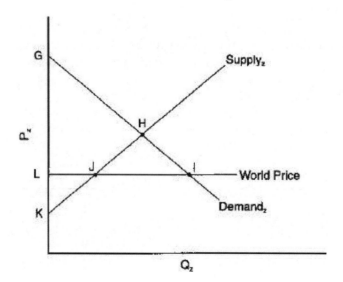

9.    Which one of the following explains what Alphaland should do in order to maximize total surplus?
   a.  It should increase exports of good Z until the domestic price falls to the world price.
   b.  It should increase exports of good Z until the world price rises to the domestic price.
   c.  It should increase imports of good Z until the world price rises to the domestic price.
   d.  It should increase imports of good Z until the domestic price falls to the world price.

10.   After trade, total surplus will increase by which one of the following graph areas?
   a.  GHK
   b.  GIJK
   c.  HIJ
   d.  LJK

11.   Which one of the following describes the status of good Z's consumers and producers in Alphaland, as a result of trade?
   a.  Consumers will be better off, but the producers will be worse off.
   b.  Consumers will be worse off, but the producers will be better off.
   c.  Consumers and producers will be worse off.
   d.  Consumers and producers will be better off.

12.   Which of the following statements is supported by the infant-industry argument?
   a.  new industries should be discouraged because they cannot compete with established firms
   b.  protecting a new industry from foreign competition may be desirable in the short term in order to give it time to become competitive
   c.  new industries may require permanent subsidies from the government in order to be competitive with established foreign firms
   d.  protecting industries that produce products for young children can be a worthwhile investment in the nation's human capital

13.   Which of the following is the best response if Mexico subsidizes its textile production, making it impossible for Canadian producers to compete?
   a.  a high tariff on textiles would improve economic well-being in Canada
   b.  Canada's most appropriate response would be to retaliate with an identical subsidy
   c.  the ideal response would be to threaten retaliation without actually following through on the threat
   d.  Canada would maximize its economic well-being by purchasing the subsidized textiles from Mexico

14. Some opponents of free trade argue that when Canadians buy shirts from Bangladesh, Canadian workers lose their jobs. Which one of the following is a good counterargument?
    a. The jobs lost as a result of free trade pay salaries below the poverty line.
    b. Free trade creates jobs, many of which pay more than the jobs lost.
    c. Imports from Bangladesh create more handling and distributing jobs than they lose.
    d. The jobs lost are concentrated in restricted geographic areas.

Use the following table to answer question 15.

| Good | Canada | Japan |
|------|--------|-------|
| X | 5 | 4 |
| Z | 10 | 5 |

15. Which one of the following is the best advice?
    a. Japan should produce good Z and Canada should produce good X, and they should trade with each other.
    b. Japan should produce good X and Canada should produce good Z, and they should trade with each other.
    c. Japan should produce both X and Z and export them to Canada.

16. Which one of the following is the advantage held by Japan?
    a. an absolute advantage in producing good X only
    b. an absolute advantage in producing good Z only
    c. an absolute advantage, but not a comparative advantage, in producing both goods
    d. a comparative advantage, but not an absolute advantage, in producing both goods

17. Which one of the following describes how Japan's combined consumer and producer surplus will be maximized?
    a. if Japan specializes according to its comparative advantage
    b. if Japan specializes according to its absolute advantage
    c. if Japan uses tariffs to protect its domestic industries
    d. if Japan subsidizes good Z, which requires 25% more labour than good X to produce

## C. Short-Answer Questions

1. Suppose that Alphaland and Utopia can provide widgets and frinzels according to the following production possibilities.

### Daily Output Per Worker

| Country | Widgets | Frinzels |
|---------|---------|----------|
| Alphaland | 20 | 20 |
| Utopia | 40 | 80 |

a. Which country is the lower opportunity cost producer of widgets? Of frinzels? Explain. _____

_____

_____

_____

_____

_____

b. Alphaland seems to be generally less productive than Utopia in terms of both goods. How can Alphaland hope to compete internationally with Utopia? _____

_____

_____

_____

_____

2. International trade *can* make everyone better off, but will it?

_____

_____

_____

_____

3. Rebut the following claim.
   Imposing tariffs on imported goods will increase employment, and hence income, in Canada. There is a double advantage here. If the tariff moves production to Canada, there will be a reduction in unemployment and an increase in government revenue. If, on the other hand, production is not moved to Canada, the government still gets revenue from tax on imported goods. _____

_____

_____

_____

_____

_____

## D.  Practice Problems

1.  The graph below shows a country before and after the imposition of a tariff.

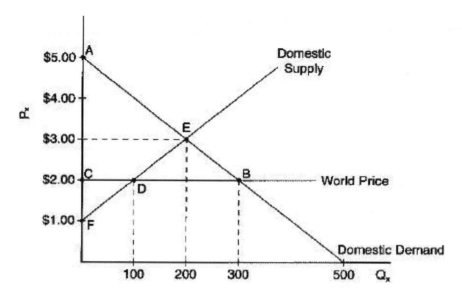

a.  Show graphically and calculate the actual change in consumer surplus and producer surplus as a result of the tariff. (Hint: Remember that the area of a triangle = 0.5 × base × height.) What is the change in the total surplus? How was the result calculated? _____

_____

_____

_____

_____

b.  Why did total surplus change in response to the tariff?

_____

_____

_____

_____

2.  Economists are generally critical of tariffs and quotas, even though such trade restrictions are often popular with the general public.

a.  Who wins and who loses from tariffs and other trade restrictions?

_____

_____

_____

_____

b.  What effect does a tariff have on economic well-being? Why?

_____

_____

_____

c.  In light of the answer to part (b) above, why are trade restrictions so popular?

_____

_____

_____

_____

d.  List the arguments for trade restrictions and evaluate each briefly.

1.  _____

_____

_____

2.  _____

_____

_____

3.  _____

_____

_____

4.  _____

_____

_____

5.  _____

_____

_____

## E.  Advanced Critical Thinking

Recently, a representative of the Canadian Auto Workers' union said, in support of protection for the Canadian auto industry, "we want free trade, but we want fair trade." He argued that Japanese automakers are subsidized by their government, and therefore should not be allowed free entry into the Canadian auto market.

a.    Given the large number of Canadian autoworkers who have lost their jobs in recent decades due to foreign competition, should Canada act to reduce the number of imported cars if other countries are creating artificial advantages for their industries? Who would win and who would lose? What would happen to society's overall economic well-being? Explain. What if another country subsidized every industry? Could they put Canada out of business? _____

_____

_____

_____

_____

_____

_____

b.    In the supply and demand diagram below, fill in the world price, and label the equilibrium quantity and the price with free international trade, as well as after import restrictions eliminate all imported cars.

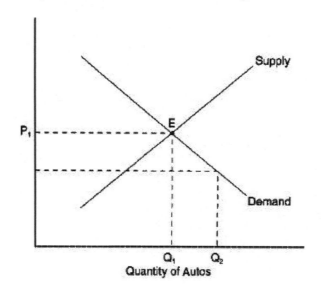

## III.  Solutions

### A.  True/False Questions

1.   F; tariffs save some domestic jobs (those in competition with imports) at the expense of other domestic jobs (those in export industries).
2.   T
3.   F; international trade redistributes jobs from less productive to more productive uses.
4.   F; domestic producers of a good are better off while domestic consumers are worse off.
5.   T
6.   F; if a country has a price of steel that is less than the world price, this indicates that the country has a comparative advantage in steel.
7.   F; any trade restriction, including a tariff, reduces gains from trade.
8.   T
9.   T
10.   T

### B.  Multiple-Choice Questions

| | | | | |
|---|---|---|---|---|
| 1. a | 5. a | 9. d | 13. d | 17. a |
| 2. d | 6. c | 10. c | 14. b | |
| 3. d | 7. c | 11. a | 15. a | |
| 4. b | 8. a | 12. b | 16. c | |

### C.  Short-Answer Questions

1.   Alphaland and Utopia can provide widgets and frinzels according to the following production possibilities.

Daily Output Per Worker

| Country | Widgets | Frinzels |
|---|---|---|
| Alphaland | 20 | 20 |
| Utopia | 40 | 80 |

a.   Alphaland is the lower opportunity cost producer of widgets, even though its workers are only half as productive as Utopia's (20 per day vs. 40 per day). This is because Alphaland's opportunity cost of producing widgets is the frinzels that it could have produced instead. At a ratio of 20:20, the opportunity cost of a widget is one frinzel. In Utopia, the ratio is 40:80, for an opportunity cost of 2 frinzels per widget. Utopia, however, is the lower opportunity cost producer of frinzels (80 frinzels to 40 widgets, or 2 frinzels to 1 widget) vs. 20 frinzels to 20 widgets or 1 frinzel for 1 widget in Alphaland. As a result, even though Utopia has an absolute advantage in either good, it has a comparative advantage only in producing frinzels. Alphaland has the comparative advantage in widgets. Both countries gain if they specialize according to their comparative advantages.

b.  Even though Utopia has an absolute advantage in producing both goods, it nevertheless gives up more to produce widgets than if it produces frinzels and trades them for Alphaland's widgets at any relative price less than 2:1. Similarly, Alphaland would gain at any relative price greater than 1:1. At any relative price between 1 and 2 frinzels per widget, both countries gain.

2.  Trade will probably *not* make everyone better off. Compensation for those who lose as a result of trade is rare. In the absence of such compensation, trade expands the size of the economic pie, but might leave some groups in the economy with a smaller slice.

3.  Imposition of tariffs will raise the price of goods to consumers but will not necessarily increase employment, and hence income, to compensate for this increased cost. Countries affected by the tariff may retaliate by imposing their own protective measures against Canadian exports, which may lead to more unemployment and less government revenue.

## D.  Practice Problems

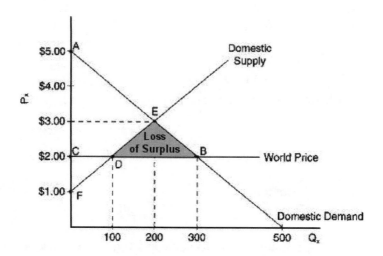

1.  a.  Total surplus falls from $500 to $400. With trade, the equilibrium is at point B, with a price of $2 and consumption (including imports) of 300. Of this quantity of 300, 100 are produced by domestic firms and 200 are imported. The original surplus, with trade, is the area ABC, representing consumer surplus, plus area CDF, which is producer

surplus. Numerically, this surplus is ½ ($5–$2)(300) + ½ ($2–$1)(100) = $500. After eliminating trade, the equilibrium shifts to point E, at a price of $3 and a total domestic output of 200. The total surplus is triangle AEF, or ½ ($5–$1)(200) = $400. Thus, the total surplus falls by $100, which is also the area of triangle DEB = ½ ($3–$2)(300–100).

    b.   Total surplus falls because buyers and sellers are prevented from making all of the exchanges that are in their best interests. Cutting consumption of good X back from 300 to 200 units means that consumers will not be able to buy 100 units that had a marginal value (or benefit) to society which exceeded the marginal cost of producing it.

2.   a.   Winners include domestic producers, who face less competition, and foreign consumers, who have more of their products left to consume at home. Losers include domestic consumers, who face a restricted supply, and foreign producers, whose foreign markets are restricted by tariffs.

    b.   A tariff lowers overall economic well-being by reducing the sum of producer and consumer surplus, just as any other tax would do—by distorting behaviour and reducing output below the competitive market equilibrium.

    c.   The winners from trade restrictions are highly visible and tend to be quite vocal in their opposition to free trade. The losers—the general public—are more diffused and harder to identify. If consumers in general pay slightly higher prices, it may not be obvious that trade restrictions are the cause, even though the total loss is great.

    d.  1.  Trade restrictions can protect some jobs in industries that compete with imports, but at the expense of others that are in export-related industries. Canada's imports provide the dollars that our trading partners use to buy our exports.

        2.  Trade restrictions can also provide temporary protection for new or "infant" industries until they get established, but the problem is that infant industries never want to grow up.

        3.  National security is another possibly valid argument, but every industry tries to claim that it is vital.

        4.  Retaliation against unfair competition is another argument, but retaliation ends up hurting the economic welfare of the retaliating country.

5.   The threat of protectionism can be used to encourage trading partners to reduce their trade barriers, but it can also backfire and lead to trade wars that make both trading partners worse off.

## E.  Advanced Critical Thinking

a.    Although it would be politically popular to protect autoworkers, it would actually reduce our total surplus from automobiles. It would help autoworkers and auto companies in Canada, but it would hurt Canadian auto buyers and foreign auto producers. It would also help foreign consumers of automobiles, who would find that more of their supply would stay at home, thus holding down the price they pay. Most industries seem to make the claim that imports are subsidized, but it is not possible for another country to subsidize everything and drive all industries out of business. When a country subsidizes one industry and makes it more competitive internationally, it makes it harder for its other industries to compete. Jobs are not created, but merely redistributed from less subsidized to more subsidized industries.

b.

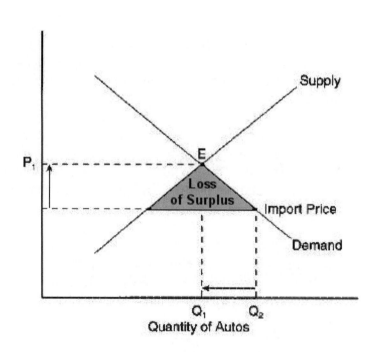

# CHAPTER 10 Externalities

## I. Chapter Overview

### A. Context and Purpose

Markets do many things well, but they do not do everything well; at times markets fail. This chapter considers the situation in which the market does not perform efficiently—when decision makers do not bear all of the costs or realize all of the benefits of their actions. The chapter also looks at the role of government in correcting such market imperfections.

### B. Helpful Hints

1. *Externality* refers to a positive or negative effect on a third party as a result of a transaction between a buyer and a seller.

2. *Internalizing an externality* means altering incentives (through a tax or other market-based schemes or regulations) so that people take account of the external effects of their actions.

3. *Transactions costs* refer to the costs of negotiating and implementing an agreement between buyers and sellers.

4. The *Coase theorem* states that for any initial distribution of property rights, if transactions costs are relatively small, the affected parties can negotiate to internalize the externality and reach a bargain that will make everyone better off.

5. *Corrective* or *Pigovian taxes* are taxes set equal to the external cost of pollution in order to internalize the negative externality.

6. *You really can have too much of a good thing.* We live life at the margin, so even if people put a high value on a clean environment, at some point they are likely to decide that a little more cleanup costs more than it is worth (at the margin). Suppose that Canadians choose to clean up 99% of the air pollution that results from producing paper. Even though Canadians put a high value on a clean environment, they may choose to leave the remaining 1% if it is discovered that eliminating the last 1% of air pollution will cost as much to clean up as the first 99% did. That is, the marginal cost exceeds the marginal benefit for the final 1%.

7.    *It is difficult to identify the most efficient level of environmental cleanup because many of the benefits are hard to measure.* For example, how much value is put on a life saved through pollution control? The typical reaction is that each life has an infinite value, but people do not behave that way. Rational people take risks with their lives every day as they drive cars, eat, work, and play. The economic value of a human life is difficult to measure, but it is nevertheless a real factor to consider in evaluating environmental cleanup or other government programs.

## II. Self-Testing Challenges

### A. True/False Questions

_____1.    Because buyers and sellers neglect the external effects of their actions when deciding how much to demand or supply, the market equilibrium is not efficient.

_____2.    Tradeable pollution permits have the same effects on output and the level of pollution as a Pigovian tax on polluters.

_____3.    "Do unto others as you would have them do unto you," tells people to internalize externalities.

_____4.    A corrective or Pigovian tax reduces economic efficiency by distorting taxpayer behaviour.

_____5.    A disadvantage of market-based policies designed to clean up the environment is that they treat the environment as if it were a commodity rather than a priceless resource.

_____6.    If studded snow tires do an estimated $10 damage to the highways per vehicle each year, then the most efficient outcome for society would be to ban the use of studded snow tires.

_____7.    According to the Coase theorem, negative externalities require government action because the market fails to take into account external social costs.

_____8.    When correcting for a negative externality, command-and-control policies are preferable because they are more efficient.

_____9.    Patent protection internalizes technology spillovers by giving the inventors property rights over their inventions.

_____10.    Positive externalities lead markets to produce a smaller quantity than is socially desirable and to charge a price that is too low to be optimal.

## B.    Multiple-Choice Questions

1.   Which one of the following describes when private solutions to negative externalities are **LEAST** likely to be effective?
     a.   when the costs of pollution are high
     b.   when the costs of pollution cleanup are high
     c.   when property rights are clearly assigned to one party
     d.   when transactions costs are high

2.   Pulp and paper mills not only produce paper but they also create dioxin, a byproduct of the manufacturing process. Therefore, which one of the following can be said about this market?
     a.   equilibrium price and equilibrium output are too high to be socially desirable
     b.   equilibrium price and equilibrium output are too low to be socially desirable
     c.   equilibrium price is too low and equilibrium output is too high to be socially desirable
     d.   equilibrium price is too high and equilibrium output is too low to be socially desirable

3.   A market economy has a tendency to _____ goods with positive externality and _____ goods with negative externality.
     a.   overproduce, underconsume
     b.   overproduce, underproduce
     c.   underproduce, overproduce

4.   Which of the following is supported by the Coase theorem?
     a.   The market can internalize external costs and benefits, and achieve efficiency, if private parties can negotiate solutions to the externalities.
     b.   Government can improve upon the operation of the market by using environmental controls.
     c.   The market can internalize externalities if all parties involved have roughly equal bargaining power.
     d.   Correcting externalities through the market can work, but only if the innocent third parties have clearly established and enforceable property rights.

5.   Which one of the following is **NOT** a plausible example of market failure due to externalities?
     a.   a beekeeper who benefits from being next to an apple orchard
     b.   the high salaries of professional hockey players
     c.   long traffic jams every day on Whitemud Drive in Edmonton
     d.   the production of a lighthouse

6.  Which one of the following negative externalities would be a target for correction by a gasoline tax, which is a waste tax?
    a.  construction
    b.  accidents
    c.  pollution
    d.  pedestrian safety

7.  Relative to market-based pollution control policies, which one of the following statements can be made about direct regulation?
    a.  requires less detailed information to set the pollution limits
    b.  provides more of an incentive to develop better technology to clean up beyond the minimum
    c.  allows polluters to pollute at no charge, up to the limits set by the government
    d.  makes it easier to fine-tune regulations for different situations

8.  Which one of the following is the essential problem with the existence of externalities?
    a.  a discrepancy between private and social cost
    b.  a discrepancy between private benefit and social cost
    c.  a discrepancy between private cost and social benefit
    d.  government failure

9.  Many goods with negative externalities are overproduced, relative to the socially optimal level. Which one of the following is this an example of?
    a.  market failure
    b.  government failure
    c.  producer failure

10. Which one of the following is an example of internalizing an externality?
    a.  The municipal government offers subsidies to homeowners to offset the cost of beautifying their front yards.
    b.  A restaurant no longer serves imported wine, having decided to offer only domestic wine.
    c.  A beekeeper buys extra hives to expand the business.

11. Which of the following describes when a deadweight loss from pollution cleanup occurs?
    a.  whenever pollution cleanup imposes costs on society
    b.  whenever society puts a price tag on pollution, thus providing a "licence to pollute"
    c.  when government gets involved
    d.  whenever some units of pollution cleanup cost more than their marginal benefit to society

12.	Suppose the last unit of output produced at a paper mill has a value to society of $10 and a social cost of $15, but the private cost to the company is $10, and the current price is $10. Which one of the following is true?
   a.	Market is in equilibrium, but a lower output would make society better off.
   b.	Market is in equilibrium, but a higher output would make society better off.
   c.	Output is too low, and price is too high, for equilibrium.
   d.	Output is too high, and price is too low, for equilibrium.

13.	In the presence of technology spillovers, the market tends to _____ and _____ the product relative to society's best interest.
   a.	overproduce, underprice
   b.	overproduce, overprice
   c.	underproduce, underprice
   d.	underproduce, overprice

14.	Which one of the following is an example of a private solution to the problem of externalities?
   a.	Greenpeace Canada
   b.	Canadian National Parks
   c.	Canada Post
   d.	Natural Resources Canada

15.	Which one of the following would be achieved by the **MOST** efficient pollution control system?
   a.	It would ensure that each polluter cleans up to the point where total social benefits are maximized.
   b.	It would ensure that each polluter cleans up just to the point where that the polluter's last unit of cleanup has a social value exactly equal to its social cost.
   c.	It would ensure that each polluter meets exactly the same pollution standards as all the other polluters.
   d.	It would ensure that each polluter cleans up to the maximum level that is technically feasible.

16.	Heavy trucks travelling on the Trans-Canada Highway cause noise pollution in nearby neighbourhoods. Which one of the following is an efficient policy to deal with this?
   a.	Rely on the "invisible hand" to take care of the problem.
   b.	Provide a subsidy to each trucking company, depending on the total amount of noise its trucks create in the affected neighbourhoods.
   c.	Impose a tax on each trucking company, depending on the total amount of noise its trucks create in the affected neighbourhoods.
   d.	Subsidize trucking companies that install noise-abatement devices.

17.    Which one of the following is an important question to address in defining an anti-pollution policy?
    a.  How do we reduce pollution to the appropriate level?
    b.  How do we eliminate pollution?
    c.  How do we learn to live with pollution, rather than worry about its growth?
    d.  How do we design a policy, not to be used today, but instead when it is needed later in the decade?

18.    Which one of the following outcomes is supported by the Coase theorem when transaction costs are low and property rights exist?
    a.  deadweight losses result due to positive externalities
    b.  deadweight losses result due to negative externalities
    c.  private transactions cannot be efficient
    d.  private transactions are efficient

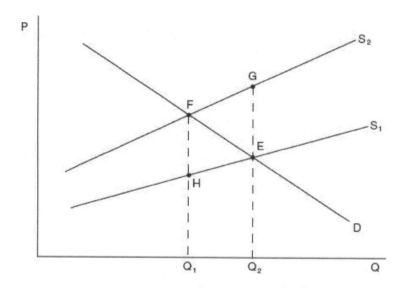

Refer to the above figure to answer questions 19 and 20. In the above figure, D represents the demand curve; $S_1$ represents the supply curve and indicates private marginal cost at each level of output, and $S_2$ indicates the marginal cost to society at each level of output when the marginal external cost of the pollution created by the production of this good is taken into account.

19.    Which one of the following is demonstrated in the above figure?
    a.  A competitive industry will produce $Q_2$ units of this good, and the efficiency loss to society is given by area EFH.
    b.  A competitive industry will produce $Q_2$ units of this good, and the efficiency loss to society is given by area EFG.
    c.  A competitive industry will produce $Q_2$ units of this good, and the efficiency loss to society is given by area EHFG.

20.    Given the conditions described by the above figure, which one of the following is the appropriate government policy to pursue?
    a.    Levy a tax on this good equal to FH per unit.
    b.    Levy a tax on this good equal to EG per unit.
    c.    Levy a tax on this good equal to FG per unit.

## C.    Short-Answer Questions

1.    According to the Coase theorem, the market can often solve problems of negative externalities on its own.

    a.    What conditions must hold for the market solution to work?

_____
_____
_____

    b.    When the private parties involved can negotiate a solution to a negative externality, does it matter for economic efficiency who pays whom? For example, if the problem is water pollution, does it matter whether the polluter is penalized for polluting or the victim subsidizes the polluter for not polluting? Or, if government is involved, will a pollution tax have a different effect than a subsidy to polluters to not pollute? Include an explanation of how such different assignments of property rights to the environment affect the opportunity cost to the polluter of continuing to pollute.

_____
_____
_____
_____
_____

2.    Reducing pollution using pollution permits is quite different from using Pigovian taxes. Would an economist agree? Why or why not?

_____
_____
_____
_____

3.    Because positive externalities harm no one, there is no need for government intervention. Would an economist agree? Explain.

_____
_____
_____
_____

4. Critics argue that carbon credits look like a good idea at first glance, but there are several reasons why they are not likely to work. (1) It would be very difficult to decide who should get them because some firms with older factories may not be able to clean up as much as newer firms. (2) Credits would give firms a licence to pollute, thus putting a dollar value on a priceless resource. (3) Some firms might make money by selling their credits rather than using them themselves. How would an economist respond? Are these criticisms valid for explaining why such a system would not be efficient for society?_____

_____

_____

_____

_____

_____

_____

_____

## D.   Practice Problems

An economics consultant has been hired by the city of Sydney, Nova Scotia. The city is faced with a massive cleanup bill for benzopyrene, which has been found in the town's drinking water. A local manufacturer dumped solvents into a pit on its property for a number of years because it cost the firm less than proper disposal. The firm has gone out of business, leaving contamination with an estimated cleanup cost of $6.5 million. The Nova Scotia Department of Environment (NSDOE) has presented the following options: (a) do nothing—live with the problem or move out; (b) boil water for drinking and otherwise avoid contact with water; (c) drill new water wells and cap the old, contaminated wells; or (d) find the source of contamination and clean it up completely. The following table shows estimated costs and benefits of each cleanup option. The cost is the cost of cleanup, not the cost of pollution itself. The benefit is the reduction in the damage due to the contamination. Note that the maximum potential benefit is $6.5 million, which represents total elimination of the damage from benzopyrene. Fill in the missing blanks.

NSDOE Cleanup Options for Sydney, Nova Scotia

|  | Option | Total cost (millions) | Total benefit (millions) | Marginal cost (millions) | Marginal benefit (millions) | Net benefit (millions) |
|---|---|---|---|---|---|---|
| a. | Do nothing | 0 | 0 | $_____ | $_____ | $_____ |
| b. | Boil water | $1 | $4 | $_____ | $_____ | $_____ |
| c. | Drill new wells | $2 | $5.5 | $_____ | $_____ | $_____ |
| d. | Complete cleanup | $5 | $6.5 | $_____ | $_____ | $_____ |

Note: All benefits and costs are social rather than private. Specifically: marginal cost = the marginal cost to society of one additional level of cleanup; marginal benefit = the marginal benefit to society (social value) of one additional level of cleanup; and net benefit = total benefit − total cost (to society). Total benefit is the reduction in pollution damage, up to the point of complete elimination of the $6.5 million in damage from benzopyrene contamination.

1. Based on these numbers, what level of cleanup should the economics consultant recommend and why?

2. How might an economics consultant interpret the total benefit column? That is, what kinds of benefits would be included here? What kinds of problems would be anticipated in measuring the benefits of such an environmental cleanup project?

3. What would be the dollar value of the deadweight loss from total cleanup (option d)? Why would total cleanup result in a deadweight loss to society even though the people would like to have a clean environment?

4. If total cleanup (option d) were the only alternative to doing nothing (option a), would the economics consultant recommend it? Explain why or why not.

5. The economics consultant has just discovered that the polluter could have disposed of the solvent properly for $1 million, and thus would have avoided all contamination of the water supply.

   a. Why did the market not take care of the problem before the contamination occurred? Would that not have been more efficient?

b.   What conditions would have been required to achieve a market solution so that the victims and the polluters could have avoided this problem? _____

_____

_____

_____

c.   Would the contamination have occurred if the polluter had also owned the Sydney Water Company? Why or why not? _____

_____

_____

_____

## E.   Advanced Critical Thinking

The Optimal Level of Crime Prevention: How Many Robberies Are Too Many?

A public official recently argued that society's goal should be to eliminate crime that society should not stop until there is not a single occurrence of a robbery or murder. His assertion is that even one robbery is one too many. Even if society has enough resources to make it feasible to eliminate crime, would it make sense? Or is this bad economics? Is it possible to make an analogy with pollution control? Write a short essay explaining what is wrong with this way of thinking.

_____

_____

_____

_____

_____

_____

_____

_____

_____

_____

_____

In order to answer these and other questions, consider the hypothetical case study of the small town of Dry Coulee, Manitoba. The number of robberies has increased over the past decade, and the town council is under pressure from the voting public to clean up crime. The town has hired a consultant to estimate the economic effects of forming a professional police department instead of relying on a volunteer who works part-time when he is not working at his regular job as a clerk at the local hardware store. The council has just received the consultant's report and must decide how many police officers to hire.

According to the consultant, the projected social cost of crime without any police protection at all is $200 000 per year. This includes explicit costs such as property loss, medical costs, and lost earnings due to injuries, as well as intangible costs such as loss of peace of mind or reduced quality of life due to the higher crime rate. The benefit from each additional police officer hired is the estimated reduction in the total social cost of crime in the village; therefore, the maximum possible benefit from crime prevention is $200 000, which represents the total elimination of crime (and its social costs) in the village. The consultant has found that the village can hire police officers at an annual cost of $30 000 each, including salary and fringe benefits.

The consultant's estimates of costs and benefits follow. Fill in the missing numbers and answer the questions that follow. The first line is already filled in.

**Consultant's Report: Annual Costs and Benefits of Various Levels of Police Protection for Dry Coulee, Manitoba**

| Number of police officers | Total social cost | Marginal social cost | Total social benefit | Marginal social benefit | Net social benefit |
|---|---|---|---|---|---|
| 0 | $0 | $ — | $0 | $ — | $0 |
| 1 | $30 000 | $ | $30 000 | $ | $ |
| 2 | $60 000 | $ | $70 000 | $ | $ |
| 3 | $90 000 | $ | $105 000 | $ | $ |
| 4 | $120 000 | $ | $134 000 | $ | $ |
| 5 | $150 000 | $ | $160 000 | $ | $ |
| 6 | $180 000 | $ | $180 000 | $ | $ |
| 7 | $210 000 | $ | $190 000 | $ | $ |
| 8 | $240 000 | $ | $196 000 | $ | $ |
| 9 | $270 000 | $ | $200 000 | $ | $ |
| 10 | $300 000 | $ | $200 000 | $ | $ |

1. Some people argue that the town should hire enough police officers to eliminate crime. Based on the consultant's report, how should the town respond? How many police officers should the town hire and why?

2.  Plot marginal social cost (MSC) and marginal social benefit (MSB) on the graph below, and label the socially optimal amount of crime prevention. Plot the total cost (TC) and total benefit (TB) on the graph on the next page, and identify the point that maximizes net benefit (TB − TC). (This point should coincide with your answer to question 1.)

Marginal Social Cost (MSC) and Marginal Social Benefit (MSB) of Crime Prevention

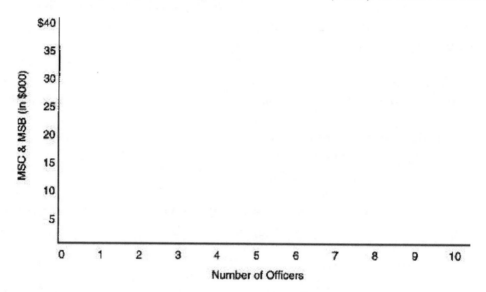

Total Cost (TC), Total Benefits (TB), and Net Benefits (TB−TC) of Crime Prevention

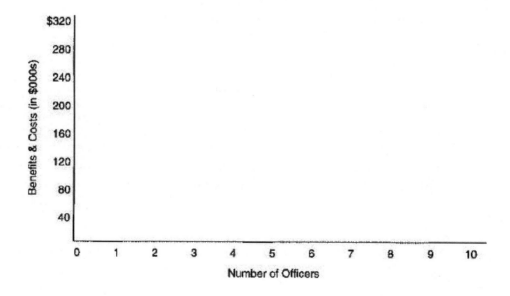

## III. Solutions

### A. True/False Questions

1.  T
2.  T
3.  T
4.  F; it improves efficiency by eliminating a distortion of behaviour caused by not pricing a scarce resource.
5.  F; an advantage of market-based policies is that they put a price on a scarce resource that had previously been treated as a free good.
6.  F; even if the studded snow tires do $10 in damage to the highways, it is efficient to use them if their benefit exceeds their cost, including the $10 in external cost to society. A $10 tax would let the market determine whether or not they were worth their full cost to society.
7.  F; according to the Coase theorem, the market may be able to internalize externalities when negotiating costs are not excessive.
8.  F; market-based policies such as a corrective tax or a Pigovian tax internalize an externality more efficiently.
9.  T
10. T

### B. Multiple-Choice Questions

| 1. d | 5. b | 9. a | 13. d | 17. a |
|------|------|------|-------|-------|
| 2. c | 6. c | 10. a | 14. a | 18. d |
| 3. c | 7. c | 11. d | 15. b | 19. b |
| 4. a | 8. a | 12. a | 16. c | 20. a |

### C. Short-Answer Questions

1. a. The affected parties must be able to negotiate a settlement. For this to happen, the transactions costs must be low enough to make it worthwhile. As a result, the market is more likely to work efficiently when the affected population is small. With a large population, it is difficult to identify everyone and work out a settlement.

   b. According to the Coase theorem, if the affected parties can negotiate a solution to an externality, the result will be the same improvement in economic efficiency regardless of who pays whom. If the victims of pollution own the property rights to the environment, they can charge the polluter for using their scarce resource. If the polluter owns the rights, the victims can subsidize the polluter in order to cut back on pollution. Either way, the polluter will internalize the pollution cost. Losing a subsidy has the same opportunity cost as paying an equivalent pollution charge.

2.  Disagree, because the two policies have much in common. In both cases, polluting firms pay for the pollution they generate. In the case of pollution permits, firms must pay to buy the permit. Even for those firms that already own permits, there is an opportunity cost of polluting that exists in terms of what they could have received by selling their permits. With Pigovian taxes, firms must pay a levy to the government based on the amount of pollution they generate. The pollution permits and Pigovian taxes both internalize the externality of pollution by making it costly for firms to pollute.

3.  Positive externalities lead markets to produce a smaller quantity and charge a lower price than is socially desirable. Therefore, government intervention will internalize this externality.

4.  These arguments are invalid. First, if newer factories can clean up more easily than older factories, then it is more efficient for the new factories to clean up relatively more. A cleanup should be undertaken wherever it can be done at the lower cost. Second, credits put a price on a scarce resource that had been underpriced (free to the user) in the past, which encouraged overconsumption. Prices are put on other scarce resources, so why exclude this one? Third, if some firms sell their credits, it means that other firms put a higher value on them. As long as the total number of credits issued equals the amount of pollution that society will accept, why not let the firms decide who can clean up at the lowest cost?

## D.  Practice Problems

### NSDOE Cleanup Options for Sydney, Nova Scotia

| Option | Total cost (millions) | Total benefit (millions) | Marginal cost (MC) (millions) | Marginal benefit (MB) (millions) | Net benefit (millions) |
|---|---|---|---|---|---|
| a.  Do nothing | $0 | $0 | — | — | $0 |
| b.  Boil water | $1 | $4 | $1 | $4 | $3 |
| c.  Drill new wells | $2 | $5.5 | $1 | $1.5 | $3.5 |
| d.  Complete cleanup | $5 | $6.5 | $3 | $1 | $1.5 |

Note: All benefits and costs are social rather than private. Specifically: marginal cost = marginal cost to society; marginal benefit = marginal benefit to society (social value); and net benefit = total benefit − total cost (to society)

1. The most efficient level of cleanup is option (c):, drill new wells. To maximize social well-being, every action that has a marginal benefit greater than the marginal cost should be taken. This means that option (c) is the best choice: its marginal benefit is $1.5 million while its marginal cost is only $1 million. Society gains another $0.5 million (MB – MC) by moving from option (b) to (c). Even though society would like to have total cleanup—option (d)—it is not worth the cost to society. Option (d) has a marginal cost of $3 million, which exceeds its marginal benefit of $1 million to society.

2. The total benefit from pollution cleanup is actually the reduction in the cost of pollution to society. In this example, the total benefit from eliminating the source of pollution is $6.5 million, which represents the benefits from avoiding the damage by the pollutant. These benefits would include such factors as reduced risk to property or human health, including lost hours of work and medical bills, as well as pain and suffering. Measurement of the factors is difficult because the health effects are uncertain and likely to be long term. Even if the health effects are known, it is difficult to estimate the full dollar value of pain and suffering and other intangible health costs.

3. Total cleanup would reduce net benefits from $3.5 million to $1.5 million, making society $2 million worse off. Another way to see this is to look at the marginal benefit and marginal cost of option (d); at that point, the marginal cost of $3 million exceeds the MB of $1 million by $2 million. This $2 million shortfall reduces the net benefit of the cleanup program by $2 million relative to the previous option.

4. If the choice were all or nothing, then total cleanup would make sense because the net benefit is positive. A $1.5 million net benefit is better than nothing.

5. a. To the polluter, dumping the chemical was costless even though it imposed a $6.5 million cost on society. Clearly, it would have been more efficient to spend $1 million to avoid a $6.5 million cost rather than spending much more later without even being able to clean things up completely. The problem is that the $6.5 million is an external cost, leading to excessive pollution. If the polluter had been paying the full social cost of pollution, it would have paid the $1 million to avoid contamination rather than $6.5 million in environmental damage.

   b. If property rights to the environment had been defined clearly, and if the victims had been identified, then the victims could have negotiated with polluters not to pollute. The cost of pollution would have been internalized, and the polluters would have paid the $1 million to avoid contamination rather than bearing the full $6.5 million in environmental damage.

c.  If the same company owned both the polluter and the water supply, then the company would have had an incentive to pay the $1 million in disposal costs for the benzopyrene rather than do $6.5 million in damage to a resource that it owned. This would have internalized the cost, i.e., which is similar to the answer to 5(b) above.

## E.  Advanced Critical Thinking

This is bad economics. Because society cannot have everything it wants, society has to make choices. Marginalist thinking says that no matter how much people value something, they should still stop at the point at which the next unit provides an additional benefit that is less than its cost. People would like to stop crime, but society should never use more resources to prevent an additional crime than that prevention is worth to society. The cure should never cost more than the problem being solved. Pollution is similar to crime: in both cases, society would like less of the activity, but society does not want to spend $100 000, for example, to save $10 000 in social costs.

### Consultant's Report: Annual Costs and Benefits of Various Levels of Police Protection for Dry Coulee, Manitoba

| Number of police officers | Total social cost | Marginal social cost | Total social benefit | Marginal social benefit | Net social benefit |
|---|---|---|---|---|---|
| 0  | $0        | —         | $0        | —         | $0          |
| 1  | $30 000   | $30 000   | $30 000   | $30 000   | $0          |
| 2  | $60 000   | $30 000   | $70 000   | $40 000   | $10 000     |
| 3  | $90 000   | $30 000   | $105 000  | $35 000   | $15 000     |
| 4  | $120 000  | $30 000   | $134 000  | $29 000   | $14 000     |
| 5  | $150 000  | $30 000   | $160 000  | $26 000   | $10 000     |
| 6  | $180 000  | $30 000   | $180 000  | $20 000   | $0          |
| 7  | $210 000  | $30 000   | $190 000  | $10 000   | ($20 000)   |
| 8  | $240 000  | $30 000   | $196 000  | $6 000    | ($44 000)   |
| 9  | $270 000  | $30 000   | $200 000  | $4 000    | ($70 000)   |
| 10 | $300 000  | $30 000   | $200 000  | $0        | ($100 000)  |

1.  The town should hire police officers as long as the last officer hired costs no more than the estimated value of that officer to the town. That is, keep hiring as long as MB > MC, and stop hiring when MB = MC. This means hiring three officers because the first three officers have marginal benefits greater than the $30 000 marginal cost, but even one additional officer would have a marginal benefit to the town of less than the $30 000 marginal cost. Note that hiring three officers also maximizes the net benefit to society.

2. Marginal Social Cost (MSC) and Marginal Social Benefit (MSB) of Crime Prevention

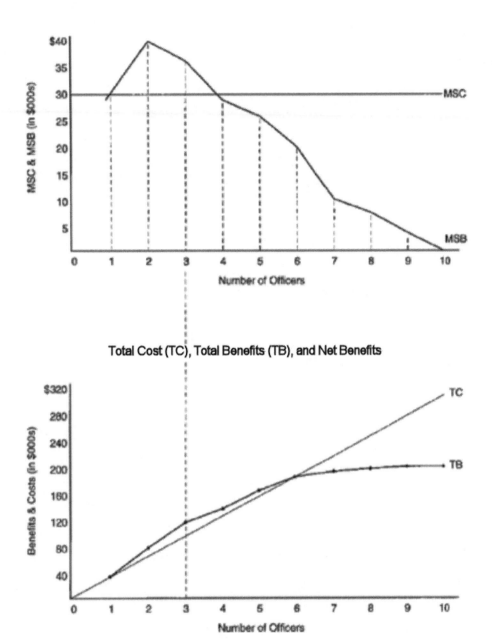

# CHAPTER 11 — Public Goods and Common Resources

## I. Chapter Overview

### A. Context and Purpose

The market works well at allocating resources when everyone bears the costs and benefits of their actions. Unfortunately, this restriction does not always hold, which leads to imperfections in the market. Chapters 10–12 analyze the role of government in correcting for such market imperfections.

The previous chapter investigated the role of government in correcting the problems that externalities cause for the market. The next chapter covers the tax system. This chapter extends the analysis of the role of government to cover public goods and common resources, which are those goods that are consumed simultaneously by multiple users, even by those who do not pay for the goods.

### A. Helpful Hints

1. *Excludable and rival goods.* An excludable good is one that others can be prevented from using. A rival good is a good of which one person's consumption takes away from another's enjoyment.

2. *Private goods.* These are goods that are both excludable and rival, such as hamburgers.

3. *Public goods.* These are goods that are neither excludable nor rival, such as national defence.

4. *Common resources.* These are goods that are rival but not easily excludable, such as fish in the ocean.

5. *Natural monopoly.* This is the market for a good that is excludable but not rival, such as cable television signals.

6. *Not all public goods are provided by government, and not all private goods are provided by markets.* However, in those cases where markets provide public goods, finding an efficient way to pay for the good can be tricky. Consider commercial television as an example. Exclusion is not feasible with present technology, and consumption is nonrival. In short, a commercial television signal is a public good. Because of the difficulty in excluding free riders, the broadcast companies have turned to another way to generate revenues: they sell advertising.

7. *It is possible to satisfy the demand for public goods without providing a separate good for each consumer.* Suppose 30 million Canadians would like to have one nuclear submarine for protection. Only one submarine is required to satisfy the entire demand. Conversely, if 30 million Canadians each demand a private good such as one hamburger, then 30 million hamburgers are required to satisfy the market demand. Because of the nonrival nature of consumption, Canadians can "pass the hat" or ask everyone to contribute toward the purchase of a public good for the group. Because of the free-rider problem, that "contribution" may have to be mandatory in the form of taxes.

8. *Some essentially private goods share characteristics with public goods.* The same logic about "passing the hat" to pay for a public good applies to some goods that are neither purely public nor purely private. Suppose that a few friends would like to rent a new video. As long as everyone wants to see the same movie, only one copy needs to be rented in order to meet everyone's demand. Up to the point that the room gets crowded, the video rental behaves in part like a public good in that it has nonrival consumption. One more person viewing the film does not take away from the enjoyment of the other viewers.

9. *Public goods differ from private goods not because of who provides them, but because of innate characteristics of the goods themselves.* Government may provide goods that are essentially private (excludable and rival), such as a congested provincial campground. Similarly, markets may provide goods that are essentially public (nonexcludable and nonrival). Commercial television signals, for example, are essentially public goods, with infeasible exclusion (without using different broadcast technology) and nonrival consumption (additional viewers do not detract from others' enjoyment). To avoid the free-rider problem, broadcasters use commercial advertising to pay for the good.

10. *Common resources tend to be overproduced and overconsumed.* If it seems unlikely that common pools of petroleum would lead to overproduction and consumption of oil, consider two children who must share a box of popcorn or a soft drink at the movies. Granted, drilling for oil is a bit more difficult than sipping pop through a straw, but the basic analysis is the same. In each case, property rights are not assigned clearly, causing the parties involved to use the resource at a faster than desirable rate. With the popcorn, one child might prefer to eat slowly, making the popcorn last for the entire movie. However, if he waits, the other child may finish off the popcorn. Both eat faster to make sure that they get their share. Similarly with oil, companies that choose to leave oil in the ground for later use will be left out as others drill the wells dry.

## II.  Self-Testing Challenges

### A.  True/False Questions

_____1.    Private decisions about consumption and production of nonexcludable goods lead to an efficient allocation of resources.

_____2.    Contrary to what the musicians maintain, downloading music from the Internet is not a free-rider problem.

_____3.    An uncongested road is a common resource.

_____4.    To avoid inefficient exclusion, the government often provides excludable, but not rival, goods and services.

_____5.    A good or service that is excludable and rival is known as a private good and is most efficiently provided by the market.

_____6.    The main weakness of national defence as an example of a public good is that defence is actually provided privately in a market economy through aerospace companies and other defence contractors.

_____7.    Human life is priceless.

_____8.    The socially optimal price for admission to our national parks is zero.

_____9.    A private good is one that is always provided by the market.

_____10.    General knowledge, as opposed to specific technological knowledge, is an excludable good.

### B.  Multiple-Choice Questions

1.  Which one of the following are sidewalks an example of?
    a.  public good
    b.  private good
    c.  common resource
    d.  public or private good depending on who provides it

2. The whaling industry has hunted some species of whales nearly to extinction. Cattle, however, continue to thrive on farms throughout the world. Which one of the following is the major reason for this difference between cattle and whales?
   a. Whales are a common resource and cattle are private property.
   b. Whales are more valuable than cattle, and whalers are simply responding to economic incentives.
   c. The technology for harvesting whales has improved faster than that for cattle.
   d. Whaling is an international industry but cattle are raised locally.

3. Which one of the following is a reason that more litter occurs along highways than in private driveways?
   a. because there is more traffic on highways
   b. because nobody cares about litter along highways
   c. because highways are a common resource
   d. because there are not enough tax dollars to clean the highways

4. Which one of the following are flood control dams?
   a. public goods
   b. private goods
   c. natural monopolies
   d. common resources

5. Which one of the following is the **BEST** example of the Tragedy of the Commons?
   a. an AIDS epidemic
   b. overconsumption when McDonald's misjudges and underprices its basic hamburger
   c. when tomatoes in a community garden are picked before they are fully ripe
   d. the failure of communism and the downfall of the Soviet Union

6. Which one of the following describes a good that is neither rival nor excludable?
   a. it generates positive externality
   b. it generates negative externality
   c. It is a public good
   d. It is a private good

7. The free-rider problem is associated with _____ and is a consequence of their consumption being _____.
   a. public goods, excludable.
   b. public goods, not excludable.
   c. private goods, excludable.
   d. private goods, not excludable.

8. Which of the following statements can be made about public goods?
   a. cost nothing to produce.
   b. can be consumed by additional people without additional cost once they are produced.
   c. tend to be overconsumed from the standpoint of society.
   d. are overproduced by the market.

9. Which one of the following explains why private firms are **NOT** likely to fund the socially optimal amount of basic research?
   a. because basic research has no payoff
   b. because basic research yields benefits that cannot be measured in dollars
   c. because basic research provides long-term but not short-term benefits
   d. because basic research produces benefits to society as a whole, including those who do not pay for it

10. Which of the following occurs when someone consumes a common resource, (unlike the case with public goods)? ,?
    a. engages in rival consumption
    b. increase the benefits received by other consumers
    c. tends to underconsume it from the standpoint of society
    d. does not impose a negative externality on others

11. Which one of the following refers to the provision of an education in a public school?
    a. it is excludable and rival
    b. it is nonexcludable but rival
    c. it is excludable but nonrival
    d. it is nonexcludable and nonrival

12. Which one of the following explains why markets are **NOT** likely to produce a public good?
    a. because of the cost of producing the public good
    b. because the technology is too expensive for private firms to produce the public good
    c. because of the negative externalities associated with these goods
    d. because it is almost impossible to prevent a person not willing to pay for the good from receiving benefits from the good

13. Which one of the following features does a common good share with a private good?
    a. rival consumption
    b. excludability
    c. efficient provision by the market
    d. nonrival consumption

14. Which one of the following features is common to both private goods and natural monopolies?
    a.  they are both excludable
    b.  they are both nonrival
    c.  they are both produced efficiently by the market
    d.  they are both consumable by additional users without making existing users worse off

15. Which one of the following is an example of the Tragedy of the Commons?
    a.  a crime is committed in a public place
    b.  a common resource becomes rival in consumption
    c.  law enforcement in public places is enhanced
    d.  property rights are ignored
    e.  common resources are divided equally among their users.

16. Which one of the following explains why cost benefit analysis is difficult?
    a.  because analysts cannot estimate the explicit cost of a project that has not been completed
    b.  because analysts do not have access to information about typical cost overruns
    c.  because analysts do not typically observe prices when evaluating the benefits of a public good
    d.  because analysts are not able to consider the opportunity cost of resources

17. Many species of animals with commercial value are threatened with extinction. Which one of the following explains why the cow, a valuable source of food, does not face this threat?
    a.  because cows are a common resource
    b.  because cows are privately owned
    c.  because veterinary practices have protected cows from diseases
    d.  because their hides fetch less money than other species

18. Which one of the following is the simplest way to solve the problem of congested roads?
    a.  build more roads
    b.  offer more public transportation
    c.  levy a gasoline tax
    d.  institute tolls

## C.  Short-Answer Questions

1.  From 1850 to 1950, the annual average catch of northern cod, a population
    of cod located on the eastern shores of Newfoundland and Labrador, was
    250 000 tonnes. By 1968, the size of the annual catch reached a peak of
    800 000 tonnes, but the stock of northern cod was not large enough to
    support this level of fishing. The federal government set a limit of 120 000
    tonnes on the catch of the species in 1991 and closed this fishery in 1992.
    In 1999, the federal government reopened it with a limit of 7000 tonnes,
    only to halt it again later. Why did the government limit and/or halt the size
    of the catch? Would it not be rational for fishers to cut back voluntarily on
    the quantity of fish they catch, when it is obvious that everyone benefits if
    they all agree to some restraint in order to avoid exhaustion of this
    resource? _____

    _____

    _____

    _____

    _____

2.  A lighthouse is often given as an example of a public good. Why? (How
    does it satisfy the criteria for a public good?) Are there any reasons why a
    lighthouse might fail to meet the test for a public good? Explain. ___

    _____

    _____

    _____

    _____

3.  Food is more of a basic necessity than highways, yet governments build
    roads for the general public and normally do not provide food for everyone.
    Why?

    _____

    _____

    _____

    _____

## D.  Practice Problems

1.  Consider the following goods and services. Identify their characteristics in
    terms of rivalry and excludability, then categorize each as either private,
    public, natural monopoly, or common resource. Explain the answers.
    a.  Commercial television signals. _____

        _____

        _____

        _____

    b.  Congested city streets. _____

_____

_____

_____

    c.  A poem. _____

_____

_____

_____

    d.  General medical research on the relationship between lifestyle and heart disease.

_____

_____

_____

    e.  A congested public swimming pool. _____

_____

_____

_____

    f.  An uncongested private swimming pool. _____

_____

_____

_____

2.  The following table shows four possible categories of goods according to degree of rivalness and excludability.

    a.  Label the four types as either public goods, private goods, common resources, or natural monopolies.

    b.  Give an example not already used in the text of a good in each category.

    c.  Explain briefly under each example why it belongs in the category.

**Categories of Good**

RIVAL?

| | YES | NO |
|---|---|---|
| **YES**<br><br><br>**EXCLUDABLE?**<br><br><br>**NO** | TYPE: _____<br><br>EXAMPLE: _____<br><br>EXPLAIN: _____<br><br>_____<br>_____<br>_____<br>_____<br>_____<br>_____<br>_____<br>_____<br>_____<br><br>TYPE: _____<br><br>EXAMPLE: _____<br><br>EXPLAIN: _____<br><br>_____<br>_____<br>_____<br>_____<br>_____<br>_____<br>_____<br>_____ | TYPE: _____<br><br>EXAMPLE: _____<br><br>EXPLAIN: _____<br><br>_____<br>_____<br>_____<br>_____<br>_____<br>_____<br>_____<br>_____<br>_____<br><br>TYPE: _____<br><br>EXAMPLE: _____<br><br>EXPLAIN: _____<br><br>_____<br>_____<br>_____<br>_____<br>_____<br>_____<br>_____<br>_____ |

3.  Why does free access to a common resource generate an inefficient solution?

_____

_____

_____

### E.  Advanced Critical Thinking

1.  According to the late Jacques Cousteau, "our goal for the environment should be total cleanup: We should not stop until all effluent should be drinkable and all smokestack gases should be breathable."

    a.  Do you agree? If we had achieved 99.9% cleanup, would you agree that our goal should be to eliminate the final 0.1% pollution? Would it change your opinion if there were clear evidence that cleaning up the final 0.1% residual pollution would save 10 lives per year? What if the cost to society for the final 0.1% cleanup were $1 trillion? Write a critique of Cousteau's statement, explaining clearly why you agree or disagree. _____

    _____

    _____

    _____

    _____

    _____

    _____

    b.  In what sense is the environment a common resource? Does this help to explain why achieving the optimal level of environmental cleanup tends to require government action? _____

    _____

    _____

    _____

    _____

    _____

    _____

2. Irving Kristol, in a *Wall Street Journal* article entitled "The Hidden Cost of Regulation," wrote that environmental cleanup is an "economically unproductive expenditure" because it does not contribute to profit. Kristol argued that "cleaner water is a 'free social asset' to the population in the neighbourhood." He also argued that environmental regulations "render . . . economic costs invisible." Write a critique of Kristol's statement, in the form of a Letter to the Editor of a major newspaper, explaining clearly the ways in which you agree or disagree. Include a discussion of whether or not environmental cleanup is a "productive expenditure." Could it be productive for society overall but not for the individual firm? What is Kristol assuming about the property rights to the environment? In what sense is he right that regulation renders costs invisible? In what sense does environmental regulation have the opposite effect, i.e., in making explicit some existing costs that had been invisible to polluters?

_____

_____

_____

_____

_____

_____

_____

_____

_____

_____

_____

## III. Solutions

### A. True/False Questions

1. F; such decisions regarding nonexcludable goods lead to an inefficient allocation of resources due to externalities—something of value has no price attached to it.
2. F; downloading music from the Internet is not excludable and the musicians are not paid for their creations; downloaders get a free ride.
3. F; an uncongested road is not a common resource because the consumption is not rival; rather, if exclusion is not practical, it is a public good (until it becomes crowded).
4. T
5. T
6. F; this is irrelevant: nonrivalness and nonexclusion make national defence a public good, which would be true even if an aerospace firm ran the military as a private company.
7. F; at least in an economic sense, society does not put an infinite value on life; people take risks with human life every day in a variety of ways.

8.    F; at a zero price, Canada's national parks would be hopelessly overcrowded, indicating that the price is too low for equilibrium; price serves to ration scarce resources efficiently, including space in national parks.
9.    F; private goods are sometimes provided by government (surplus food, for example); some goods are private because of their innate characteristics of rivalness and excludability.
10.   F; general knowledge is a public good; one person's use of an item of general knowledge does not prevent any other person from using the same knowledge.

## B.  Multiple-Choice Questions

| | | | | |
|---|---|---|---|---|
| 1. a | 5. c | 9. d | 13. a | 17. b |
| 2. a | 6. c | 10. a | 14. a | 18. d |
| 3. c | 7. b | 11. a | 15. b | |
| 4. c | 8. b | 12. d | 16. c | |

## C.  Short-Answer Questions

1.    Because northern cod is a common resource, there is a tendency toward overfishing, and it illustrates an important example of an externality. Even if every fisher would like to cut back in order to maintain the cod stocks over time, this will not happen without collective action such as regulation. If a fisher tries to conserve the stock by leaving the cod in the ocean, someone else will probably catch that cod. Although there will be fewer fish to catch in the future, the cost will be borne by all. Without enforceable property rights and in the absence of regulations, there is no incentive for rational people to conserve. Or, in other words, there is an incentive to overfish.

2.    Traditionally, a lighthouse has been used as an example of a public good. Consumption is nonrival in the sense that the light is available for everyone simultaneously; additional users do not diminish the value received by others. Supposedly it is also very difficult to exclude those who refuse to pay. However, the claim of nonexclusion may be overstated: it is certainly possible for a lighthouse owner to contract with ship owners to turn on the light only when their ships are passing, while leaving the light off at other times to avoid free riders.

3.    Food is a private good subject to rival consumption and easy exclusion of nonpayers. As such, food lends itself easily to efficient provision by the market. Highways, however, are nonrival, at least during uncongested periods, and exclusion is difficult for other than limited-access highways. Although there are some strong arguments for pricing roads to ration their usage during congested periods, it is still more challenging to price roads than to price food.

## D.  Practice Problems

1.  a.  Commercial television signals. This good is nonrival because an additional viewer does not reduce the strength of the signal received by other viewers. Nonexcludable (with current equipment) because anyone with a tuner can receive the signal without paying. This makes it a public good even though it is provided privately.

    b.  Congested city streets. This good is rival because additional users impose costs on other drivers by increasing the congestion. Nonexcludable because it would be very difficult to charge tolls on city streets with virtually unlimited access. This is a common resource that tends to be overconsumed.

    c.  A poem. This good is nonrival because many people can enjoy the same poem at the same time. Nonexcludable because users can read the poem or even memorize it and enjoy it without paying for it. As such, it is a classic case of a public good.

    d.  General medical research on the relationship between lifestyle and heart disease. Consumption is nonrival because the same research can benefit one or one billion people simultaneously. It is also nonexcludable because once knowledge is gained, it is virtually impossible to keep it away from people who do not pay for it. Basic research is a public good.

    e.  A congested public swimming pool. This good is rival because of the crowding. More users clearly will detract from the benefits received by existing users. It is also excludable because it is very easy to admit only those who buy an admission ticket. It meets both criteria for a private good even though it is publicly provided.

    f.  An uncongested private swimming pool. This good is nonrival because it is not crowded. As long as it is not crowded, additional swimmers do not impose costs on other users. It is also excludable, not because it is privately owned, but because it is easy to require the purchase of a ticket for admission. Therefore, it meets the requirements for a natural monopoly. The fact that it is privately owned is irrelevant.

2.

# Categories of Goods

## RIVAL?

|  | YES | NO |
|---|---|---|
| **YES** **EXCLUDABLE?** | TYPE: Private<br>EXAMPLE: sirloin steak<br><br>EXPLAIN: My consumption of a steak prevents you from consuming it, and those who do not pay can be excluded (any similar example would work here). | TYPE: Natural Monopoly<br>EXAMPLE: a nearly empty theatre<br><br>EXPLAIN: Because it is not crowded, consumption is nonrival, yet exclusion is still possible (those who do not buy tickets are not admitted) |
| **NO** | TYPE: Common Resource<br>EXAMPLE: wild mushrooms<br>EXPLAIN: People who pick wild mushrooms tend to pick all that they can find because they know that if they leave any to regenerate, someone else will come along and pick them anyway. The pickers would be more likely to do a controlled harvest if they could keep the mushroom patch to themselves. | TYPE: Public Good<br>EXAMPLE: a song<br>EXPLAIN: A song can be enjoyed by additional people without taking away enjoyment by others. It is also very difficult to exclude nonpayers from enjoying it, although copyright owners try to collect royalties from public use (an action that is not always successful). |

3. Common resources are rival but nonexcludable. As a result, the use of these resources by one consumer reduces the amount available for others, and externalities associated with the use of common resources are generally negative. Because these resources are not priced ($P = 0$), people tend to overuse and, as a result, the socially optimal quantity is less than the actual quantity consumed.

## E. Advanced Critical Thinking

1.  a.  Although the goal is noble, it is impractical and would actually make society worse off. Even without factories, cars, furnaces, or even campfires, human beings themselves cannot even meet the standard of zero effluent. Zero tolerance on the environment would mean cleaning up every vestige of pollution, even if the residual pollution were trivial, yet would cost billions of dollars to correct. Even if society had the technology, society would be worse off by cleaning up pollution beyond the point at which the last dollar spent provided a dollar's worth of benefit to society. Even when lives are involved, costs and benefits need to be weighed. Suppose that society could eliminate the residual pollution and save 10 lives per year at a social cost of $1 trillion per year. More lives could be saved each year by reallocating that $1 trillion to other lifesaving activities, such as making highways safer or medical research. The $1 trillion has to come from somewhere; nothing is free. If the alternative is other lifesaving activities, then spending the $1 trillion on the environment may actually cost lives!

    b.  Unless property rights to the environment are established, clean air and water are owned by nobody, and, therefore, they tend to be treated as free goods. If the marginal cost of using the environment is zero to the individual, then in the absence of restrictions, he or she will use it as long as an additional unit has any positive marginal benefit. Although rational for the individual, it is overconsumption from the standpoint of society.

2.  Kristol makes a valid point that environmental cleanup is not free; it takes resources away from other uses. To call it unproductive, however, suggests that it has no value. He glosses over the distinction between private and public benefits. Certainly, a clean environment has benefits to society, even if cleanup does not add to profit. The fact that pollution is a negative externality is, of course, the rationale for government intervention: the individual polluter does not consider the social good in making a decision about environmental cleanup. Kristol argues that regulation hides some costs to society in the sense that, unless forced to do so by law, regulators will not measure the costs of their regulations to business and society as a whole. However, the purpose of environmental

policy is to make explicit some costs that polluters traditionally ignored because they were able to shift those costs to others. When regulators internalize negative externalities, they actually make visible to the polluter some costs that had been invisible. Kristol apparently treats the property rights to the environment as "first come, first served." Otherwise, it makes no sense to state that when a polluter cleans up after itself, it is providing a "free social asset" to the community. Only if one accepts the argument that the polluter owns the environment does it follow that restoring it to its original state is somehow a gift to the victims of pollution.

# CHAPTER 12 The Design of the Tax System

## I. Chapter Overview

### A. Context and Purpose

The last two chapters looked at the role of government in correcting the problems caused by externalities and public goods in a market economy. The emphasis was on government expenditures, with little consideration of how the government generates the revenue to pay for those spending programs.

This chapter concludes the three-chapter sequence on the role of government by analyzing the characteristics and economic impact of the Canadian tax system. The chapter explores the efficiency cost or deadweight loss from taxes, the incidence of taxes (who actually bears the burden), and the equity effects of taxation.

### A. Helpful Hints

1. *Taxes impose efficiency costs on the economy in the form of deadweight losses when they (i) alter people's behaviour and incentive and (ii) impose administrative costs.* Taxes alter behaviour if they discourage someone from buying a good or service and, as a result, no tax revenue is generated from that taxpayer. The deadweight loss results because there is a loss for one person without a corresponding gain for another. Taxes are not costless to administer. Like the deadweight loss, the administrative cost is an efficiency loss because there is a cost to one person without an offsetting gain to someone else. The time that a person spends filling out a tax return benefits no one.

2. *The equity of a tax system concerns the fair distribution of the tax burden among the population.* Equity is difficult to assess because fairness is very subjective. One way to determine the fairness of a tax is through the *benefits principle*: benefits that taxpayers receive from the government programs that these taxes finance. An alternative is the *ability-to-pay principle*: taxes should be assessed according to taxpayers' financial capability; that is, those who earn more should pay more. The goals are *vertical equity* and *horizontal equity*. Vertical equity means that taxpayers with a higher ability to pay should pay more taxes. Horizontal equity means that taxpayers with the same ability to pay should pay the same amount. In evaluating the equity of a tax system, it is important to remember that the distribution of tax burdens is not the same as the distribution of tax bills.

3. *Taxes are designed to transfer real resources—land, labour, and capital— from the private to the public sectors.* For those who are skeptical, keep in mind that government has printing presses and could always print more money to pay for its spending. The problem is that printing money would not make scarcity go away. Printing money is essentially another way to tax people to pay for government expenditures. Everything has an opportunity cost. If society wants more public roads or schools or parks, it must be willing to give up something else to get them. Taxes are simply a way to reduce private spending when public spending goes up.

4. *If society wants more of something, subsidize it. If society wants less of something, tax it.* Taxes distort behaviour by increasing the opportunity cost of doing whatever is taxed. Sometimes this is desirable, for example, when cigarette taxes are raised to discourage smoking. Other times, taxes discourage behaviour that is desirable. For example, payroll taxes like Employment Insurance contributions are essentially taxes on employment. As such, they introduce a wedge between the wage paid and the wage received (after taxes), resulting in fewer people working.

5. *People pay taxes.* This may seem obvious, but often one hears of arguments for taxing rich corporations. Corporations are neither rich nor poor, rather, they are merely conduits through which money flows from people to other people. Corporate taxes are paid by people—owners, customers, and/or employees. The actual mix, or tax incidence, is determined by the elasticities of supply and demand in the relevant markets for the corporation's products, labour, and capital.

## II. Self-Testing Challenges

### A. True/False Questions

_____ 1. The average tax rate is the most important factor in how much a particular tax will distort behaviour.

_____ 2. Horizontal equity means that everyone should pay the same dollar amount of taxes regardless of income.

_____ 3. A tax that collects more dollars from a rich person than a poor person is known as a progressive tax.

_____ 4. A marginal tax rate is equal to the actual taxes paid divided by income.

_____ 5. One tax system is more efficient than another if it raises the same amount of revenue at a higher cost to taxpayers, and imposes small deadweight losses and small administrative burdens.

_____6.   Replacing the income tax with a consumption tax would encourage saving.

_____7.   A regressive tax takes a smaller fraction of income from a rich person than from a poor person.

_____8.   The deadweight loss is the inefficiency that a tax creates as people allocate resources according to the tax incentive, rather than according to the true costs and benefits of the goods and services that they produce and consume.

_____9.   The Canadian tax system, when viewed in its totality, is roughly proportional except for very low-income and very high-income levels.

_____10.  The degree of efficiency loss from an excise tax varies between markets, depending on the price elasticities of demand and supply.

## B.  Multiple-Choice Questions

1.   Which one of the following specifies the **MOST** important sources of tax revenue for the federal and provincial governments, respectively?
     a.   personal income tax, corporate income tax
     b.   personal income tax, personal income tax
     c.   corporate income tax, personal income tax
     d.   personal income tax, provincial sales tax

2.   Which one of the following explains why deadweight losses occur?
     a.   because of the distortion of behaviour caused by taxes
     b.   because of the inevitable inefficiency caused by all government programs
     c.   because of the inherent reduction in standard of living caused by the payment of taxes
     d.   because of the inequities caused by taxes

3.   Which one of the following is the **BEST** example of a tax justified under the benefits principle?
     a.   a gasoline tax used to pay for highways
     b.   a sales tax used to build a sports arena
     c.   a provincial payroll tax to help fund health care
     d.   an income tax used for defence spending

4.   Which one of the following would be an effect of replacing income tax with a flat-rate consumption tax?
   a.   It would encourage less saving.
   b.   It would make the tax system more progressive.
   c.   It would mean that two families with the same income would not necessarily have the same tax bill.
   d.   It would decrease the after-tax interest rate received on bank accounts.

5.   Which one of the following levels of government is where **MOST** of the growth in the size of the Canadian government sector has taken place over the past 40 years?
   a.   at the government agency level
   b.   the provincial government level
   c.   the federal government level

6.   If a person pays $2000 tax on an income of $10 000 and $3000 on an income of $20 000, which one of the following is the tax structure?
   a.   average
   b.   marginal
   c.   regressive
   d.   progressive

7.   Suppose a person's average tax rate is 25 percent and the marginal tax rate is 40 percent. If the person receives an additional $100 of income, which one of the following would be the amount of the implied additional tax payment?
   a.   $10
   b.   $25
   c.   $40
   d.   $65

8.   Which one of the following is the entire burden or the incidence of the corporate income tax on?
   a.   consumers
   b.   owners
   c.   workers
   d.   people

9.   Which one of the following describes the **MOST** basic tradeoff in economics?
   a.   between efficiency and equity
   b.   between vertical and horizontal equity
   c.   between business taxes and individual taxes
   d.   between the needs of the many and the desires of the few

10.  Which one of the following is the **BIGGEST** source of revenue for the Canadian federal government?
   a.  payroll taxes
   b.  corporate income taxes
   c.  excise taxes
   d.  individual income taxes

11.  Which of the following is characteristic of a tax system that satisfies the principle of vertical equity?
   a.  the average tax rate is higher for those with higher incomes
   b.  the marginal tax rate is the same for all
   c.  those with high incomes pay more taxes
   d.  those in similar situations pay the same amount in taxes

12.  Which one of the following is the **BIGGEST** single source of revenue for Canada's provincial governments?
   a.  property taxes
   b.  individual income taxes
   c.  corporate income taxes
   d.  sales taxes

13.  Which one of the following is the **LARGEST** budget item for provincial governments?
   a.  transportation
   b.  social services
   c.  education
   d.  health care

14.  Which one of the following is the **MOST** efficient tax?
   a.  lump-sum tax
   b.  individual income tax
   c.  corporate income tax
   d.  consumption tax

15.  Which one of the following is the **BEST** example of a tax that is usually justified on the grounds of ability to pay?
   a.  sales tax
   b.  property tax
   c.  corporate income tax
   d.  progressive income tax

16.  Which one of the following defines an efficient tax?
   a.  one that raises large amounts of money quickly
   b.  one that generates revenues at the least cost to the taxpayers
   c.  one that satisfies both vertical and horizontal equity
   d.  one that is easy to administer

17.   Which one of the following is associated with vertical equity and horizontal equity?
    a.   the benefits principle of taxation
    b.   the ability-to-pay principle of taxation
    c.   falling marginal tax rates
    d.   rising marginal tax rates

18.   The structure of the Canadian federal income tax is progressive. Which one of the following best explains what this means?
    a.   average tax rates that rise and marginal tax rates that are constant at most income levels
    b.   average tax rates that are more than marginal tax rates at most income levels
    c.   average tax rates that are less than marginal tax rates at most income levels
    d.   average and marginal tax rates are equal and rise at most income levels

## C.  Short-Answer Questions

1.   Lump-sum taxes are sometimes promoted as superior to other forms of taxation, yet they are rarely included in real-world tax structures.

    a.   What are lump-sum taxes and what are their advantages over traditional taxes? Explain. _____

       _____
       _____
       _____
       _____

    b.   What characteristics of lump-sum taxes keep them from becoming more commonly used? _____

       _____
       _____
       _____
       _____
       _____

2.   The benefits principle seems much more objective as a measure of equity than the ability-to-pay principle. In spite of this, the benefits principle is not used very often to justify a tax proposal. Why is not it used more often? (Why is it easier to justify most taxes on ability-to-pay grounds?)

     _____
     _____
     _____

3.  Parliament has built many incentives into the tax code to encourage certain types of behaviour, such as deductions for charitable giving and contributions to Registered Savings Plans (RSPs). Even if these inducements are socially desirable on efficiency grounds (as either public goods or positive externalities), are there any ways that they might interfere with the achievement of equity? _____

_____
_____
_____
_____
_____
_____

4.  What do economists mean when they argue that the tax system should be both efficient and equitable? _____

_____
_____
_____

## D. Practice Problems

1.  The table below presents a case study of taxable consumption by income bracket for taxpayers in a hypothetical province with a 5% sales tax.

    a.  Fill in the blanks in the table.

    ### Tax Paid and Effective Tax Rate under a 5% Provincial Sales Tax

| Income | Taxable consumption | Tax paid | Average tax rate (% of income) |
|---|---|---|---|
| $10 000 | $10 000 | $_____ | _____% |
| $20 000 | $18 000 | $_____ | _____% |
| $30 000 | $26 000 | $_____ | _____% |
| $40 000 | $34 000 | $_____ | _____% |
| $50 000 | $42 000 | $_____ | _____% |

    b.  Is the tax regressive, progressive, or proportional? Why? _____

_____
_____
_____
_____
_____
_____
_____

c.  Would the numbers and your answer to part (b) change if the province exempted certain basic necessities like food and clothing? Explain.

_____

_____

d.  Is a consumption tax, such as the sales tax, likely to be more or less efficient than an income tax with a comparable yield? Would exempting food and clothing make the sales tax more or less efficient? Explain. _____

_____

_____

_____

_____

_____

_____

2.  Calculate the marginal tax rates from the following hypothetical example.

| Taxable income | Tax rate |
| --- | --- |
| $10 000 | 10% |
| $50 000 | 20% |
| $100 000 | 30% |

## E.  Advanced Critical Thinking

Before World War II, the corporate income tax was the second largest revenue source for the federal government, behind only the individual income tax. In recent decades it has fallen in importance to third place behind federal payroll taxes. In spite of the movement away from this tax, the general public continues to support the corporate income tax under the belief that rich corporations should pay their share of the tax burden. On the other hand, some critics argue that the corporate income tax could be integrated into the individual income tax by eliminating the corporate tax and raising individual income tax rates to make up for the lost tax revenue. They argue that equity and efficiency could be improved and the tax system streamlined by combining both income taxes into a single individual income tax.

What do you think? Would corporations get away without paying their fair share of taxes if the two income taxes were combined? Who really pays business taxes? The corporations themselves? Write a critique of the corporate income tax, addressing the issues raised by both the critics and the supporters. Be sure to include the following issues: vertical and/or horizontal equity, administrative costs, and deadweight losses. Conclude with a summary evaluation of the prospects for integrating the corporate and individual income taxes. _____

_____

_____

_____

_____

_____

_____

## III.  Solutions

### A.  True/False Questions

1.  F; the marginal tax rate has the primary effect on behaviour because people make decisions at the margin.
2.  F; it means that people with equal incomes should pay the same taxes.
3.  F; only if the rich person pays a higher tax *rate* (not just more dollars) is it progressive.
4.  F; marginal tax rate is *additional* dollars as a percent of *additional* income.
5.  F; a tax system is efficient if it raises the same amount of revenue at a *lower* cost to taxpayers.
6.  T
7.  T
8.  T
9.  F; the system is roughly proportional for all income levels.
10.  T

### B.  Multiple-Choice Questions

| | | | | |
|---|---|---|---|---|
| 1. b | 5. b | 9. a | 13. d | 17. b |
| 2. a | 6. c | 10. d | 14. a | 18. c |
| 3. a | 7. c | 11. c | 15. d | |
| 4. d | 8. d | 12. b | 16. b | |

### C.  Short-Answer Questions

1.  a.  A lump-sum tax is one that requires everyone to pay the same number of dollars in taxes regardless of their economic status or behaviour. By their nature, lump-sum taxes do not distort behaviour because there is no behaviour change that can alter them; therefore, they are a model of efficiency. The cost to the taxpayer is the tax itself, without any deadweight loss.

b. In spite of their efficiency advantages, lump-sum taxes have a major drawback in terms of equity. Because everyone pays exactly the same amount, the tax is highly regressive. The millionaire pays exactly the same number of dollars in taxes as the homeless person. Few people would accept this on vertical equity grounds. In fact, it is not even possible for a person at the subsistence level to pay taxes without starving.

2. In general, it is difficult to link most taxes to the benefits of the government programs that they fund. In most cases, tax revenues go directly into general revenues to fund programs in general. The income tax, for example, can be defended based on ability to pay but would be hard to link to specific programs and their beneficiaries. Only in a few cases, such as the gasoline tax used to build and maintain highways, can beneficiaries be identified closely enough to use the benefits principle.

3. Such tax breaks can interfere with both vertical and horizontal equity. Because higher-income taxpayers are more likely to give to charity and to save for retirement, this tax break will tend to reduce the tax burden more for them, reducing the progressivity of the income tax. It also means that two taxpayers with identical incomes (ability to pay) may have different tax bills if one gives more to charity or saves more for his or her retirement. This violates the criterion of horizontal equity.

4. It means that taxes should impose as small a cost on society as possible and that the burden of the taxes should be distributed fairly.

### D.  Practice Problems

1.  a.   **Tax Paid and Effective Tax Rate under a 5% Provincial Sales Tax**

| Income | Taxable consumption | Tax paid | Average tax rate (% of income) |
|---|---|---|---|
| $10 000 | $10 000 | $500 | 5.0% |
| $20 000 | $18 000 | $900 | 4.5% |
| $30 000 | $26 000 | $1300 | 4.33% |
| $40 000 | $34 000 | $1700 | 4.25% |
| $50 000 | $42 000 | $2100 | 4.2% |

b.  The tax is regressive: the average tax rate falls from 5% to 4.2% as income rises from $10 000 to $50 000. This occurs because consumption rises at a slower rate than income. Taxpayers earning only $10 000 spend their entire income and, therefore, pay the 5% sales tax on their whole income. Taxpayers earning $50 000 spend only 84% of it, so the 5% tax is on only a part of their income, making the effective rate on income less than 5%. Note that 84% of 5% is 4.2%, which is the average sales tax for those earning $50 000.

c.  Exempting necessities would reduce taxes for all taxpayers, but the biggest percentage reduction would be for lower-income taxpayers, who spend proportionately more on such goods. This would make the tax less regressive, although it would be unlikely to eliminate regressivity completely.

d.  Consumption taxes tend to be more efficient than income taxes in the sense that they do not discourage saving by taxing interest received. The income tax introduces a tax wedge between suppliers and demanders of saving. A consumption tax avoids this source of inefficiency, and resulting deadweight loss, when the interest received by savers is less than the interest paid by banks because of taxes on interest. However, exempting food and clothing to improve equity introduces a new source of inefficiency by distorting consumer behaviour away from taxable and toward nontaxable consumption.

2.  Taxes paid on $10 000 are $1000.
    Taxes paid on $50 000 are $10 000.
    Therefore, additional taxes paid on $40 000 additional income are $9000.
    The marginal tax rate is 22.5% ($9 000/$40 000).
    Taxes paid on $100 000 are $30 000.
    Therefore, additional taxes paid on $50 000 additional income are $20 000.
    The marginal tax rate is 40% ($20 000/$50 000).

## E.  Advanced Critical Thinking

The corporate income tax is an inefficient way to raise revenue for the federal government. As revenues decline, the administrative costs for the government and the taxpayers continue. In some cases, the administrative cost to the taxpayers is actually greater than the tax payment itself. This is not efficient. Integrating the corporate tax into the individual income tax with the same revenue yield would eliminate an entire layer of bureaucracy and administrative cost. Generating the same revenue from the individual income tax would reduce the distortion caused by taxing some businesses (corporations), but not others. This additional taxation of corporations distorts their behaviour. Eliminating the corporate tax would end a distortion of behaviour caused by treating incorporated and unincorporated businesses differently. On equity grounds, the corporate income tax is ambiguous, mainly because society cannot agree entirely on who pays it. It is known, however, that it is not rich corporations that pay the tax. Corporations are neither rich nor poor. Only people pay taxes. When a corporation is taxed, the tax may be shifted to consumers in the form of higher prices, or workers in the form of lower wages, or owners (stockholders) in the form of lower profits leading to lower dividends and lower value of their shares of stock. Under the individual income tax, the degree of progressivity is controlled by society in setting tax rates. Under the corporate tax, the market controls tax incidence, which makes it harder for policymakers to achieve vertical and horizontal equity goals.

# 13 The Costs of Production

## I. Chapter Overview

### A. Context and Purpose

Earlier chapters introduced the workings of the market system (Chapters 1–7), and then explored the role of government in improving efficiency when the market is less than perfect (Chapters 8–12). The focus now returns to the analysis of the market system by examining business structure and operation in the next five chapters (13–17).

This chapter looks at a firm's cost of production and the firm's revenue and profit, and it distinguishes economic cost and profit from accounting cost and profit. The chapter explains that cost and profit take on very specific meanings in economics that differ from the everyday use of the terms. The analysis in this chapter will provide the tools necessary to understand how all firms, from the largest to the smallest, behave under different types of market conditions.

### A. Helpful Hints

1. *Economic cost is not the same as accounting cost.* The concept of cost used by economists is not quite the same as that used by accountants. By cost, economists mean "opportunity cost," that is, all those things that must be forgone to acquire an input or the return that a particular resource could get in its best alternative use. Thus, economists include not only the explicit accounting costs, but also implicit costs of production.

2. *The distinction between short run and long run in economics is somewhat arbitrary.* Economists define the short run as a period in which some inputs (typically capital and land) are fixed, while at least one input (typically labour) is variable, and the long run as a period long enough for firms to vary all inputs or even enter or exit the industry. Although arbitrary, it makes a lot of sense: a firm desiring to increase output quickly could expand labour immediately, but it would take a while to build a new factory.

3. *Diminishing marginal product is the rule, not the exception.* As long as only labour can vary, it should not be surprising that output will not rise in proportion with labour input. Imagine growing strawberries in your backyard in a plot that is only 20 × 10 metres. You might be able to pick 3 pints of strawberries in 15 minutes. However, additional workers in the same small plot could not be expected to maintain that level of output per

worker. Eventually, the marginal product of an additional worker will fall because land and capital are fixed. With enough workers, the marginal product actually becomes negative when the patch is so crowded that people are getting in each others' way and trampling the berries.

4. *Diminishing marginal product is not the same thing as negative marginal product.* The average person often confuses the two concepts. In the strawberry patch, diminishing marginal product is not bad—even if all workers are identical, not every worker should be expected to add the same amount to output. In addition, hiring more workers adds to total product, albeit at a decreasing rate. Negative marginal product, on the other hand, means that another picker actually reduces total product and should not be hired, or even be allowed to help for free.

5. *Marginal cost always intersects average total cost and average variable costs at their lowest points.* The marginal value contributes to the average, so if marginal is less than average, it pulls the average down, and if marginal is greater than average, it pulls the average up. Think about what happens to the overall GPA (grade point average) of the class when another student adds the course. The marginal GPA of the additional student either raises or lowers the average. Overall, GPA for the class falls as long as the marginal GPA is below the average, and rises when the marginal GPA exceeds the average.

6. *Economies of scale and diseconomies of scale* refer to technological conditions under which long-run average cost decreases or increases, respectively, as output increases.

## II.  Self-Testing Challenges

### A.  True/False Questions

_____1.    Economic profit is typically higher than accounting profit.

_____2.    The marginal product of an input is the last unit of output that it produces.

_____3.    Implicit costs are opportunity costs for which there is no actual money outlay.

_____4.    Whenever marginal cost is less than average variable cost, average variable cost is falling.

_____5.    Average fixed cost does not vary with output.

_____6.    All costs are variable in the short run.

_____7.    Marginal cost is defined as the additional cost incurred as a result of hiring one more unit of input.

_____8.    The average-total-cost curve has the most pronounced U-shape in the short run.

_____9.    Average total cost reaches a minimum where it intersects average variable cost.

_____10.    Diseconomies of scale are caused by problems of coordination and communication that are inherent in large organizations.

_____11.    If marginal product is negative, output decreases whenever one more unit of the variable input is hired.

_____12.    Diminishing marginal product is the property whereby the marginal product of an input declines as the quantity of the input decreases.

## B.    Multiple-Choice Questions

1.    Which one of the following costs is variable in the short run?
    a.    wages paid to labour
    b.    payments to suppliers to buy new capital equipment
    c.    rent on land
    d.    interest on business loans to buy capital equipment

2.    Which one of the following costs is variable in the long run?
    a.    wages paid to labour
    b.    grants to suppliers to buy new capital equipment
    c.    purchase price of land
    d.    interest on business loans to buy capital equipment

3.    Which one of the following would an economist say is the definition of the opportunity cost of an input used in production?
    a.    the money paid to acquire that input
    b.    the benefit forgone by not using that input in its best alternative
    c.    the accounting cost of that input
    d.    the benefit forgone by not using that input in its worst alternative

4.    Which one of the following is the point at which marginal cost always equals average total cost?
    a.    at minimum average total cost
    b.    at minimum marginal cost
    c.    at maximum average total cost
    d.    at average variable cost

Use the following data for Jalali's Auto Trader to answer questions 5–11.

| Number of automobiles sold per week | Total cost of operation (excluding the value of automobiles) |
|:---:|:---:|
| 0 | $1000 |
| 10 | $1400 |
| 20 | $1600 |
| 30 | $1700 |
| 40 | $2000 |
| 50 | $2600 |

5.    Which one of the following is the variable cost of selling 30 automobiles?
   a.  $700
   b.  $1400
   c.  $1600
   d.  $1700

6.    Which one of the following is the fixed cost of selling 40 automobiles?
   a.  $1000
   b.  $1400
   c.  $1600
   d.  $1700

7.    Which one of the following is the marginal cost of the 20th automobile?
   a.  $10
   b.  $20
   c.  $30
   d.  $40

8.    Which one of the following is the average total cost of selling 40 automobiles?
   a.  $25
   b.  $30
   c.  $32
   d.  $50

9.    Which one of the following is the average variable cost of selling 20 automobiles?
   a.  $25
   b.  $30
   c.  $32
   d.  $50

10.  Which one of the following is the average fixed cost of selling 50 automobiles?
  a.  $20
  b.  $25
  c.  $30
  d.  $50

11.  Which one of the following is the efficient scale of operation for Jalali's Auto Trader?
  a.  20 automobiles sold
  b.  30 automobiles sold
  c.  40 automobiles sold
  d.  50 automobiles sold

12.  Which one of the following explains when diminishing marginal product occurs?
  a.  whenever business is operating inefficiently, resulting in high per-unit costs
  b.  whenever the quality of the available labour pool deteriorates and production costs rise
  c.  whenever business becomes so large that it is unwieldy to manage and productivity declines
  d.  whenever additional workers add less to output than did the workers who came before

To answer questions 13–16, use the following information for Freischütz's Fabulous Franks, a hot dog stand that has been a downtown institution for 50 years.

| | |
|---|---|
| Cost of supplies and other materials | $10 000 |
| Rent | $20 000 |
| Wages paid | $25 000 |
| Interest on a $10 000 bank loan | $1000 |
| Freischütz's salary offer from a competitor | $20 000 |

13.  Which one of the following is the total explicit (accounting) cost of running Freischütz's Franks?
  a.  $11 000
  b.  $36 000
  c.  $56 000
  d.  $76 000

14.  Which one of the following is the total opportunity (economic) cost of running Freischütz's Franks?
   a. $36 000
   b. $56 000
   c. $75 000
   d. $76 000

15.  If Mr. Freischütz pays off the bank loan and invests $10 000 of his own money in the business, thus giving up the chance to earn $1000 in interest elsewhere, which one of the following will occur?
   a. Accounting and economic costs will both rise by $1000.
   b. Accounting and economic costs will both fall by $1000.
   c. Accounting cost will fall by $1000, but economic cost will not change.
   d. Accounting cost will not change, but economic cost will fall by $1000.

16.  If Mr. Freischütz has a job offer of $50 000 per year to manage his competitor's business, which one of the following will occur?
   a. The implicit cost of staying in business will rise.
   b. The explicit cost of staying in business will rise.
   c. The implicit cost of staying in business will fall.
   d. The explicit cost of staying in business will fall.

17.  Which one of the following statements is true?
   a. If fixed costs are positive, the average variable cost and the average total cost move further apart as output increases.
   b. If there are no fixed costs, the average variable cost is constant.
   c. If there are no fixed costs, the average variable cost and the average total cost are the same.

18.  Which one of the following statements is true?
   a. Diseconomies of scale is a short-run concept.
   b. Diminishing marginal product is a short-run concept.
   c. Diminishing marginal product results when the firm doubles in size without doubling output.
   d. Diseconomies of scale results when only one input increases and output fails to keep up.

19.  Which one of the following describes the behaviour of marginal cost when marginal product is rising?
   a. cost is rising
   b. cost is falling
   c. cost is constant

20.    With the law of diminishing returns, which of the following occurs as output increases in the short run?
a.   fixed cost will eventually fall
b.   fixed cost will eventually rise
c.   marginal cost will eventually fall
d.   marginal cost will eventually rise

## C.   Short-Answer Questions

1.   Consider the following production function for a pet supply manufacturer, Linh's Lemming Runs.

| Number of workers hired | 0 | 1 | 2 | 3 | 4 | 5 | 6 | 7 | 8 | 9 | 10 |
|---|---|---|---|---|---|---|---|---|---|---|---|
| Output | 0 | 10 | 25 | 40 | 50 | 59 | 61 | 62 | 62 | 62 | 60 |
| Marginal product | — | — | — | — | — | — | — | — | — | — | — |

a.   Fill in the missing values for marginal product.

b.   With which worker does diminishing marginal product set in? When does marginal product actually become negative? Compare the two cases in terms of the effect on total output. _____

_____
_____
_____
_____

2.   What is the connection between the U-shaped nature of the average total cost curve and (a) the property of diminishing marginal product, and (b) fixed costs? Explain your answer._____

_____
_____
_____

3.   Explain in your own words the difference between accounting profit and economic profit. Include discussion of the distinction between explicit and implicit costs and how they relate to economic cost and opportunity cost.

_____
_____
_____
_____
_____

## D.    Practice Problems

1.    Wendell's Widget Works faces the following cost schedule.

| Quantity (Q) | Fixed cost (FC) | Variable cost (VC) | Total cost (TC) | Marginal cost (MC) | Average variable cost (AVC) | Average fixed cost (AFC) | Average total cost (ATC) |
|---|---|---|---|---|---|---|---|
| 0 | $46 | $ 0 | $ | $ | $ | $ | $ |
| 1 | $ | $30 | $ | $ | $ | $ | $ |
| 2 | $ | $50 | $ | $ | $ | $ | $ |
| 3 | $ | $58 | $ | $ | $ | $ | $ |
| 4 | $ | $64 | $ | $ | $ | $ | $ |
| 5 | $ | $84 | $ | $ | $ | $ | $ |
| 6 | $ | $114 | $ | $ | $ | $ | $ |
| 7 | $ | $150 | $ | $ | $ | $ | $ |
| 8 | $ | $190 | $ | $ | $ | $ | $ |
| 9 | $ | $240 | $ | $ | $ | $ | $ |

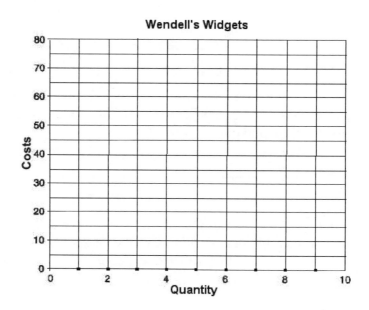

a. Fill in the table and graph the results.

b. Based on these cost curves, where does the diminishing marginal product set in? Explain. _____

_____

_____

_____

c. What is the relationship between total cost, variable cost, and fixed cost? Explain. _____

_____

_____

d. What is the relationship between average total cost, average variable cost, and AFC? Explain. _____

_____

_____

_____

e. What is the relationship between average total cost and marginal cost? Between average variable cost and marginal cost? Explain.

_____

_____

_____

f. What is Wendell's efficient scale? Explain. _____

_____

_____

_____

2.    Bob's Burger Box has been operating continuously since 1962. The original investment was $100 000, but the business is worth a lot more today. In fact, Bob's chief competitor would like to buy him out and has made a standing offer of $1 million any time that Bob wants to sell. He is also willing to hire Bob for $50 000 per year if Bob sells out. Bob has been tempted because he figures that he could earn 10% on the $1 million if he invests it wisely. You need to help him decide. Currently, Bob figures that he is earning a profit of $100 000 per year based on the following information:

Total Revenue: $200 000 (from 100 000 hamburgers @$2)
Total Money Outlays: $100 000 (wages paid, materials, utilities)

a.    What are his explicit (accounting) costs? What are his implicit costs? What is his total economic (opportunity) cost? Explain. _____
_____
_____

b.    If his goal is to maximize profit, should he stay in business or sell out? Is he earning any money? Would an accountant and an economist give the same answer to the question about how much he is earning? Explain. _____
_____
_____
_____
_____

c.    Would it affect your answer to (b) above if he inherited the business from his uncle and, therefore, had no money of his own invested in the business?
_____
_____

d.    Suppose that instead of owning the business free and clear, Bob owed $1 million to the bank on a 10% loan, or $100 000 per year, in interest. What effect would this have on your answer to (a)? Specifically, would it affect his explicit (accounting) cost? His implicit cost? His total economic (opportunity) cost? How would this affect his economic and accounting profit? Explain. _____
_____
_____
_____
_____
_____

3. Farbod Manufacturing has an opportunity to invest $1500 in Project A or Project B. Project A promises to generate $500 profit at the end of the first year, $550 at the end of two years, $600 at the end of three years, and $625 at the end of four years. Project B promises to generate $25 profit at the end of the first year, $100 at the end of two years, $600 at the end of three years and $1000 at the end of four years. Determine which investment promises to be the better of the two for the company, assuming that Farbod Manufacturing has a weighted average cost of capital of 9%.

## E.  Advanced Critical Thinking

Your uncle, who farms 1000 hectares in central Manitoba, has always claimed that he is losing money in farming. However, according to his tax returns, he earns a decent profit. Is someone not telling the truth, or does he simply need a better tax accountant? Why do you suppose he stays in agriculture if he is incurring losses as he claims?_____

_____
_____
_____
_____
_____
_____
_____
_____
_____
_____
_____

# III.  Solutions

## A.  True/False Questions

1.  F; economic profit is accounting profit minus implicit cost.
2.  F; the marginal product of an input is the additional output forthcoming from employing an additional unit of that input, other inputs held constant.
3.  T
4.  T
5.  F; average fixed cost always declines as output increases.
6.  F; all costs are variable in the *long run*.
7.  F; marginal cost is the extra cost incurred as a result of producing an additional unit of output.
8.  T
9.  F; average total cost reaches a minimum where it intersects *marginal* cost.
10.  T
11.  T
12.  F; it implies that the marginal product of an input declines as more (not less) of an input is employed.

## B.    Multiple-Choice Questions

| | | | | |
|---|---|---|---|---|
| 1. a | 5. a | 9. b | 13. c | 17. c |
| 2. a | 6. a | 10. a | 14. d | 18. b |
| 3. b | 7. b | 11. c | 15. c | 19. b |
| 4. a | 8. d | 12. d | 16. a | 20. d |

## C.    Short-Answer Questions

1.    a.    Consider the following production function for a pet supply manufacturer, Linh's Lemming Runs.

| Number of workers hired | 0 | 1 | 2 | 3 | 4 | 5 | 6 | 7 | 8 | 9 | 10 |
|---|---|---|---|---|---|---|---|---|---|---|---|
| Output | 0 | 10 | 25 | 40 | 50 | 59 | 61 | 62 | 62 | 62 | 60 |
| Marginal product | — | 10 | 15 | 15 | 10 | 9 | 2 | 1 | 0 | 0 | −2 |

      b.    Diminishing returns set in with the 4th worker hired because this is the first drop in marginal product (from 15 to 10). When marginal product begins to decline, total output continues to rise, although at a slower rate. With the 10th worker hired, the marginal product actually becomes negative, which means that *total* product begins to fall.

2.    The U-shaped nature of average total cost arises from the forces of both diminishing marginal product and declining average fixed cost (AFC). Initially, as output increases, the marginal productivity of the variable input rises, causing average variable cost (AVC) to fall. Falling average variable cost and declining AFC cause average total cost (which is the sum of AFC and average variable cost) to fall. Thus, as output increases, marginal productivity of the variable input diminishes, causing average variable cost to rise. Eventually, average variable cost rises faster than average fixed cost falls, causing average total cost to increase.

3.    Accounting profit is based on money flows; it equals the firm's total revenues minus all of the explicit money outlays required to generate those revenues. Economic profit takes into account all opportunity costs, even those that did not result in money outlays. Economic profit equals the firm's total revenues minus the full opportunity cost of earning those revenues, including both money outlays and any implicit opportunity costs of production.

## D.   Practice Problems

1.   a.   Wendell's Widget Works faces the following cost schedule:

| Quantity (Q) | Fixed cost (FC) | Variable cost (VC) | Total cost (TC) | Marginal cost (MC) | Average variable cost (AVC) | Average fixed cost (AFC) | Average total cost (ATC) |
|---|---|---|---|---|---|---|---|
| 0 | $46 | $0 | $46 | — | — | — | — |
| 1 | $46 | $30 | $76 | $30 | $30 | $46 | $76 |
| 2 | $46 | $50 | $96 | $20 | $25 | $23 | $48 |
| 3 | $46 | $58 | $104 | $8 | $19.3 | $15.3 | $34.7 |
| 4 | $46 | $64 | $110 | $6 | $16 | $11.5 | $27.5 |
| 5 | $46 | $84 | $130 | $20 | $16.8 | $9.2 | $26 |
| 6 | $46 | $114 | $160 | $30 | $19 | $7.7 | $26.7 |
| 7 | $46 | $150 | $196 | $36 | $21.4 | $6.6 | $28 |
| 8 | $46 | $190 | $236 | $40 | $23.8 | $5.8 | $29.5 |
| 9 | 46 | 240 | $286 | $50 | $26.7 | $5.1 | $31.8 |

b.   Yes, diminishing marginal product sets in at the output level at which marginal cost begins to rise, with the fifth unit of output. It is diminishing marginal product that causes marginal cost to rise by increasing the labour cost of each additional unit of output.

c.   Costs are either variable or fixed. Therefore, total cost = variable cost + fixed cost.

d.   If TC = VC + FC, then dividing both sides by Q maintains the equality and gives the following identity: ATC = AVC + AFC.

e.   Marginal cost always intersects ATC and average variable cost at their minimum points. In each case, the average is influenced by the marginal value: if MC > ATC or AVC, then the average rises, and if MC < ATC or AVC, then the average is pulled down by the low marginal cost.

f.   Wendell's efficient scale is an output of 5. At this quantity, average total cost reaches a minimum at 26.

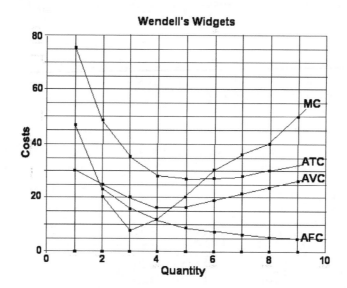

**Wendell's Widgets**

2.   a.   Bob's accounting cost = $100 000. These are the explicit costs or money outlays required to stay in business. His implicit costs include forgone earnings of $50 000 by not accepting the job offer + $100 000 in lost interest by not selling out and investing the $1 million at 10% interest. His total economic cost is the total opportunity cost of staying in business, including both explicit and implicit costs. This opportunity cost equals $250 000 ($100 000 in explicit costs + $50 000 in forgone wages + $100 000 in forgone interest).

     b.   To maximize his profit, he should sell out. When he takes into account all of the costs of staying in business, he is losing money. His economic profit is negative: $200 000 in total revenue minus $250 000 in total (opportunity) cost equals a profit (loss) of ($50 000). To an accountant (and the Canada Customs and Revenue Agency), however, he is earning $100 000 ($200 000 in revenues minus $100 000 in explicit cost).

     c.   The answer would be unchanged. The opportunity cost of staying in business would still include the interest on the $1 million because, regardless of its source, it is available for him to invest if he sells out.

     d.   If Bob owes $1 million to the bank, the $100 000 in interest becomes an explicit cost that would be deducted from accounting profit. However, his economic cost already included the $100 000 in interest as an implicit cost, so his economic profit (in this case a loss) would be unchanged at ($50 000). His accounting profit would be 0 ($200 000 in revenues minus $200 000 in explicit cost).

3.  For each project we need to calculate the net present value (NPV).
    Project A

$$NPV_A = -1500 + \frac{500}{1.09} + \frac{550}{(1.09)^2} + \frac{600}{(1.09)^3} + \frac{625}{(1.09)^4}$$

$$= -1500 + 458.72 + 462.18 + 461.54 + 443.26$$

$$= \$325.70$$

Project B

$$NPV_B = -1500 + \frac{25}{1.09} + \frac{100}{(1.09)^2} + \frac{600}{(1.09)^3} + \frac{1000}{(1.09)^4}$$

$$= -1500 + 22.94 + 84.03 + 461.54 + 709.22$$

$$= -\$222.27$$

Project B, having a negative NPV, should not be undertaken. Farbod
Manufacturing should invest in Project A.

## E.  Advanced Critical Thinking

This is not inconsistent. His tax returns show his accounting profit equal to
total revenue minus total explicit cost. Accounting profit fails to consider any
implicit cost of production, such as the value of his time or the interest on his
investment in the business. The farmland alone could be worth millions of
dollars. If he were not in farming, this money could be invested elsewhere
earning hundreds of thousands of dollars per year. His economic profit reflects
these implicit costs. If the implicit costs are substantial enough to offset the
positive accounting profit, then economic loss will result. If he stays in business
in spite of incurring an economic loss, this could mean that he gets enough
utility out of working (and owning) the land to make him willing to incur the
loss. Another possibility is that he is willing to hold the land as an investment.
Every year that the land appreciates in value, it earns a return equal to its rate of
appreciation.

# 14 Firms in Competitive Markets

## I. Chapter Overview

### A. Context and Purpose

The previous chapter provided an overview of costs of production. This chapter extends that analysis to cover profit maximization by competitive firms in the short and long run. The next three chapters adapt this model to cover other types of firms.

### A. Helpful Hints

1. *The competitive firm's output, price, and profit in the short run is determined by industry supply and demand.* Competitive firms take the price as given and produce the level of output that maximizes profit. In the short run, each competitive firm can earn an economic profit, incur an economic loss as long as loss is less than its fixed cost, or break even.

2. *The competitive firm's output, price, and economic profit in the long run is zero.* In a competitive market with free entry and exit, profits are driven to zero in the long run. All firms produce at the efficient scale, price equals the minimum of average total cost, and the number of firms adjusts to satisfy the quantity demanded at this price.

3. *Sunk costs are sunk.* That is, fixed costs cannot be recovered and, therefore, are irrelevant for future decisions. In the short run, a business cannot avoid its fixed costs even by shutting down. This is why it is rational for a business to continue to produce at a loss in the short run as long as its revenues cover the variable costs. Any revenues in excess of the variable cost will offset part of the fixed cost and reduce losses. However, if the firm shuts down, it will incur losses equal to the full fixed cost.

4. *Sunk costs are really sunk.* This is worth a second hint. Thinking at the margin is what distinguishes economists from noneconomists. Even if you now accept this axiom, its implications still may not be obvious. A business that is maximizing profit ignores fixed costs. This means that in the short run (when there are some fixed costs), a business that just replaced an expensive piece of equipment or made an expensive repair will not find it profitable to raise price even by a slight amount. This is probably counterintuitive, but remember that the firm is already charging whatever the market will bear, up to the point at which MC = MR. Just ask yourself this question: if it is profitable for the firm to raise price now to recoup the cost, why was it not

profitable to raise price before the big investment just to make more profit? The answer is that if the firm can raise price to make more profit, it would have already done so! If it is rational, however, it will not make the decision based on sunk costs. Similarly, if you go to a concert that turns out to be a waste of time, you should not stay until the end just because you paid $50 for a ticket. The $50 is gone; do not make yourself even more miserable by sitting through a worthless concert.

## II. Self-Testing Challenges

### A. True/False Questions

_____1.    A firm earning zero economic profit will exit the industry in the long run.

_____2.    For all firms, average revenue and marginal revenue equals the price of the good.

_____3.    A firm facing a price that is less than average total cost will shut down temporarily until the situation improves.

_____4.    Because a competitive firm's marginal cost curve determines the quantity of the good the firm is willing to supply at any price, it is also the competitive firm's supply curve.

_____5.    A profit-maximizing competitive firm will produce until P = MC.

_____6.    A firm producing where MC > MR is producing more than the profit-maximizing quantity.

_____7.    Long-run supply is always horizontal for competitive industries.

_____8.    For a competitive firm, total revenue is proportional to the amount of output.

_____9.    A firm that is not covering its variable cost should shut down unless it is at least covering fixed cost.

_____10.   In the long-run equilibrium, competitive firms must operate at their minimum efficient scale.

_____11.   The demand curve perceived by an individual competitive firm is perfectly inelastic, while the market demand curve is perfectly elastic.

_____12.    In the long-run equilibrium, the price received by a perfectly competitive firm is equal not only to marginal revenue and marginal cost but also to average total cost.

## B.  Multiple-Choice Questions

1.    Which one of the following explains why a perfectly competitive firm is **NOT** likely to earn economic profit in the long run?
    a.  because the demand curve for the firm will not remain horizontal in the long run
    b.  because all economic resources are variable in the long run, causing the firm to face uncertainty
    c.  because the existence of economic profit will attract new firms into the industry and reduce the price

2.    Which one of the following is marginal profit equal to?
    a.  marginal revenue minus marginal cost
    b.  marginal revenue plus marginal cost
    c.  marginal cost minus marginal revenue
    d.  marginal cost plus marginal revenue

3.    A profit-maximizing competitive firm will produce up to the point at which
    a.  total revenue is maximized
    b.  marginal revenue is maximized
    c.  total cost is minimized
    d.  marginal revenue equals marginal cost

4.    Bärbel's Bäckerei is a competitive firm producing where MR = $4 and MC = $2. Which one of the following strategies should the firm pursue to maximize profit?
    a.  expand output
    b.  cut back on output
    c.  raise price to increase total revenue
    d.  cut price to increase total revenue

5.    Which one of the following describes the supply curve for a competitive firm?
    a.  the upward-sloping portion of the firm's marginal cost curve
    b.  the portion of the firm's marginal cost curve that lies above the average variable cost
    c.  the portion of the firm's marginal cost curve that lies above the average total cost

6.   Which one of the following describes when the long-run market supply curve is likely to slope upward?
     a.   if additional firms are attracted into the industry in the long run
     b.   if not all firms have the same costs of production
     c.   if diminishing marginal product sets in
     d.   if there are no barriers to entry into the industry

7.   Which one of the following describes how a profit-maximizing competitive firm determines output?
     a.   by equating marginal revenue and marginal cost
     b.   by equating marginal cost and average revenue
     c.   by equating average cost and marginal revenue

8.   Which one of the following situations should cause a firm to shut down in the short run?
     a.   if it is not covering its variable costs
     b.   if it is not covering its fixed costs
     c.   if it is not covering its total costs
     d.   if it is not covering its money outlays or explicit costs

9.   Which one of the following situations should cause a firm to shut down in the long run?
     a.   if it is not covering its fixed costs
     b.   if it is not covering its accounting costs
     c.   if it is not covering its money outlays
     d.   if it is not covering its economic costs

10.  In a perfectly competitive market, the market price of the product is $10. A firm in this market is producing the output level at which average total cost equals marginal cost, both of which are $8. Which one of the following strategies should the firm pursue in order to maximize profit?
     a.      expand output
     b.      reduce output
     c.      leave output unchanged
     d.      change the price of the product

11.  Which one of the following describes when a rational entrepreneur should enter a competitive industry?
     a.   only if price exceeds average variable cost
     b.   only if price exceeds average total cost
     c.   only if price exceeds marginal cost
     d.   only if price exceeds average fixed cost

12.    Suppose that demand increases for the output of a competitive industry, thus driving up price. Each of the 1000 current firms is willing to increase quantity supplied by 2 units in response to the higher price. Assuming free entry and exit, which one of the following amounts is the increase in total quantity supplied that the industry will eventually experience?
    a.   less than 2000
    b.   exactly 2000
    c.   more than 2000

13.    Which one of the following is a reason that a perfectly competitive firm will not try to sell more by lowering its price below the market price?
    a.   because its marginal revenue will exceed its price
    b.   because its average total cost will exceed its marginal cost
    c.   because its average variable cost will exceed its marginal cost
    d.   because its demand is perfectly elastic

14.    Which one of the following will be satisfied by a competitive firm in long-run equilibrium?
    a.   $P = MR$
    b.   $MR = MC$
    c.   $P = AR$
    d.   $P = AC$

Use the following graph for a competitive firm to answer questions 15–17.

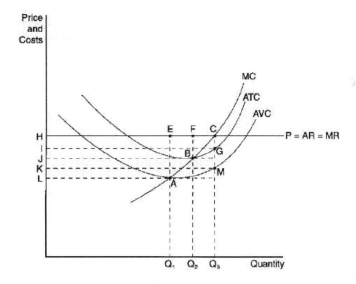

15.    Which one of the following is the output level at which the firm will produce?
    a.   $Q_1$
    b.   $Q_2$
    c.   $Q_3$
    d.   $Q_4$

16.    Which of the following statements represents what the firm is realizing?
    a.  profit equal to area HCGI
    b.  profit equal to area HCMK
    c.  profit equal to area HFBJ
    d.  loss equal to area ECMA

17.    Which one of the following describes what will happen to this firm in the long run?
    a.  More firms will enter the industry, thus driving down price until profit equals zero.
    b.  More firms will enter the industry, thus lowering cost and raising profit because of economies of scale.
    c.  More firms will enter the industry, thus increasing average total cost but leaving price unchanged until profit equals 0.
    d.  Firms will leave the industry, thus increasing price until profit equals zero.

18.    The market for maple syrup is perfectly competitive. Currently, each producer is making a profit. Which one of the following can be expected to occur in the long run?
    a.  the market demand will increase
    b.  the market demand will decrease
    c.  the market supply will increase
    d.  the market supply will decrease

## C.  Short-Answer Questions

1.    How can the long-run industry supply curve be horizontal even though the short-run supply has a positive slope for both individual firms and the industry?

_____

_____

_____

2.    What is the difference between the exit price and the shutdown price?

_____

_____

3.    A Canadian maple syrup producer knows that an additional carload (120 cases) of its famous Old Recipe Maple Syrup would bring an additional $12 888 in revenue. Production of an additional carload, however, would cost $10 580. Should the producer increase production by one carload? Would selling an additional carload raise or lower the producer's profit from the current $238 000? By how much?

_____

_____

_____

4.    If a competitive firm makes zero profit, why does it stay in business?

_____

_____

_____

5.    How would a rational, profit-maximizing, competitive firm respond in the short run to an increase in fixed costs? Will there be any change in equilibrium price or quantity in the short run? Why or why not?

_____

_____

_____

6.    During the 1990s, most of the major airlines reported large losses. In one year, Air Canada lost more than $400 million. However, Air Canada and other airlines continued their operations despite these losses. Why did these airlines not shut down their operations?

_____

_____

_____

## D.  Practice Problems

1.    The graph below shows a competitive firm maximizing profits. However, the curves are not labelled.

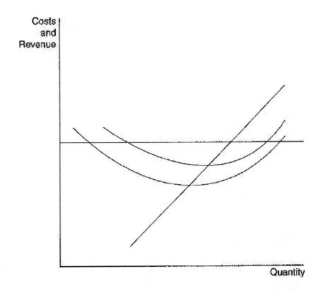

a.    Label the following: price (P), AR, marginal revenue (MR), marginal cost (MC), average total cost (ATC), and average variable cost (AVC). Show the equilibrium quantity and price as $Q_e$ and $P_e$. Label the short-run shutdown point as point A and the breakeven point as point B.

b.  Why is it rational for the firm to produce at $Q_e$? Should it continue to produce temporarily if the price falls below point B but stays above point A? Why or why not? Would your answer be different in the long run? Explain. _____

_____

_____

_____

_____

_____

c.  Is the firm in short-run equilibrium? Long-run equilibrium? How can you tell?

_____

_____

_____

d.  What is likely to happen to the price in the long run? Why? Show the new price line on the graph and explain what happened in the market to cause this shift.

_____

_____

_____

_____

Ecow 10/
$
Ecwn 281

2.  a.  In Chapter 13 you calculated production costs for Wendell's Widget Works. Below is the cost schedule.

| Quantity (Q) | Variable cost (VC) | Total cost (TC) | Marginal cost (MC) | Average variable cost (AVC) | Average total cost (ATC) | Marginal revenue (MR) | Profit (TR–TC) |
|---|---|---|---|---|---|---|---|
| 0 | $0 | $46 | — | — | — | $____ | $____ |
| 1 | $30 | $76 | $30 | $30 | $76 | $____ | $____ |
| 2 | $50 | $96 | $20 | $25 | $48 | $____ | $____ |
| 3 | $58 | $104 | $8 | $19.3 | $34.7 | $____ | $____ |
| 4 | $64 | $110 | $6 | $16 | $27.5 | $____ | $____ |
| 5 | $84 | $130 | $20 | $16.8 | $26 | $____ | $____ |
| 6 | $114 | $160 | $30 | $19 | $26.7 | $____ | $____ |
| 7 | $150 | $196 | $36 | $21.4 | $28 | $____ | $____ |
| 8 | $190 | $236 | $40 | $23.8 | $29.5 | $____ | $____ |
| 9 | $240 | $286 | $50 | $26.7 | $31.8 | $____ | $____ |

b.  Wendell is selling in a competitive market at a price of $40. Fill in the missing blanks for marginal revenue and profit.

$P = \$40$

c.  What is the profit-maximizing output for Wendell? What is his profit or loss? Should he continue to produce in the long run? _____

_____

_____

_____

_____

$P =$

d.  If the price falls to $20, what is Wendell's profit-maximizing output in the short run? What is his profit or loss? What should he do in the long run?

$P = 20$

_____

_____

_____

_____

e.  If Wendell's price falls to $15, what would be his profit or loss if he continued to produce at a price of $15? What would be his profit or loss if he temporarily shut down in the short run? Which action should he take in the short run? Explain. _____

_____

_____

_____

_____

Econ.
281

3.  The following graph shows the effects of a tax hike on a competitive industry that shifts the short-run supply curve from Supply₁ to Supply₂.

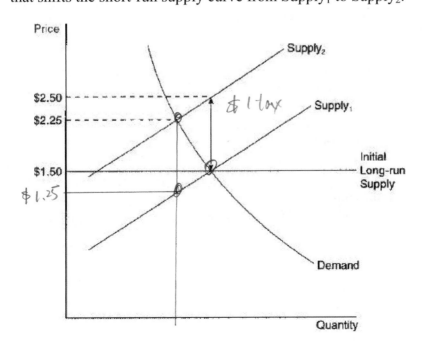

a.  How much is the tax? How much will price rise in the short run? (Who pays the tax in the short run?)

_____

_____

b.  What happens to quantity in the short run? Identify the initial equilibrium quantity and the new short-run equilibrium quantity after the tax.

_____

_____

_____

c.  If the industry was initially in long-run equilibrium at a price of $1.50, what will happen to profit (or loss) in the short run? Explain. _____

_____

_____

_____

d.  How will firms respond in the long run? What are the implications for long-run industry supply and the resulting price? Who pays the tax in the long run? Explain. _____

_____

_____

_____

e.  Show the new long-run supply curve on the graph.

## E.  Advanced Critical Thinking

Your campus newspaper has run an editorial attacking the fast-food restaurants in the food court for anticompetitive behaviour when they raised prices simultaneously last week. Demanding equal time, the restaurants responded that the higher prices were necessitated by a rent hike by the university for all restaurants in the food court. They argued further that they were behaving perfectly competitively by raising price because, under competition, all costs are passed along to the consumer. Evaluate both sides of this argument. Are the restaurants behaving like perfect competitors? Should a profit-maximizing business consider the rent in setting the price of its product? Would your answer vary depending on the length of time involved? Explain. __

_____

_____

_____

_____

## III. Solutions

### A. True/False Questions

1.  F; zero profit covers all costs of doing business, including a normal return on investment; therefore, there is no reason to enter or exit the industry.
2.  F; although average revenue equals the price of the good for all firms, marginal revenue equals the price for competitive firms only.
3.  F; a firm facing a price that is less than average *variable* cost will shut down temporarily.
4.  T
5.  T
6.  T
7.  F; a competitive market can have an upward-sloping long-run supply curve.
8.  T
9.  F; a firm that is not covering its variable cost should shut down regardless of fixed cost.
10. T
11. F; the demand faced by a competitive firm is perfectly elastic, while the market demand curve is downward sloping.
12. T

### B. Multiple-Choice Questions

| | | | | |
|---|---|---|---|---|
| 1. c | 5. c | 9. d | 13. d | 17. a |
| 2. a | 6. b | 10. a | 14. b | 18. c |
| 3. d | 7. a | 11. b | 15. c | |
| 4. a | 8. a | 12. c | 16. a | |

### C. Short-Answer Questions

1.  Long-run supply is horizontal if all firms have identical cost curves and there are constant returns to scale. The positive slope of the short-run supply curve results from diminishing returns when some inputs are fixed. In the long run, all inputs are variable.

2.  The exit price is a long-run concept, and it coincides with the minimum point on the average total cost curve, while the shutdown price is a short-run concept that coincides with the minimum point on the average variable cost curve.

3.  The producer should increase its production by an additional carload. Its profit will increase by $2308 ($12 888 – $10 580).

4.    Profit equals total revenue minus total cost, and total cost includes all the opportunity costs of the firm. That is, total cost includes the opportunity cost of the time and money that the owner(s) of the firm devote to the business. Thus, it is worthwhile for the firm to stay in business, because the owner(s) are doing better than, or at least as well as, they could do in any other activity.

5.    A rational firm would ignore fixed cost in setting its output. Firms maximize profit where MC = MR. Fixed cost affects neither because sunk costs are irrelevant. They do not affect the cost of producing an additional unit of output. Neither price nor quantity will change in the short run.

6.    Many of the airlines' costs are sunk in the short run. The cost of an airplane that an airline has bought and cannot resell is sunk. The opportunity cost of a flight includes only the variable costs of operation, that is, the costs of fuel, the wages and salaries of pilots, flight attendants and the ground crew, among others. As long as the total revenue from flying exceeds these variable costs, the airlines should continue operating.

## D.  Practice Problems

1.    a.

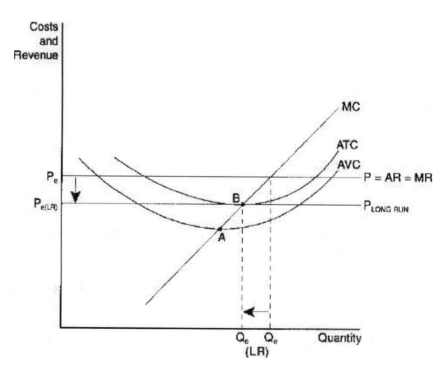

      b.    Output level $Q_e$ maximizes profit because it means producing every unit of output that adds more to revenue than it adds to cost. If price falls below point B, the firm will have negative profit (incur a loss). However, in the short run the firm should continue to produce as long as it is above point A, the average variable cost curve. Any price in excess of average variable cost contributes to fixed cost, reducing the losses that result below point B. In the long run, the firm can avoid all costs (nothing is fixed); therefore, it should not produce at a loss (below point B). It can go out of business and avoid all losses.

c.  The firm is in short-run equilibrium only. It is earning an economic profit. In long-run equilibrium, entry of new firms will continue until all firms are earning zero economic profits.

d.  In the long run, the profit will encourage new firms to enter the industry. The additional industry supply will drive down price until the profit is eliminated. Each firm then will produce at minimum average total cost (its efficient scale) in order to survive. The new price line will be tangent to average total cost (at point B).

2.  a.  Costs and revenues for Wendell's Widget Works at price $40.

| Quantity (Q) | Variable cost (VC) | Total cost (TC) | Marginal cost (MC) | Average variable cost (AVC) | Average total cost (ATC) | Marginal revenue (MR) | Profit (TR–TC) |
|---|---|---|---|---|---|---|---|
| 0 | $ 0 | $46 | — | — | — | — | ($46) |
| 1 | $30 | $76 | $30 | $30 | $76 | $40 | ($36) |
| 2 | $50 | $96 | $20 | $25 | $48 | $40 | ($16) |
| 3 | $58 | $104 | $8 | $19.3 | $34.7 | $40 | $16 |
| 4 | $64 | $110 | $6 | $16 | $27.5 | $40 | $50 |
| 5 | $84 | $130 | $20 | $16.8 | $26 | $40 | $70 |
| 6 | $114 | $160 | $30 | $19 | $26.7 | $40 | $80 |
| 7 | $150 | $196 | $36 | $21.4 | $28 | $40 | $84 |
| 8 | $190 | $236 | $40 | $23.8 | $29.5 | $40 | $84 |
| 9 | $240 | $286 | $50 | $26.7 | 31.8 | $40 | $74 |

b.  Wendell maximizes profit by producing up to the point at which MC = MR, or Q = 8. Because the eighth unit adds $40 each to cost and revenue (MC = MR = $40), Wendell is indifferent between stopping with Q = 7 and continuing to Q = 8. Either way, his profit is $84. Because it is greater than zero, he should continue to produce in the long run.

c.  At a price (and marginal revenue) of $20, MR = MC at an output of 5. He should produce up to 5 units for a loss of $30 (TR – TC = $100–$130 = -$30). Because it exceeds his average variable cost of $16.80, he is better off producing in the short run to avoid losing his entire fixed cost of $46. A $30 loss is $16 better than a $46 loss. Note that his $20 price exceeds his average variable cost by $3.20, leaving $3.20 times 5 units, or $16, to contribute to fixed cost. In the long run, however, all costs are variable, and Wendell would be better off leaving the widget industry rather than continuing to lose money.

d.  At a price of $15, if Wendell continued to produce, his output would be 4 (this is the most he could produce without MC > MR). However, this does not even cover his variable cost. His loss would be $50 (TR − TC = $6 − $110), which is worse than the $46 that he would lose if he shut down. Therefore, he should shut down and lose only his fixed cost.

3. a.    The tax is $1. It will raise the price to $2.25 in the short run, which means that the consumer pays $0.75 ($2.25–$1.50), and the seller pays the remaining $0.25.

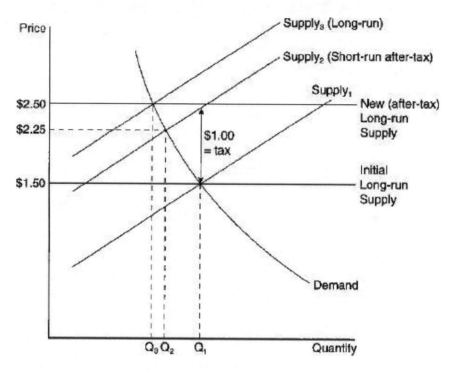

b.  Equilibrium quantity falls from $Q_1$ to $Q_2$ as a result of the tax.

c.  If the industry was in long-run equilibrium, profit was zero. The $0.25 portion of the tax absorbed by the sellers will result in losses in the short run.

d.  In the long run, firms will respond to losses by leaving the industry until price rises by the full $1 tax. The long-run industry supply curve will shift upward by $1, which is the price hike required to restore long-run equilibrium at zero profit. Therefore, the consumer pays the full tax in the long run.

e.  The new long-run supply curve is Supply₃.

### E.  Advanced Critical Thinking

The fast-food restaurants are not behaving perfectly competitively. Under competition, the consumer ultimately pays all costs of production, but this occurs in the long run through free entry and exit. If competitive firms are losing money, they cannot raise prices to recoup the losses. Some firms eventually go out of business, and price rises because of the reduction in supply in the long run. Profit-maximizing firms do not consider rent and other fixed costs in setting price in the short run because fixed costs are sunk and do not affect marginal cost or marginal revenue.

# 15 Monopoly

## I. Chapter Overview

### A. Context and Purpose

The previous chapter introduced market structure by investigating the characteristics of perfect competition. This chapter extends the analysis to monopoly, the case in which barriers to entry protect a single seller from competition. These barriers to entry allow monopolists to earn economic profit in the long run.

### A. Helpful Hints

1. *A monopolist is the sole seller of a product without close substitutes.* Monopolies occur because of barriers to entry. Barriers to entry arise for one of the following three reasons:
   (a) *monopoly resources*; that is, control over a key resource
   (b) *government regulation*; that is, government gives a single firm the exclusive right to produce some good (legal monopoly), and
   (c) *the production process* or *economies of scale*; that is, a single firm can produce output at a lower cost than can a large number of producers (natural monopoly).

2. *In general, a monopolist maximizes profit by producing up to, but not beyond, the point at which marginal revenue is equal to marginal cost (MR = MC).* The monopolist then chooses the price at which that quantity is demanded. The primary difference between monopoly and competition is control over price; a monopolist's price exceeds its marginal revenue, so its price exceeds its marginal cost.

3. *No firm, not even a monopoly, can charge whatever it wants (at least not if it cares about the quantity it sells).* Monopolists charge "whatever the market will bear" rather than set price unilaterally. Even monopolists are constrained by the demand curve.

4. *The monopolist must cut price in order to sell more.* If it seems puzzling that price is greater than marginal revenue for monopolists, keep in mind that, unlike the perfect competitor, the monopolist lowers price in order to move along the demand curve and increase sales. Therefore, an extra unit sold adds less than its price to total revenue. Instead, it adds its price minus the loss of revenue caused by cutting price on the earlier units. The net addition to revenue is the marginal revenue. The only reason that this does not hold for competitive firms is that they can sell all that they want at the market price.

5. *Monopoly imposes efficiency costs* on society in the form of deadweight losses from underproduction of the good.

6. *Governments attempt to limit the inefficiency associated with monopoly in a variety of ways.* Policies include making monopolies behave more competitively, regulating monopoly pricing and other behaviour, and converting monopolies into public enterprises (Crown corporations).

7. *Monopolists often charge different prices for the same good based on a buyer's willingness to pay and, therefore, raise their profits.* This practice of price discrimination can increase economic welfare by eliminating part or all (as in the case of perfect price discrimination) the deadweight losses associated with monopoly.

## II.   Self-Testing Challenges

### A.  True/False Questions

_____1.   Unlike competitive producers, a monopolist restricts output below the level at which MR = MC.

_____2.   A monopolist produces the socially efficient quantity of output.

_____3.   For monopoly, price exceeds marginal revenue.

_____4.   A natural monopoly is a single firm that can supply a product to an entire market at a lower cost than could two or more firms.

_____5.   In the long run, a monopolist is guaranteed a positive economic profit.

_____6.   In the short run, a monopolist would never produce where P < ATC.

_____7.   For price discrimination to be effective, a monopolist must be able to separate consumers into different markets.

____8.   Discount coupons are actually irrational behaviour by firms because it would be more efficient for them simply to cut price than to incur the added cost of producing coupons.

____9.   A natural monopolist cannot earn a profit while producing at the competitive output and price levels.

____10.  A monopolist has an upward-sloping supply curve.

____11.  A monopolist can charge as high a price as it likes.

____12.  A monopolist has to accept a lower price if it wants to sell more output.

## B.  Multiple-Choice Questions

1.   Which one of the following shows where a monopolist produces?
     a.   MC = MR
     b.   MC = P
     c.   P = ATC
     d.   P > ATC

2.   Which one of the following explains why an unregulated monopoly is inefficient?
     a.   because it equates marginal cost with demand, rather than with marginal revenue
     b.   because it equates marginal revenue with demand, rather than with marginal cost
     c.   because it equates marginal revenue with average cost, rather than with marginal cost
     d.   because it equates marginal cost with marginal revenue, rather than with demand

3.   Which one of the following indicates where a monopolist sets price?
     a.   where MC = MR
     b.   from the demand curve at the quantity for which MC = MR
     c.   where supply = demand
     d.   where marginal revenue = demand

4.   Suppose a monopolist is producing at the point where marginal revenue exceeds marginal cost by the greatest amount. Which one of the following should the monopolist do in order to maximize profit?
     a.   increase output and lower price
     b.   decrease output and raise price
     c.   increase both output and price
     d.   decrease both output and price.

5.    Which one of the following makes zero economic profit?
    a.  a monopoly regulated by marginal cost pricing
    b.  a monopoly regulated by average cost pricing
    c.  a monopoly regulated by variable cost pricing
    d.  a monopoly regulated by fixed cost pricing

6.    Which one of the following explains why monopoly occurs?
    a.  because of barriers to entry into the industry
    b.  because of greed by the seller
    c.  because of lack of interest by potential competitors
    d.  because of inadequate regulation by government

7.    As the only seller, which of the following will a monopolist do?
    a.  avoid economic losses
    b.  earn an accounting profit
    c.  earn an economic profit
    d.  Set MR=MC

8.    Which one of the following tends to occur with price discrimination by a monopolist?
    a.  increases in deadweight loss
    b.  decreases in economic efficiency
    c.  leads to output closer to that of the competitive firm
    d.  increases the gap between marginal revenue and price

9.    Which of the following does price discrimination allow a monopolist to do?
    a.  charge more to people based on personal characteristics rather than differences in demand
    b.  take more of the total surplus than they otherwise would have received
    c.  increase their own welfare at the expense of reduced net social welfare
    d.  lower price when costs of production are lower

10.    Which one of the following describes the supply curve of the monopolist?
    a.  It is the whole marginal-cost curve.
    b.  It is the marginal-cost curve above the average variable cost.
    c.  It is the average-total-cost curve.
    d.  It does not exist.

11.    Compared with a perfectly competitive industry with the same cost structure, which one of the following would a monopolist tend toward?
    a.  lower price and output
    b.  lower price and higher output
    c.  higher price and lower output
    d.  higher price and output

12.    Suppose a monopolist can sell 20 units of output per week for a price of $30 each, and 21 units of output per week for $29 each. Which one of the following is its marginal revenue for the 21st unit sold?
   a.   $1
   b.   $9
   c.   $29
   d.   $30

13.    Which one of the following would a price-discriminating monopolist probably produce?
   a.   a higher output with average revenue higher than the best single price
   b.   a lower output with average revenue higher than the best single price
   c.   a higher output with average revenue lower than the best single price
   d.   a lower output with average revenue lower than the best single price

Use the following graph to answer questions 14–15.

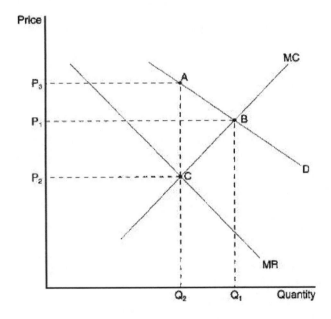

14.    Which one of the following describes how the firm would maximize profit?
   a.   by producing output $Q_1$ at price $P_1$
   b.   by producing output $Q_2$ at price $P_2$
   c.   by producing output $Q_2$ at price $P_3$
   d.   by producing output $Q_2$ at price $P_1$

15.    Which one of the following describes deadweight loss from the monopoly?
   a.   ABC
   b.   $P_3ABCP_2$
   c.   $P_3ACP_2$
   d.   $ABQ_1Q_2$

Use the graph below to answer questions 16 and 17.

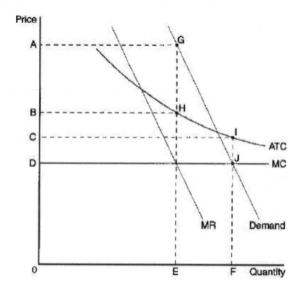

16.    Which one of the following would the profit-maximizing natural monopolist realize?
    a.  AGE0
    b.  AGHB
    c.  DJF0

17.    If the natural monopolist were forced to produce the competitive output and price, which one of the following describes the outcome?
    a.  AGE0
    b.  AGHB
    c.  (CIJD)
    d.  DJF0

18.    If a monopolist produces where its marginal revenue is zero, which of the following has happened?
    a.  maximized its profit
    b.  minimized its cost
    c.  maximized its revenue

19.    Which one of the following statements describes price discrimination in action?
    a.  Movie theatres charge a lower price for children and senior citizens.
    b.  Airlines charge a lower price for a round-trip ticket if the traveller stays over a Saturday night.
    c.  Colleges and universities give financial aid to all students.
    d.  Minimize its average cost.

20. Which one of the following describes how government policymakers can respond to the problem of monopoly?
    a. by making monopolies less competitive
    b. by de-regulating the behaviour of monopolies
    c. by turning monopolies into public enterprises

## C. Short-Answer Questions

1. Explain why a monopolist produces a lower output than a competitive industry produces, even though both maximize profit by producing where $MC = MR$.

    _____
    _____
    _____
    _____

2. What are the advantages and disadvantages of price discrimination for the monopolist and for society as a whole? _____

    _____
    _____
    _____
    _____

3. What are competition laws and what are their advantages and disadvantages for economic efficiency? _____

    _____
    _____
    _____
    _____

4. a. Show equilibrium price and output for the firm in the following graph. Label the profit or loss.

    b. What type of firm is represented in the diagram? How can you tell? Explain.

    _____
    _____
    _____

    c. What would happen if this firm produced where price equals marginal cost? Explain. _____

    _____
    _____
    _____

## D.  Practice Problems

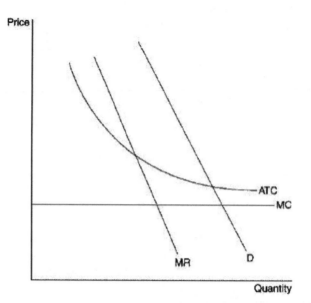

1.  The chart below provides cost and revenue data for Tara's Greenhouse:

| Quantity (Q) | Fixed cost (FC) | Variable cost (VC) | Total cost (TC) | Marginal cost (MC) | P | Total revenue (TR) | Marginal revenue (MR) | Average variable cost (AVC) |
|---|---|---|---|---|---|---|---|---|
| 0 | $40 | $0 | $__ | $__ | $25 | $__ | $__ | $__ |
| 1 | $__ | $30 | $__ | $__ | $24 | $__ | $__ | $__ |
| 2 | $__ | $50 | $__ | $__ | $23 | $__ | $__ | $__ |
| 3 | $__ | $58 | $__ | $__ | $22 | $__ | $__ | $__ |
| 4 | $__ | $64 | $__ | $__ | $21 | $__ | $__ | $__ |
| 5 | $__ | $70 | $__ | $__ | $20 | $__ | $__ | $__ |
| 6 | $__ | $80 | $__ | $__ | $19 | $__ | $__ | $__ |
| 7 | $__ | $94 | $__ | $__ | $18 | $__ | $__ | $__ |
| 8 | $__ | $114 | $__ | $__ | $17 | $__ | $__ | $__ |
| 9 | $__ | $144 | $__ | $__ | $16 | $__ | $__ | $__ |

a.  Fill in the blanks.

b.  Is this firm a competitive firm? How can you tell? _____

    _____

    _____

c.  What price should Tara's Greenhouse charge and what output should it produce? What profit or loss will result? Is this a long-run equilibrium? Explain.

_____

_____

_____

_____

_____

_____

2.  Use the following diagram to answer the questions that follow.

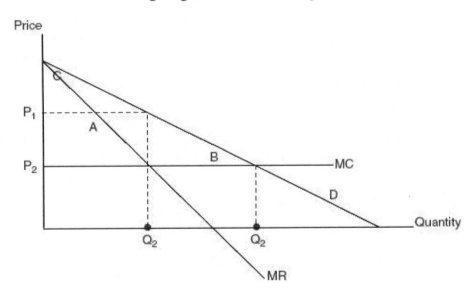

a.  What is the equilibrium output under perfect competition and under a monopoly market structure?

b.  What is the producer surplus under competition and under monopoly?

c.  What is the consumer surplus under competition and under monopoly?

d.  What is the deadweight loss under competition and under monopoly?

### E.  Advanced Critical Thinking

1.  The production and distribution of electric power traditionally has been treated as a natural monopoly subject to government regulation of pricing.

    a.  Explain clearly why this is so. Would this industry still be a natural monopoly without regulation? _____

    _____
    _____
    _____
    _____
    _____
    _____
    _____
    _____

    b.  Recently, there has been a move to deregulate the power industry in some provinces and allow competition among producers, who could buy and sell electricity through a nationwide power grid similar to the pipelines used to transport petroleum or natural gas. How would this affect the industry's status as a natural monopoly? _____

    _____
    _____
    _____
    _____
    _____
    _____
    _____
    _____
    _____

2.  Pharmaceutical companies and their discovery of new drugs can be treated as monopolies.

    a.  The laws governing patents on drugs have benefits and costs. Explain the effects of those laws. _____

    _____
    _____
    _____
    _____
    _____
    _____

b. Some patented drugs are quite expensive. The annual cost of AZT, a drug used in the treatment of AIDS, was about $10 000. Wellcome PLC of Britain, the manufacturer of AZT, was forced by AIDS lobby groups to reduce the cost of the drug. Should drug manufacturers be allowed to profit from disease?

_____

_____

_____

_____

_____

_____

## III. Solutions

### A. True/False Questions

1. F; monopolists produce at MR = MC, below the competitive output where P = MC.

2. F; because a monopolist charges a price above marginal cost, some potential customers who value the product more than its marginal cost but less than the monopolist's price end up not buying the good. Thus, the monopolist produces *less* than the socially efficient quantity of output.

3. T

4. T

5. F; monopolists typically earn economic profits, but only if demand is sufficient to charge a price greater than average total cost.

6. F; in the short run, a monopolist might produce at a loss, as long as variable costs are covered, if demand will not support a higher price.

7. T

8. F; discount coupons are a form of price discrimination that enables firms to capture part or all of consumer surplus; they are a rational strategy whenever the benefit outweighs the cost of the coupons.

9. T

10. F; a monopoly has no supply curve. For a monopolist, the price and amount supplied depend on its demand, and therefore its marginal revenue. Hence, there is no unique relationship between price and quantity supplied.

11. F; no firm, not even a monopoly, can charge what it wants. Monopolists cannot set their prices unilaterally. Rather, they charge whatever the market will bear.

12. T

## B.  Multiple-Choice Questions

| | | | | |
|---|---|---|---|---|
| 1. a | 5. b | 9. b | 13. a | 17. c |
| 2. d | 6. a | 10. d | 14. c | 18. c |
| 3. b | 7. d | 11. c | 15. a | 19. d |
| 4. a | 8. c | 12. b | 16. b | |

## C.  Short-Answer Questions

1.    A competitive industry will produce the level of output at which that industry's marginal cost curve intersects the demand curve facing the industry, that is, $P = MR = MC$. A monopolist will produce the level of output at which the industry's marginal cost curve intersects the monopoly's marginal revenue curve, that is, $MR = MC$. Because the marginal revenue curve lies below the demand curve (i.e., $MR < P$), this implies a lower level of output in the monopoly industry.

2.    The advantage of price discrimination to the monopolist is that it is a means to capture consumer surplus. This is accomplished by charging different prices for the same good based on a buyer's willingness to pay, that is, charging higher prices to those with low-demand elasticity and lower prices to those with high-demand elasticity. The disadvantage is that it is costly for the monopolist to identify and separate the different groups of consumers. For society, price discrimination can reduce or eliminate the incentive for the monopolist to underproduce because of the price effect of increasing output and moving down the demand curve. Perfect price discrimination would eliminate the deadweight loss from monopoly because marginal revenue would reflect the price paid, leading to output coinciding with society's valuation of the additional product. The discriminating monopolist would be willing to produce whenever the marginal consumer's price is equal to or greater than the cost of producing the additional output.

3.    Competition laws are intended to prevent firms or groups of firms from gaining and using monopoly power. For example, they prohibit price fixing by the firms in an industry. They can be useful in promoting competition, but they can also be detrimental when they protect inefficiency rather than competition. Competition laws have been used, for example, to prevent large chain stores from undercutting small stores on price, even when the large stores were simply more efficient and passing along savings to the consumer.

4.    a.

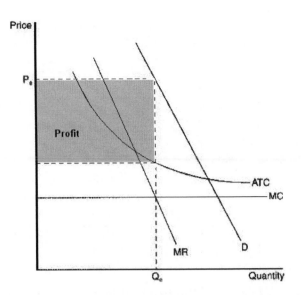

b.  The firm is a natural monopoly, as evidenced by the declining average total cost. The declining average total cost occurs because marginal cost is less than average total cost.

c.  A competitive firm would produce where MC = P. Because MC < ATC, price would be less than average total cost as well. This means that losses are inevitable, and the firm cannot survive in the long run with marginal-cost pricing.

### D.  Practice Problems

1.  a.

| Quantity (Q) | Fixed cost (FC) | Variable cost (VC) | Total cost (TC) | Marginal cost (MC) | P | Total revenue (TR) | Marginal revenue( MR) | Average variable cost (AVC) |
|---|---|---|---|---|---|---|---|---|
| **0** | $40 | $0 | $40 | ~~$0~~ | $25 | $0 | ~~$0~~ | $0 |
| 1 | $40 | $30 | $70 | $30 | $24 | $24 | $24 | $30.00 |
| 2 | $40 | $50 | $90 | $20 | $23 | $46 | $22 | $25.00 |
| 3 | $40 | $58 | $98 | $8 | $22 | $66 | $20 | $19.33 |
| 4 | $40 | $64 | $104 | $6 | $21 | $84 | $18 | $16.00 |
| 5 | $40 | $70 | $110 | $6 | $20 | $100 | $16 | $14.00 |
| 6 | $40 | $80 | $120 | $10 | $19 | $114 | $14 | $13.33 |
| 7 | $40 | $94 | $134 | $14 | $18 | $126 | $12 | $13.43 |
| 8 | $40 | $114 | $154 | $20 | $17 | $136 | $10 | $14.25 |
| 9 | $40 | $144 | $184 | $30 | $16 | $144 | $8 | $16.00 |

b.  No, if it were a competitive firm it would be a price taker. Tara's Greenhouse faces a downward-sloping demand curve from which it can pick the price-quantity combination that it prefers.

c.  Tara's Greenhouse should expand output as long as marginal revenue exceeds the increasing portion of marginal cost without going beyond the point at which they are equal. This means producing an output of 6 at a price of $19. Producing 7 units would be less profitable because the marginal revenue of $12 is less than the marginal cost of $14. The firm would lose $2 on the 7th unit of output. The firm will lose $6 (TR − TC = $114 − $120), so this cannot be a long-run equilibrium. In the long run the firm will sell out if business does not improve.

2.  a.  $Q_2$ and $Q_1$, respectively.
    b.  Zero under competition; area of the rectangle A under monopoly.
    c.  A + B + C under competition; area C under monopoly.
    d.  None under competition; area B under monopoly.

### E. Advanced Critical Thinking

1.  a.   The electric power industry has been traditionally characterized by sufficient economies of scale so that one firm has been able to satisfy the market demand at a lower cost than would have been the case with two or more firms. Building more than one power plant for a region would have raised the average total cost. Government regulation of price was a response to natural monopoly, not a cause.

    b.   Such a nationwide power grid makes it possible for firms to buy and sell electric power between regions. This means that power companies in different regions can compete even though the market demand within a region is not sufficient to justify building more than one plant. This change means that the production of electric power will no longer fit the natural monopoly case, although the transmission lines remain so. It is still inefficient for competing firms to build multiple transmission lines to serve a specific area.

2.  a.   Because patents give one producer a monopoly, they lead to higher prices than would occur under competition. Thus, the benefit of these laws is the increased incentive for creative activity. This benefit is offset, to some extent, by the costs of monopoly pricing. Because a monopolist charges a price above marginal cost, it produces less than the socially efficient quantity of output. As a result, some potential consumers who value the good at more than its marginal cost but less than the monopolist's price will not buy the good. Thus, monopoly pricing causes deadweight losses by preventing some mutually beneficial trades from taking place.

    b.   If drug manufacturers were not allowed to profit from their inventions and discoveries, would they be interested in developing new drugs? The profits made from the discovery of a new drug are likely to attract new competitors into the field. Where would the sufferers of AIDS and other diseases be without drugs? People respond to incentives. The incentive to improve on existing drugs needs to be present.

# 16 Monopolistic Competition

## I. Chapter Overview

### A. Context and Purpose

Earlier chapters introduced the notion of market structure, which can range from competition, with many buyers and sellers, to monopoly, with a single seller. The extreme cases are useful for analyzing implications of various assumptions about markets, but they may seem unrealistic for the real world, which is rarely that black and white.

We continue our discussion of the grey area between monopoly and competition with Chapter 17, which deals with the market structure of monopolistic competition. This category includes fast-food restaurants, gasoline service stations, and corner markets— in short, most of the businesses that we deal with every day. You will see that monopolistic competition shares some of the characteristics of a monopoly and some of a perfectly competitive industry.

### A. Helpful Hints

1. *Monopolistic competition is characterized by three attributes: (i) a great number of firms, (ii) differentiated products, and (iii) free entry into the industry.* Each firm in this market charges a price above its marginal cost of production; this mark-up is associated with the normal deadweight loss of monopoly pricing. Each firm has excess capacity; that is, it operates on the downward-sloping portion of its average-total-cost curve. A monopolistically competitive firm, unlike a perfectly competitive one, could increase the quantity it produces and lower the average total cost of production.

2. *The underproduction of monopolistic competition is a source of inefficiency.* Remember that even though price in monopolistic competition is higher than would be the case in perfect competition, price itself is not the source of inefficiency. Rather, it is the lower quantity that results from the higher price. By itself, the higher price merely redistributes income from buyers to sellers; the efficiency effect occurs because people buy fewer units of the product at the higher price.

3. *The product differentiation inherent in monopolistic competition leads to the use of advertising and brand names.* On the one hand, advertising and brand names are defended on the grounds that they inform customers and allow the firms to compete on price and quality. On the other hand, critics argue that firms use advertising and brand names to take advantage of consumer irrationality and to reduce competition.

## II.    Self-Testing Challenges

### A.    True/False Questions

_____1.    Advertising is inherently inefficient because it adds an additional layer of cost to the product price.

_____2.    Long-run profit disappears under monopolistic competition because new firms enter the industry and drive down price and profit.

_____3.    Monopolistic competitors in the long run produce at minimum average total cost due to free entry into the industry.

_____4.    Monopolistic competitors set output and price at the point where marginal revenue equals marginal cost.

_____5.    Brand names can be advantageous to society by providing an incentive for firms to maintain quality.

_____6.    Policymakers have come to accept the view that advertising can make markets less competitive and that it usually leads to an increase in the price of advertised goods.

_____7.    Excess capacity and mark-up over marginal cost are two noteworthy differences between monopolistic and perfect competition.

_____8.    Monopolistic competitors are able to differentiate their products enough to maintain modest long-run economic profit.

_____9.    Critics of advertising argue that much advertising is psychological rather than informational; firms advertise in order to manipulate people's tastes.

_____10.    Most economists agree that, because of the problem of excess capacity, monopolistic competition is detrimental to society's well-being.

_____11.    Proponents of advertising argue that it fosters competition and would make a firm's demand curve less elastic, which would lead to lower prices.

_____12.    Product differentiations have economic significance whether the differences are real or merely imaginary.

## B.    Multiple-Choice Questions

1.    Which one of the following statements is true regarding monopolistic competition?
    a.    Unlike the oligopolist, the monopolistic competitor sells a product that is different from those of other firms.
    b.    Like the perfect competitor, the monopolistic competitor must sell at the prevailing market price.
    c.    Like the monopolist, the monopolistic competitor sells at a price that is greater than marginal cost and marginal revenue.

2.    Which one of the following describes the rivals of firms in monopolistic competition?
    a.    They set their price equal to MR = MC.
    b.    They set their price according to the demand they face.
    c.    They will always match their price increases.
    d.    They will always match their price decreases.

3.    Which one of the following explains why, in the long run, monopolistically competitive firms may earn only zero economic profit?
    a.    because they must lower their price in order to sell a greater quantity
    b.    because profit encourages entry of new firms, which in turn increases the cost of production of incumbent firms
    c.    because of the existence of excess capacity
    d.    profit encourages entry of new firms, which in turn decreases the demand faced by incumbent firms

4.    Which one of the following does excess capacity predict?
    a.    that long-run equilibrium in a monopolistically competitive market occurs with all firms producing at a lower output level than that at which average total costs are minimized
    b.    that monopolistically competitive firms will achieve positive economic profits by restricting output below the economically efficient level
    c.    that profit-maximizing firms in a monopolistically competitive market restrict output to extract positive economic profit
    d.    that there are too many firms producing essentially the same product in a monopolistically competitive market

Use the information below to answer questions 5–7.

Suppose that a monopolistic competitor producing an output of 100 units faces the following revenues and costs: price = $100; marginal revenue = $50; marginal cost = $75, and average total cost = $90.

5.    Which one of the following strategies should the firm use in order to maximize profit?
    a.    reduce output and raise price
    b.    increase output and raise price
    c.    keep output the same but raise price

6.    Which one of the following shows the firm's standing with its current output of 100 units?
    a.    realizes a loss of $4000
    b.    realizes a loss of $2500
    c.    earns a profit of $1000
    d.    earns a profit of $2500

7.    If the firm were a competitive firm, with price = $100 and the same cost curves, which one of the following strategies should the firm use?
    a.    increase output and keep price the same
    b.    increase output and lower price
    c.    keep output and price the same
    d.    keep output the same but raise price

8.    Which one of the following explains how the monopolistic competitor differs from the competitive firm?
    a.    The monopolistic competitor has no demand curve in the traditional sense.
    b.    The monopolistic competitor can earn economic profit for long periods of time.
    c.    The monopolistic competitor charges a price greater than marginal cost.
    d.    The monopolistic competitor exists in an industry without free entry.

9.    Which one of the following statements is true?
    a.    Advertising is inherently inefficient because it adds to the cost of production without creating anything of value.
    b.    Advertising is inherently valuable because it increases sales and lowers overall average total cost, which leads to lower prices.
    c.    Advertising is costly, but it also provides benefits in the form of product information.
    d.    Brand names add to the price paid by consumers without providing anything of value.

Use the graphs below to answer questions 11–16.

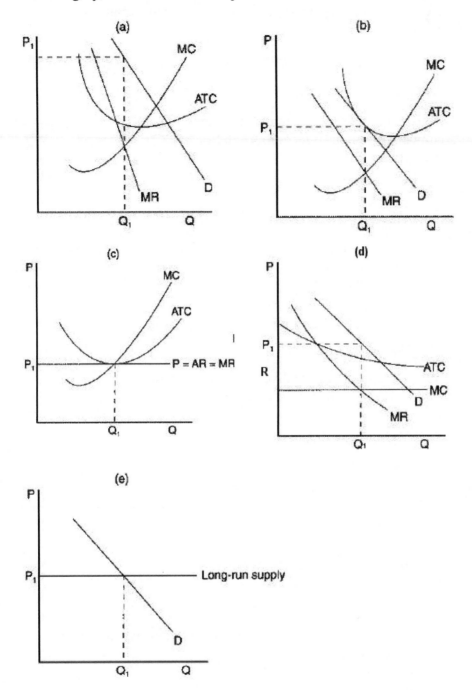

10.    Which one of the following is the diagram that shows a monopolistic competitor in short-run (but not long-run) equilibrium?
   a.  (a)
   b.  (b)
   c.  (c)
   d.  (e)

11.    Which one of the following is the diagram that shows a monopolistic competitor in long-run equilibrium?
   a.  (a)
   b.  (b)
   c.  (c)
   d.  (d)

12.    Which one of the following is the diagram that shows a competitive firm in long-run equilibrium?
   a.  (a)
   b.  (b)
   c.  (c)
   d.  (e)

13.    Which one of the above diagrams is **MOST** likely to represent a monopolist other than a natural monopolist?
   a.  (a)
   b.  (c)
   c.  (d)
   d.  (e)

14.    Which one of the following is the diagram that shows a competitive industry in long-run equilibrium?
   a.  (a)
   b.  (b)
   c.  (d)
   d.  (e)

15.    Which one of the following is the diagram that shows a natural monopoly in long-run equilibrium?
   a.  (a)
   b.  (b)
   c.  (c)
   d.  (d)

16.    Which one of the following describes what a monopolistic competitor that is losing money will do in the short run?
    a.  continue to produce as long as variable cost is being covered
    b.  raise price to reduce its losses
    c.  lower price in order to increase sales enough to end the losses
    d.  keep price the same and increase output enough to end the losses

17.    Which one of the following explains why some economists consider monopolistic competitors to be inefficient?
    a.  because they rely heavily on advertising
    b.  they produce a limited range of output
    c.  they produce an output level for which their average total cost is not at its minimum
    d.  they always realize economic profit

18.    Which one of the following explains how monopolistic competition differs from monopoly?
    a.  monopolists charge whatever the market will bear
    b.  monopolists can earn short-run profit
    c.  monopolists can earn long-run profit
    d.  monopolists produce where marginal revenue = marginal cost but use the demand curve to set price

19.    Which one of the following will occur as a result of entry into a monopolistically competitive market?
    a.  The industry demand curve will shift to the right.
    b.  The industry demand curve will shift to the left.
    c.  The demand curve faced by each existing firm will shift to the right.
    d.  The demand curve faced by each existing firm will shift to the left.

20.    Which one of the following will occur if a monopolistically competitive firm decides to raise its price?
    a.  It will increase its profit.
    b.  It will increase its revenue.
    c.  It will lose all of its customers due to the nature of the demand it faces.
    d.  It will lose some, but not all, of its customers due to product differentiation.

## B.   Short-Answer Questions

1.   How is the mark-up over marginal cost consistent with free entry and zero profit for monopolistically competitive firms? _____

_____

_____

_____

_____

_____

_____

2.   What does monopolistic competition have in common with perfect competition? In what ways does it fall short of the competitive ideal and why? _____

_____

_____

_____

_____

_____

_____

3.   What does monopolistic competition have in common with monopoly? In what ways are the outcomes in a monopolistically competitive industry preferable to those in a monopoly? _____

_____

_____

_____

_____

_____

_____

4.   There are both positive and negative externalities associated with entry of new firms in a monopolistically competitive market. What are they? Explain them.

_____

_____

_____

_____

## C.   Practice Problems

1.  The following table lists characteristics of various types of market
    structure.

| Type of market structure<br>Characteristics | _____ | _____ | _____ | _____ |
|---|---|---|---|---|
| Number of sellers | Very many | Many | One | Few |
| Type of product | Standardized | Differentiated | Standardized or differentiated | Unique |
| Barriers to entry | None | Very low | Total | High |
| Control over price | None | Some | High | Interdependent |
| Long-run profit | Zero | Zero | Typically positive | Typically positive |
| Advertising | None | Yes | Limited; often for public relations | Yes, if differentiated |
| Example: | _____ | _____ | _____ | _____ |

   a.  Fill in the blanks for types of market structure and give an example of
       each.

   b.  What accounts for the differences in long-run profit between the
       various market structures? Why is long-run profit listed as "typically
       positive" rather than simply "positive" for the last two types of market
       structure listed?

       _____
       _____
       _____
       _____
       _____
       _____

   c.  Explain why your examples are appropriate.

       _____
       _____
       _____
       _____
       _____
       _____

d.  Why do the different market structures vary in their use of advertising?

_____

_____

_____

_____

2.  A monopolistically competitive firm produces 50 units of output at a price of $10 each. The firm's average total cost and average variable cost are $8 and $6 respectively. At this level of output, the firm's marginal revenue and marginal cost are both $5 per unit.

a.  How much is the firm's profit?

_____

b.  Will the firm be able to increase its profit by charging a different price?

_____

c.  Is this firm in its long-run equilibrium? Why or why not?

_____

## D.  Advanced Critical Thinking

A newspaper columnist argued recently that the Canadian economy is much less efficient than it might be because of the large number of virtually identical competing products. He claimed that we would get much more value for our shopping dollars if we had only one brand of toothpaste, for example, rather than the dozens that now exist. Similarly with automobiles, we could produce a high-quality product at a lower price if we concentrated on producing one or two of the best designs currently available. He argues that one advantage of a command system such as the former Soviet Union is that a central planning board can make such decisions in the public interest.

In the form of a Letter to the Editor, respond to the columnist. Your letter should include an economic interpretation of his argument as well as a critique that explains the extent to which you agree or disagree with his argument. _____

_____

_____

_____

_____

_____

_____

_____

_____

_____

## III.    Solutions

### A.    True/False Questions

1.  F; advertising adds cost, but it also adds benefits by providing information about product quality and price.
2.  T
3.  F; monopolistic competitors produce at average total cost, but it is above the minimum because of the downward-sloping demand curve.
4.  F; monopolistic competitors set output at the point where marginal revenue equals marginal cost, but price is read from the demand curve.
5.  T
6.  F; they have come to accept the view that advertising fosters more competition and leads to lower prices for consumers.
7.  T
8.  F; monopolistic competitors achieve zero long-run economic profit.
9.  T
10. F; the excess capacity of monopolistic competition must be weighed against the resulting additional variety available to the consumer.
11. F; proponents of advertising argue that it enhances competition, which makes the firm's demand curve more, not less, elastic.
12. T

### B.    Multiple-Choice Questions

| | | | | |
|---|---|---|---|---|
| 1. a | 5. c | 9. a | 13. a | 17. c |
| 2. c | 6. c | 10. c | 14. a | 18. d |
| 3. c | 7. b | 11. b | 15. a | 19. d |
| 4. a | 8. b | 12. a | 16. b | 20. b |

### C.    Short-Answer Questions

1.  Zero-profit condition ensures that price equals average total cost, not marginal cost. In the long-run equilibrium, monopolistically competitive firms operate on the declining portion of their average total cost curve, so marginal cost is below average total cost. Therefore, if price is equal to average total cost, it should be greater than marginal cost.

2.  Both market structures have free entry, resulting in zero long-run profit. However, because monopolistic competitors have some control over price, their marginal revenue is less than the price and their production where MR = MC results in lower output than the socially optimal marginal-cost pricing used by competitors.

3.    Both types of firms face a downward-sloping demand curve and produce where MR = MC, which results in less than the socially optimal marginal-cost pricing of perfect competition. This occurs because both are price setters. However, the monopolistic competitor faces enough competition to eliminate long-run monopoly profits.

4.    They are the product-variety externality and the business-stealing externality. The former arises due to the introduction of a new product as a result of the entry of a new firm. This would convey a positive externality on consumers, as they gain consumer surplus from the new product. The latter, on the other hand, imposes a negative externality on the existing firms, as they lose customers and profits to the new entrants.

## D.    Practice Problems

1.    a.

| Type of market structure | Perfect competition | Monopolistic competition | Monopoly | Oligopoly |
|---|---|---|---|---|
| Characteristics: | | | | |
| Number of sellers | Very many | Many | One | Few |
| Type of product | Standardized | Differentiated | Standardized or differentiated | Unique |
| Barriers to entry | None | Very low | Total | High |
| Control over price | None | Some | High | Interdependent |
| Long-run profit | Zero | Zero | Typically positive | Typically positive |
| Advertising | None | Yes | Limited; often for public relations | Yes, if differentiated |
| Example | Wheat | Convenience marts | Cable television | Automobiles |

b.    Freedom of entry accounts for the difference in long-run profitability. Free entry eliminates long-run profits for both competition and monopolistic competition. Both monopoly and oligopoly are characterized by barriers to entry that can permit long-run profit. However, such barriers do not guarantee profit; demand may be insufficient to allow a profit.

c. Wheat is a good example of perfect competition because there are many sellers, each of whom is a price taker who cannot influence the market price. Convenience marts are monopolistic competitors: each attempts to carve out a market niche in which it has some monopoly power. It can set price within a fairly narrow range. With a government-issued franchise as a single seller, a cable television company is a good example of monopoly. Automobile companies are classic examples of oligopoly, because there are a few interdependent sellers in an industry with high barriers to entry.

d. Perfect competitors do not advertise because they can already sell all that they produce at the going market price. Monopolistic competitors advertise relatively heavily in order to differentiate their products and gain market share. Monopolists have less incentive to advertise, other than for public relations purposes. Oligopolists with differentiated products tend to advertise heavily in order to build and maintain market share. Those with standardized products, such as the steel industry, are less likely to advertise, other than to provide price information.

2. a. The firm's total revenue is $TR = P \times Q = 10 \times 50 = \$500$.
The firm's total cost of production is $TC = ATC \times Q = 8 \times 50 = \$400$.
Therefore, the firm's profit is $TR - TC = \$500 - \$400 = \$100$.

b. The firm cannot increase its profit by changing its price. It can maximize its profit by producing 50 units of output because $MR = MC$.

c. The firm is not in its long-run equilibrium. Its profit will attract new firms into the industry. Entry of new firms will lower the demand faced by this firm. Price will drop until profits are reduced to zero.

## E.  Advanced Critical Thinking

The columnist is referring to the well-documented problem of excess capacity under monopolistic competition. Each seller differentiates its product slightly, resulting in a large number of firms, each facing a downward-sloping demand curve. The result is production at less than the efficient scale of output (where average total cost is minimized). The alternative may be worse, however, because of the loss of consumer sovereignty. Under the current system, there are more alternatives available to the consumer; the best will survive in the marketplace. The price may actually be lower because of the effect of competition in pushing firms to cut costs and raise quality as much as possible. A single seller, perhaps operated by the government, would have little incentive to innovate and increase productivity. Without competition, the producers in the former Soviet Union produced products that were less innovative and of lower quality than would have been the case in the presence of competition. If we were to adopt this plan, who would make the decision regarding which toothpaste or which automobile would be produced? Who would push the seller to be more innovative or to increase productivity? Even in the former Soviet Union, sellers were encouraged to use brand names in order to promote accountability for product quality.

# **17** Oligopoly

## I. Chapter Overview

### A. Context and Purpose

Previous chapters introduced perfect competition and monopoly. These market structures provide useful information about how markets operate, even though most real-world industries are somewhere between the two extremes.

This chapter and the one that follows introduce imperfect competition, which includes the variety of firms between the two extremes. There are two types of imperfectly competitive firms—oligopolies and monopolistic competitors. This chapter deals with oligopoly, which is the market structure with few firms, each of which has a large impact on price and industry output.

### A. Helpful Hints

1. *Oligopoly is not a special case with different rules.* All firms maximize profits by producing where marginal revenue equals marginal cost. We can generalize from and extend the oligopoly model to cover most types of firms. The duopoly model with two sellers produces an outcome between competition and monopoly. However, if the two sellers cooperate to maximize their joint profits, the result is the same as the monopoly case. Similarly, as the number of firms increases, the oligopoly case begins to approach the competitive equilibrium.

2. *Game theory is the study of how people behave in strategic situations.* That is, each person or player, in deciding what action to take, must consider how others might respond to that action. In a classic game, the prisoners' dilemma, self-interest can prevent people from maintaining cooperation, even when cooperation is in their mutual interest.

3. *Policymakers use the competition laws to prevent oligopolies from engaging in behaviour that reduces competition, although the application of these laws can be controversial.* Some behaviour that may seem to infringe on competition may, in fact, have legitimate business purposes.

## II.     Self-Testing Challenges

### A.     True/False Questions

_____1.     The prisoners' dilemma shows that people do not always behave rationally.

_____2.     Forming a cartel results in output that approaches the competitive ideal.

_____3.     Most economists believe that resale price maintenance is one way to solve the free-rider problem associated with a public good.

_____4.     Oligopolists maximize profit by holding output below the point at which marginal revenue equals marginal cost.

_____5.     In a game of repeated prisoners' dilemma, the players may well be able to reach a cooperative outcome.

_____6.     Although it is not always attainable, a Nash equilibrium maximizes the well-being of the group.

_____7.     When an oligopolist sets output to maximize profit, the output effect provides an incentive to produce more.

_____8.     The price effect of an increase in production tends to increase profit.

_____9.     As the number of sellers in oligopoly grows larger, the magnitude of the output effect falls.

_____10.     Tit-for-tat strategies are essentially the biblical strategy of "an eye for an eye, a tooth for a tooth."

_____11.     An agreement among firms over production and price is called a cartel.

_____12.     A key feature of oligopoly is the tension between cooperation and self-interest.

### B.    Multiple-Choice Questions

1.     Which one of the following occurs in the prisoners' dilemma strategy game?
   a.   Self-interest leads the players to a collectively inferior outcome.
   b.   Players ignore their own self-interest.
   c.   Players operate out of misguided self-interest.
   d.   The good of the many outweighs the desires of the few.

The following table shows the possible outcomes if two oil companies drill in the same spot in the Arctic. Neither company owns the drilling rights to the entire pool of petroleum, so both have an incentive to extract what is essentially a common resource. However, if both companies drill, their overall costs are higher because of the duplication of drilling equipment, but the total amount of oil available is unchanged. Use the data to answer questions 2–4.

|  |  | **Freezoil's decision** | |
|---|---|---|---|
|  |  | <u>Drill</u> | <u>Do not drill</u> |
| **Coldzone Oil's decision** | Drill | Freezoil +$5 million <br> Coldzone +$5 million | Freezoil $0 <br> Coldzone +$30 million |
|  | Do not drill | Freezoil +$30 million <br> Coldzone $0 | Freezoil $0 <br> Coldzone $0 |

2.  Which of the following indicates the game's dominant strategy, if any?
    a.  dominant strategy for Freezoil only
    b.  dominant strategy for Coldzone Oil only
    c.  dominant strategy for both Coldzone Oil and Freezoil
    d.  dominant strategy for neither company

3.  Which one of the following is the likely outcome of the game?
    a.  drilling by either Coldzone Oil or Freezoil, but not both
    b.  no drilling by either company
    c.  drilling by both companies

4.  Which one of the following would be the **MOST** desirable outcome for the two firms combined?
    a.  drilling by either Coldzone Oil or Freezoil, but not both
    b.  no drilling by either company
    c.  drilling by both companies

5.  Which one of the following would likely lead to cooperation and the optimal joint outcome?
    a.  if both players behaved rationally
    b.  if the game were played only once
    c.  if the game were played repeatedly, with retaliation against non-cooperative behaviour
    d.  if the players split the proceeds evenly

6.  Which one of the following is characteristic of resale price maintenance?
    a.  used by government to maintain price floors
    b.  an illegal restraint of trade by retailers acting in collusion
    c.  establishes a maximum price for resale of items in short supply
    d.  involves minimum retail prices established by manufacturers in order to prevent discounting

7.  Which one of the following best defines tying agreements?
    a.  any requirement that products not be bought or sold in any manner
    b.  used to protect customer goodwill connected with a brand name
    c.  used to diminish a firm's market power

8.  Compared with perfect competition, which of the following do oligopolists tend to do?
    a.  overproduce and overprice
    b.  underproduce and overprice
    c.  overproduce and underprice
    d.  underproduce and underprice

9.  Which one of the following is the **MAIN** reason that cartels such as OPEC tend to fail?
    a.  Self-interest drives individual players to renege on their cooperative agreements.
    b.  There are too many producers for coordination to be feasible.
    c.  The players fail to behave rationally.
    d.  Demand is inadequate, resulting in falling prices in spite of the agreement to hold back output.

10. Some years ago, parliament banned cigarette advertising on television. Surprisingly, the cigarette companies did not fight the legislation. Which one of the following is the **MOST** likely reason for this inaction by the cigarette companies?
    a.  The companies did not have enough political clout to fight the ban successfully.
    b.  The legislation passed quickly, before the companies could mobilize opposition.
    c.  The ban allowed the companies to concentrate their advertising dollars in more effective media.
    d.  The ban helped the companies cooperate to end advertising that they could not agree to stop on their own.

11.    Which one of the following is a dominant strategy?
    a.  It is a strategy whereby all players comply with a collusive agreement.
    b.  It is a strategy whereby each player takes the best possible action given the strategies chosen by other players.
    c.  It is a strategy that is best for a player regardless of the strategies chosen by the other players.

12.    Which of the following explains why game theory can help to explain why countries engage in protectionist trade policies?
    a.  because when trading partners enact high tariffs, both countries end up better off
    b.  because high tariffs represent a dominant strategy for both trading partners
    c.  because Nash equilibrium maximizes the joint welfare of the two countries
    d.  because totally free trade results in one country winning at the expense of another

13.    Raising production will increase the total amount sold, which will decrease the per unit price and lower the profit on all other units sold. Which one of the following is the name of this concept?
    a.  the price effect
    b.  the output effect
    c.  the cost effect
    d.  the income effect

14.    Which one of the following may make it difficult for oligopolists to collude to set price?
    a.  a large number of firms
    b.  a standardized product
    c.  high barriers to entry
    d.  licensing restrictions by government

15.    Which one of the following can the prisoners' dilemma help to explain?
    a.  nuclear arms races
    b.  behaviour by oligopolists
    c.  overutilization of natural resources
    d.  confessions by criminals who were unlikely to be convicted if they kept quiet

16.    Which one of the following describes when Nash equilibrium occurs?
    a.  when all players comply with a collusive agreement
    b.  when each player takes the best possible action given the strategies chosen by other players
    c.  when a player selects the best strategy regardless of the strategies chosen by the other players

17.    In a prisoners' dilemma game, which one of the following makes the attainment of a cooperative outcome more likely?
    a.    Players realize that the mutual interest is served best by cooperating.
    b.    The game is played repeatedly, with the threat of retaliation against those who refuse to cooperate.
    c.    The game is played only once, and players know that there will be devastating retaliation if they fail to cooperate.
    d.    Players realize that if they fail to cooperate, so will others.

18.    Which one of the following defines predatory pricing?
    a.    pricing above cost to drive competitors out of business
    b.    pricing at cost to drive competitors out of business
    c.    pricing below cost to drive competitors out of business

19.    Which one of the following does concentration ratio measure?
    a.    the number of firms in an industry
    b.    the number of firms in a country
    c.    the proportion of the owners that is concentrated in the four largest industries
    d.    the proportion of the total output in the market supplied by the four largest firms

20.    Suppose that a cartel consisting of two firms is in collusion to maximize profit. Each firm employs a tit-for-tat strategy, and the game is repeated indefinitely. Which one of the following describes when equilibrium occurs?
    a.    when one firm cheats and the other adheres to the agreement
    b.    when both firms adhere to the agreement
    c.    when both firms produce the same amount of output
    d.    when each firm produces its maximum output possible

## C.    Short-Answer Questions

1.    Suppose that mergers in the auto industry resulted in only two surviving firms, Canadian Automotive Manufacturing and European Motor Works. Both firms are considering developing an electric automobile. Each is afraid that the other firm will develop the new automobile first, giving it a competitive edge. Even worse, the firm that fails to develop an electric automobile will lose reputation and sales in other markets as well. However, because the market is quite limited, if both companies develop an electric automobile, they will lose money. Collectively, they would be better off if neither firm develops the new technology. The table below shows the options and profits for Canadian and European.

2.

**Canadian's decision**

|  |  | Develop | Do not develop |
|---|---|---|---|
| **European's decision** | **Develop** | Canadian   —$5 million<br>European   –$5 million | Canadian  –$30 million<br>European  +$20 million |
|  | **Do not develop** | Canadian   +$20million<br>European   –$30million | Canadian   $0<br>European   $0 |

a.  Is there a dominant strategy for Canadian? For European? Explain.

_____
_____
_____
_____

b.  If the firms act independently out of individual self-interest, what outcome will result? Is it in their joint interest? Explain. _____

_____
_____
_____
_____

c.  If the firms cooperate, what outcome is likely? Explain. _____

_____
_____
_____

3.  What are tying agreements and what is their status under the Competition Act? Why would sellers use them? What are the arguments for and against tying agreements? Can you think of a product that you bought subject to a tying agreement? _____

_____
_____
_____
_____
_____

4.  Evaluate resale price maintenance or fair trade practices. What are they, and what are the arguments pro and con? _____

    _____
    _____
    _____
    _____
    _____

5.  Oligopolists face a conflict between self-interest and group interest. Self-interest tends to make them compete, even though cooperation would be more beneficial for the group. Which behaviour would be more in society's best interest, cooperation or competition, and how does society accomplish this goal? Explain. _____

    _____
    _____
    _____
    _____
    _____

## D.  Practice Problems

1.  The data below apply to the market for widgets, which has only two firms, Will's Widget Works and Wendell's Widget Wonderland.

| The Market for Widgets | | | | | | |
|---|---|---|---|---|---|---|
| Quantity (market) | Price (P) | Total revenue (TR) (mkt.) | Marginal revenue (MR) (mkt.) | Total revenue (TR) (firm) | Quantity (firm) | Average total cost (ATC) (firm) |
| 1000 | $500 | $____ | $____ | $____ | ____ | $110 |
| 1200 | 450 | $____ | $____ | $____ | ____ | $110 |
| 1400 | 400 | $____ | $____ | $____ | ____ | $110 |
| 1600 | 350 | $____ | $____ | $____ | ____ | $110 |
| 1800 | 300 | $____ | $____ | $____ | ____ | $110 |
| 2560 | 110 | $____ | $____ | $____ | ____ | $110 |

a.  Suppose that the two widget makers divide up the market so that each firm has an equal share. Fill in the missing values in the table. If they jointly set output and price to maximize their combined profit (and they must produce in multiples of 200), how much will they each produce and at what price? How much profit will each firm realize?

b.  What will be the industry output, price, and profit? How does this compare with the output, price, and profit with only one firm in the market? Explain. _____

_____

_____

_____

_____

_____

_____

_____

_____

_____

c.  If Will believes that he can cheat on the agreement without Wendell knowing, would he have any incentive to change his level of output? What would happen to his total revenue and profit if he expanded output by 200 and Wendell did not respond? What if he expanded by 400? By 600? What level of output would maximize Will's profit if Wendell does not respond? Is it likely that Wendell would ignore Will's behaviour? Explain. If Wendell responds the same way, what would be the new level of output and the resulting price for both firms combined? _____

_____

_____

_____

_____

_____

_____

d.  Does your answer to (b) help to explain the long-term prospects for survival of cartels? What is likely to happen to such agreements in the long run and why? Would the agreement be more likely to survive if the game were run repeatedly with cheating consistently subject to retaliation and cooperation rewarded by the other player? _____

_____

_____

_____

_____

_____

e.  Given that the average total cost is constant at $110, what is the marginal cost of each additional widget? What would happen to output and price if the number of firms continued to expand until there were many competitors? _____

_____

_____

_____

_____

_____

 2.  Two firms at the city's International Airport have licences to carry passengers downtown. These two firms, Airport Limo and Airport Taxi, cannot compete with price, but can compete through advertising. The table below shows the options and profits for these two companies.

**Airport limo**

|  |  | Advertise | | Do not Advertise | |
|---|---|---|---|---|---|
| Airport Taxi | Advertise | Limo | $30 | Limo | $0 |
| | | Taxi | $50 | Taxi | $60 |
| | Do not advertise | Limo | $40 | Limo | $10 |
| | | Taxi | $30 | Taxi | $80 |

a.  Does each company have a dominant strategy and if so, what is it?  *No*

b.  Is there a Nash equilibrium?

## E.  Advanced Critical Thinking

Some economists have argued that competition policy has done more harm than good. They believe that monopoly power is more likely to be created than cured by government action, and that competition laws are often aimed toward protecting competitors rather than competition. They believe that the market provides the best protection against inappropriate restraint of trade. Do you agree? Write a short essay in which you give the arguments for and against competition laws. Be specific, including, at a minimum, discussion of resale price maintenance, tying agreements, and price fixing. _____

_____

_____

_____

_____

_____

_____

_____

## III.    Solutions

### A.    True/False Questions

1.  F; the prisoners' dilemma shows that rational self-interest may not always maximize joint interest.
2.  F; forming a cartel results in monopoly output.
3.  T
4.  F; oligopolists maximize profit by setting output where marginal revenue equals marginal cost.
5.  T
6.  F; a Nash equilibrium often fails to maximize the group's interests.
7.  T
8.  F; the price effect decreases profit.
9.  F; as oligopoly grows in size, the magnitude of price effect falls.
10.  T
11.  F; it is called collusion. A cartel is a group of firms acting in unison.
12.  T

### B.    Multiple-Choice Questions

| | | | | |
|---|---|---|---|---|
| 1. a | 5. c | 9. a | 13. a | 17. b |
| 2. c | 6. d | 10. d | 14. a | 18. c |
| 3. c | 7. b | 11. c | 15. a | 19. d |
| 4. a | 8. b | 12. b | 16. b | |

### C.    Short-Answer Questions

1.  a.  Yes, both firms have "develop" as a dominant strategy because, whatever choice the competition makes, developing the electric automobile makes the firm better off. For example, if Canadian decides not to develop, then European can gain $20 million by developing, but nothing for not developing. If Canadian decides to develop, then European loses either way, but the loss is less ($5 million vs. $30 million) if European develops.

    b.  Both firms will develop electric autos because this is a dominant strategy that maximizes each firm's individual gain regardless of the other's choice. It is not in their joint interest, however, because both firms lose $5 million, which they could have avoided if neither developed an electric car.

    c.  As explained in (b), both firms could cooperate and agree not to produce an electric automobile, resulting in neither a gain nor a loss. This outcome is their best collective choice.

2.    Tying agreements are business practices under which sellers bundle two products for sale so that buyers are forced to purchase both if they want either one. This practice has been banned under the civil provisions of the Competition Act, because it can be used as a form of price discrimination, making it easier for sellers to capture part of consumer surplus without charging separate prices to different buyers. Manufacturers can also protect against inferior accessories or replacement parts by tying lease agreements to the purchase of original equipment supplies and parts. Although they do restrict consumers' options, they also protect the seller. A good example is the operating system that is bundled with new personal computers—nearly all new PC-platform machines come with Microsoft software.

3.    Resale price maintenance practices allow the manufacturer to set a minimum retail price for the product. Critics argue that they prevent competition and subsidize inefficient, high-cost retailers at the expense of big discount stores. Supporters argue that discounters get a free ride when full-service stores offer product information and advice that the discounters do not offer. Customers get advice from the full-service stores, then buy from a discounter. Also, some manufacturers prefer to avoid having their brand name associated with a discount image.

4.    Competition is better for society because it leads to price and output that are closer to the competitive ideal. Competition laws are used to limit cooperation by oligopolists in setting price and other production and sales decisions.

## D.  Practice Problems

1.    The data below apply to the market for widgets, which has only two firms, Will's Widget Works and Wendell's Widget Wonderland.

### The Market for Widgets

| Quantity (market) | Price (P) | Total revenue (TR) (mkt.) | Marginal revenue (MR) (mkt.) | Total revenue (TR) (firm) | Quantity (firm) | Average total cost (ATC) (firm) |
|---|---|---|---|---|---|---|
| 1000 | $500 | $500 000 | — | $250 000 | $500 | $110 |
| 1200 | $450 | $540 000 | $200 | $270 000 | $600 | $110 |
| 1400 | $400 | $560 000 | $100 | $280 000 | $700 | $110 |
| 1600 | $350 | $560 000 | $0 | $280 000 | $800 | $110 |
| 1800 | $300 | $540 000 | –$100 | $270 000 | $900 | $110 |
| 2560 | $110 | $281 600 | — | — | — | $110 |

a.  If the firms cooperate to maximize joint profit, they will jointly produce the monopoly output and charge the monopoly price (and earn monopoly profit). They will produce as long as marginal revenue exceeds marginal cost for the industry. Output will be 600 each at a price of $450. Each firm will earn a profit of $204 000. Industry output will be 1200 at a price of $450. Industry profit will be $408 000.

b.  Will would earn a greater profit if he could increase output while Wendell continues to produce 600. If he expanded output by 200, his total output would be 800 and industry output would be 1400 at a price of $400. His revenue would be $320 000 (800 × $400), and his total cost would be $88 000 (800 × $110), for a profit of $232 000. If Will increased output to 1000, his profit would be $240 000 (1000 × $350 less 1000 × $110). However, if he increased output to 1200, his profit would fall to $228 000 (1200 × 300 less 1200 × $110). Therefore, Will would maximize profit at output = 1000. However, Wendell is likely to do the same thing, resulting in combined output of 2000 at a price of $250. Combined profit would fall to $280 000 (2000 × $250 less 2000 × $110).

c.  Yes, the answer demonstrates the strong incentive for firms to cheat on their agreements to limit output. Each firm finds it profitable to increase output beyond the agreed-upon amount. If the game is repeated and there is the possibility of rewards for cooperation and penalties for cheating, there is a higher chance that the agreement will be honoured.

d.  If average total cost is constant at $110, then marginal cost must also be $110. With many competitors, there would be no price effect, and marginal revenue would be the same as price. Output would expand until price equals marginal cost. This occurs at an output of 2560 and a price of $110.

2.  a.  Airport Taxi does not have a dominant strategy. If Airport Limo advertises, then Taxi does best by advertising, but if Limo does not advertise, then Taxi should not advertise. Airport Limo, on the other hand, has a dominant strategy, and it should advertise.

b.  The Nash equilibrium is for both companies to advertise. Each company does best by advertising, given what the other firm does.

## E.   Advanced Critical Thinking

It is true that results under competition policy have been mixed. Some policies have actually restrained competition: for example, resale price maintenance laws that permit the manufacturer to set a minimum retail price. However, without such laws, full-service retailers would be at a disadvantage relative to discount stores that may "free ride" on the full-service stores as providers of production information and service. Similarly, tying agreements can restrict voluntary exchange, but manufacturers may need to protect their reputations by controlling the quality of supplies and accessories used along with their products. Also criticized are restrictions against predatory pricing—selling below cost just long enough to drive competitors out of business, then raising price even higher than before. Critics argue that potential competitors are available to undercut the predatory firm as soon as price rises. Perhaps the strongest case can be made for restrictions on collusion to fix prices.

# 18 The Markets for the Factors of Production

## I. Chapter Overview

### A. Context and Purpose

Previous chapters provided a framework for analysis of product markets. This chapter and the following analyze the operation of input markets—markets for the factors of production. Chapter 18 explains the behaviour of labour markets, followed in Chapter 19 by an in-depth look at how wages are determined in the Canadian economic system.

### A. Helpful Hints

1. *The demand for a factor of production is a derived demand.* A firm's demand for a factor of production is derived from its decision to supply a good in another market. For example, the demand for bakers is directly tied to the supply of bread.

2. *The price paid to a factor input is determined by the demand for and supply of that factor.* Factor demand reflects the value of the marginal product of that factor, and, in competitive markets, each factor is compensated according to its marginal contribution to the production of goods and services. In a competitive bread industry, the baker would be paid according to his value of marginal product, which is (price of the bread) × (marginal product of the baker).

3. *The profit-maximizing firm hires additional workers until it breaks even on the last worker hired.* If it seems counterintuitive that employers would hire workers until they just break even on the last worker hired, remember that this is a *marginal* decision. They are not breaking even on the *average* worker. By hiring every worker who can produce more than enough to pay his or her wage, the firm is maximizing its net gain or profit. It breaks even on the marginal worker, but it keeps the gains from all of the workers who were hired before.

## II.  Self-Testing Challenges

### A.   True/False Questions

_____1.   An increase in the demand for oranges will cause an increase in the value of the marginal product of orange pickers.

_____2.   A technological breakthrough that raises the productivity of apple pickers will have no effect on the value of the marginal product of apple pickers, although it will raise the value of the marginal product of capital.

_____3.   The demand for a factor of production by a competitive firm is the value of its marginal product.

_____4.   When a firm hires labour up to the point at which the wage equals the value of the marginal revenue product, it is producing up to the point at which price exceeds marginal cost by the greatest amount.

_____5.   The demand for a factor of production is called a derived demand because it is derived from the marginal product of that factor.

_____6.   An increase in the supply of electricians will lead to a decrease in the value of the marginal product of electricians.

_____7.   An increase in capital leads to an increase in the value of the marginal product of both capital and labour.

_____8.   The demand for labour is independent of the price of the product.

_____9.   A competitive profit-maximizing firm chooses the quantity of labour at the point at which the wage equals the marginal cost of production.

_____10.   An event that changes the supply of one factor of production alters the earning of that factor alone.

_____11.   Any event that changes the supply and demand for labour must change the equilibrium wage and the marginal product by the same amount, because these must always be equal.

_____12.   A monopsony is a market in which a single firm is the only buyer of labour.

## B.   Multiple-Choice Questions

1.   Which one of the following is reflected by the demand for labour?
     a.   the marginal product of labour
     b.   the average product of labour
     c.   the value of the average product of labour
     d.   the value of the marginal product of labour

2.   Which one of the following describes the outcome of an increase in the supply of labour in a competitive market?
     a.   It will increase the wage rate and the value of the marginal product.
     b.   It will increase the wage rate and decrease the value of the marginal product.
     c.   It will decrease the wage rate and the value of the marginal product.
     d.   It will decrease the wage rate and increase the value of the marginal product.

3.   Which one of the following will result from an increase in the demand for apples?
     a.   A decrease in apple pickers' wages
     b.   a decrease in the value of the marginal product of apple pickers
     c.   higher short-run profits for apple growers
     d.   a decrease in the number of apple pickers employed

4.   Which one of the following is **NOT** the ultimate source of the difference in productivity, wages, and standard of living?
     a.   human capital
     b.   physical capital
     c.   technological knowledge

5.   As the wage rate increases due to a decrease in labour supply, which one of the following will occur?
     a.   The value of the marginal product will fall.
     b.   The value of the marginal product will rise.
     c.   A shortage of labour will result.
     d.   A surplus of labour will result.

6.   Which one of the following is **NOT** an example of a factor of production?
     a.   steelworkers used to produce sheet metal
     b.   foundries used to produce steel
     c.   iron ore used to produce steel
     d.   share of stock in a steel company

7. Which one of the following causes a shift in the supply of labour?
   a. changes in labour laws
   b. changes in government
   c. immigration

Ken's Kamera Kiosk sells film in small booths in shopping centres. Ken must decide how many people to hire, based on the data below. Use the following table to answer questions 8–12.

| Labour hired | Output | Marginal product | Product price |
|---|---|---|---|
| 0 | 0 | — | — |
| 1 | 5 | ___ | $5 |
| 2 | 12 | ___ | $5 |
| 3 | 17 | ___ | $5 |
| 4 | 19 | ___ | $5 |
| 5 | 20 | ___ | $5 |
| 6 | 19 | ___ | $5 |

8. Which one of the following is the marginal product of the 4th unit of labour hired?
   a. 2
   b. 5
   c. 19

9. Which one of the following is the value of the marginal product of the 3rd unit of labour hired?
   a. $5.00
   b. $8.67
   c. $25.00
   d. $85.00

10. If Ken wants to maximize profit, up to how many workers should he hire if the wage is $5.00?
    a. 1
    b. 2
    c. 4
    d. 5

11. Which one of the following is the number of workers Ken should hire if the wage rises to $5.50?
    a. 1
    b. 2
    c. 3
    d. 4

12.   Which one of the following is the quantity of labour at which diminishing returns set in?
   a.   2
   b.   3
   c.   5
   d.   6

13.   Suppose that an influenza pandemic killed one-third of Earth's human population. Which one of the following would be the **MOST** likely economic effect on the survivors?
   a.   Wages would rise, and the returns to capital and land would fall.
   b.   Returns to all factors of production would fall.
   c.   Returns to all factors of production would rise.
   d.   Wages would fall, but the returns to capital and land would rise.

14.   Which one of the following categories of Canadians is **MOST** likely to support immigration restrictions to reduce the supply of labour?
   a.   workers
   b.   employers
   c.   landlords
   d.   owners of capital

Use the following information to answer questions 15–17.
Suppose that Bob's Burger Box is maximizing profit by hiring workers at $6 per hour. Bob sells hamburgers in a competitive market for $2 each. He currently employs 18 people.

15.   Which one of the following is the value of the marginal product of the 18th worker?
   a.   $0.11
   b.   $0.33
   c.   $3.00
   d.   $6.00

16.   Which one of the following is the marginal product of the 18th worker?
   a.   1
   b.   2
   c.   4
   d.   5

17.   If the price of hamburgers rises to $3, the value of the marginal product will _____ and the number of workers hired will _____.
   a.   rise to $9, increase
   b.   rise to $18, increase
   c.   fall to $6, decrease
   d.   fall to $3, decrease

18.    Which one of the following can workers who augment their stock of human capital expect to receive?
   a.  higher wages that reflect an increase in the worker's value of marginal product
   b.  the same wages but increase the worker's value of marginal product
   c.  higher wages that reflect a decrease in the worker's value of marginal product
   d.  the same wages but decrease the worker's value of marginal product

19.    As a result of an increase in the rental price of capital, _____ capital will be used in production, the marginal product of labour will _____, and the equilibrium wage will _____
   a.  less, increase, fall
   b.  more, decrease, rise
   c.  more, increase, fall
   d.  less, decrease, fall

20.    In a perfectly competitive labour market for an industry, which one of the following will result from a decrease in wages elsewhere in the economy?
   a.  an increase in wages and employment in this industry
   b.  a decrease in wages and employment in this industry
   c.  a decrease in wages and an increase in employment in this industry
   d.  an increase in wages and a decrease in employment in this industry

## C.  Short-Answer Questions

1.    A competitive firm's value of the marginal product is sometimes called that firm's marginal revenue product. Why? _____

_____

_____

_____

2.    Among the owners of the factors of production, who would win and who would lose from increasing the restrictions on immigration into Canada? Explain in terms of marginal productivity theory. _____

_____

_____

_____

_____

3.    Explain the relationship between the equilibrium wage and the value of the marginal product. _____

_____

_____

_____

4.  Should professors be concerned about the increasing demand for online and computer-based learning? _____

_____

_____

_____

## D.  Practice Problems

1.  The data below show the relationship between number of workers hired and costs and revenues for a small Italian restaurant in Hamilton, Enrico's Eggplant Emporium.

| Quantity of labour (L) | Output (Q) | Marginal product (MP$_{labour}$) | Price (P) | Value of the marginal product (VMP$_{labour}$) | Wage (W) | Marginal profit ($\Delta_{profit}$) |
|---|---|---|---|---|---|---|
| 0 | 0 | ___ | $10 | ___ | $11 | ___ |
| 1 | 5 | ___ | $10 | ___ | $11 | ___ |
| 2 | 10 | ___ | $10 | ___ | $11 | ___ |
| 3 | 14 | ___ | $10 | ___ | $11 | ___ |
| 4 | 17 | ___ | $10 | ___ | $11 | ___ |
| 5 | 19 | ___ | $10 | ___ | $11 | ___ |
| 6 | 20 | ___ | $10 | ___ | $11 | ___ |
| 7 | 20 | ___ | $10 | ___ | $11 | ___ |
| 8 | 19 | ___ | $10 | ___ | $11 | ___ |

a.  Fill in the blanks in the table.

b.  At what point do diminishing returns set in? Explain. _____

_____

_____

c.  How many workers should be hired? Explain. _____

_____

_____

d.  If the fixed cost is $100 and labour is the only variable factor, what is the firm's profit? Explain. _____

_____

_____

_____

_____

e.  If the price of the product increases to $12, how many workers should be hired? Explain. If the wage increases to $15 after the price hike, how many workers should be hired? Explain. _____

_____

_____

_____

_____

2.  A case study in the text describes the economic effects of the Black Death in 14th century Europe.

a.  Below , show graphically the effects of the plague that destroyed about one-third of the population within a few years. Indicate clearly which curves shift and in which direction, as well as the direction of the changes in factor prices and equilibrium quantities.

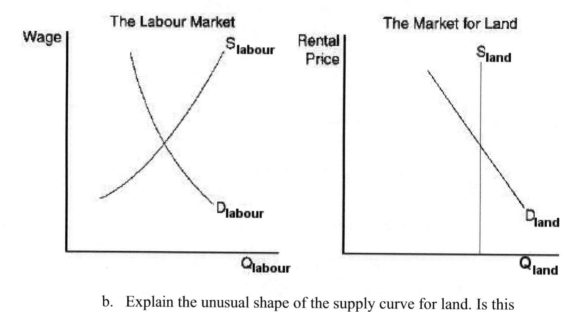

b.  Explain the unusual shape of the supply curve for land. Is this reasonable? Can you think of any way that the supply curve might have a positive slope?

_____

_____

_____

_____

c.  Explain the shifts that you identified in part (a), and include a discussion of the effects on the value of the marginal product of each of the factors of production.

_____

_____

_____

_____

## E.  Advanced Critical Thinking

Critics of the minimum wage argue that it causes unemployment by putting a floor under the price of labour in competitive labour markets, and that it hurts those whom it is designed to help—workers with the least amount of experience and job skills. Supporters of the minimum wage argue that the minimum wage has little or no negative impact on employment, because it has been kept at a very low level, typically less than half of the average wage paid by manufacturing firms. In addition, they claim that labour markets do not behave competitively; rather, they assert that big employers set wages with little regard for supply and demand. They argue further that even if the minimum wage reduces employment, the lost jobs would be the least productive, lowest paid jobs in the economy, so that society would not gain much by keeping them anyway.

1.  Evaluate the opposing arguments. What are the advantages and disadvantages of the minimum wage? Who gains and who loses under a minimum wage?

_____

_____

_____

_____

_____

_____

_____

2.  If you wanted to measure the negative impact of the minimum wage on employment, why would it be a bad idea to look at the overall level of employment in the economy before and after a change in the minimum wage? Can you think of any specific groups of workers whose employment experience before and after a minimum wage change might be a better indicator of the effects of the minimum wage? Explain. _____

_____

_____

_____

_____

_____

_____

_____

## III.    Solutions

### A.    True/False Questions

1. T
2. F; a technological breakthrough that raises the productivity of apple pickers will raise the value of the marginal product of apple pickers and raise the value of the marginal product of capital.
3. T
4. F; when a firm hires labour up to the point at which the wage equals the value of the marginal revenue product, it is producing up to the point at which price equals marginal cost.
5. F; the derived demand for a factor of production means that it is derived from the decision to supply a product in another market.
6. T
7. F; an increase in capital leads to an increase in the value of the marginal product of labour, but a decrease in the value of the marginal product of capital.
8. F; the demand for labour is dependent on the price of the product and the marginal product of labour.
9. F; a profit-maximizing employer will hire labour up to the point that the value of the marginal product equals the wage rate.
10. F; such an event can alter the earnings of *all* factors of production.
11. T
12. T

### B.    Multiple-Choice Questions

| | | | | |
|---|---|---|---|---|
| 1. d | 5. b | 9. c | 13. a | 17. a |
| 2. c | 6. d | 10. d | 14. a | 18. a |
| 3. c | 7. c | 11. d | 15. d | 19. d |
| 4. c | 8. a | 12. b | 16. c | 20. c |

### C.    Short-Answer Questions

1.  The value of the marginal product of an input is the marginal product of that input times the price of the output, i.e., $VMP = P \times MP$. The marginal revenue product is the extra revenue the firm gets from the sale of output created by the use of one additional unit of an input, i.e., $MRP = MR \times MP$. Because marginal revenue equals the price of the product, $P = MR$, for competitive firms, it follows that their VMP and MRP are the same.

2.  The reduction in the supply of labour would raise the wage and value of the marginal product for current workers. With less labour available, the value of the marginal product of capital and land would fall because of a fall in the marginal product of both capital and land. As a result, the rental price of both capital and land would fall. Owners of capital and landlords would lose, although workers would gain.

3.  The equilibrium wage must equal the value of the marginal product in competitive markets. This occurs because employers will hire additional workers as long as the wage exceeds the value of the marginal product.

4.  In the short run, the increase in demand for these types of courses may displace labour and cause a temporary decline in the demand for professors. This decrease in demand may drive professors' salaries downward. However, the enhanced use of online and computer-based learning, along with innovations in teaching, will create job opportunities for instructors with experience in these areas. There is not enough information to assess the net effect.

## D.   Practice Problems

1.  a.

| Quantity of labour (L) | Output (Q) | Marginal product ($MP_{labour}$) | Price (P) | Value of the marginal product ($VMP_{labour}$) | Wage (W) | Marginal profit ($\Delta_{profit}$) |
|---|---|---|---|---|---|---|
| 0 | 0 | — | $10 | — | $11 | — |
| 1 | 5 | 5 | $10 | $50 | $11 | $39 |
| 2 | 10 | 5 | $10 | $50 | $11 | $39 |
| 3 | 14 | 4 | $10 | $40 | $11 | $29 |
| 4 | 17 | 3 | $10 | $30 | $11 | $19 |
| 5 | 19 | 2 | $10 | $20 | $11 | $9 |
| 6 | 20 | 1 | $10 | $10 | $11 | ($ 1) |
| 7 | 20 | 0 | $10 | 0 | $11 | ($11) |
| 8 | 19 | (1) | $10 | ($10) | $11 | ($21) |

b.  The third unit of labour hired results in diminishing returns; the marginal product of the third worker is only 4, down from the marginal product of 5 for the second worker.

c.  The firm should hire five workers, following the marginal rule that they should add workers as long as additional workers add more to revenue than they add to cost. The fifth worker has a VMP of $20, but costs the firm a wage of only $11, for a marginal profit of $9 on that worker. Another worker would cost the firm $11 but add only $10 to revenues for a marginal loss of $1.

d.  The firm will earn a profit of $35. The variable cost is the wage bill of $55 (5 workers @ $11). Total cost is $155 (fixed cost of $100 plus variable cost of $55). Total revenue is $190 (19 units @ $10). The difference (TR − TC) is $35.

e.  At a price of $12, the firm should hire a sixth worker. The VMP will be $12 (MP × P = 1 × $12). The wage is still $11, so the firm makes a $1 marginal profit on the sixth worker. However, if the wage increases to $15, the sixth worker is not worth the cost ($15 > $12). The fifth worker, however, costs $15 and adds $24 (2 × $12), and should be hired.

2.  a.

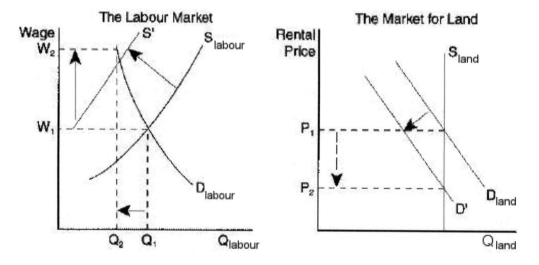

b.  The vertical slope of the supply curve for land suggests that it is totally inelastic, because it is in fixed supply. This is reasonable, unless it is possible to respond to higher land rental prices by retrieving unusable land such as swamps or land that had been under water. In the latter case, the supply curve would have a positive slope.

   c.  The supply of labour shifts to the left because of the high death rate. The wage increases because of the decreased supply. The value of the marginal product of labour rises until it is equal to the new wage rate, because in equilibrium, employment will adjust until the last worker hired has a VMP just equal to his or her wage. The drop in the number of workers will reduce the productivity of land, causing a shift to the left in its VMP curve. The rental price of land will drop as a result of the drop in demand.

## E.  Advanced Critical Thinking

1.  The minimum wage can put a floor under income for the working poor. It can provide more dignity than welfare for those who need assistance. However, it can lead to unemployment, particularly among groups with few job skills and little experience. Teenagers just entering the labour force are particularly susceptible to the negative impact of the minimum wage on their employability. An employer who might have hired an untested young worker for $4 per hour may decline to take a chance at $6/hour. The winners are those who keep their jobs and realize higher wages. The losers are those who lose their jobs or fail to be hired as a result of the minimum wage.

2.  The overall level of employment would probably hide the effect of the minimum wage on employment among the relatively hard-to-employ, such as teenagers or those with relatively low education levels. A better measure of the impact of the minimum wage would be to look at employment among teenagers, especially minorities, and others who may be at a disadvantage in the labour market. With a few exceptions, those studies generally have shown a negative effect on employment due to the minimum wage.

# CHAPTER 19 Earnings and Discrimination

## I. Chapter Overview

### A. Context and Purpose

The previous chapter introduced markets for the factors of production, with an emphasis on the labour market. Chapter 19 explores wage patterns in Canada, looking at the factors that explain differences in wages. It extends the supply and demand analysis of Chapter 18 to investigate in more depth the factors that affect the supply of and demand for labour. This chapter provides the background for a discussion of the distribution of income in Chapter 20. Understanding the factors that determine wages will help to explain why some people are rich and some are poor.

### A. Helpful Hints

1. *A person's earnings depend on the supply and demand for that person's labour*, which in turn depends on natural ability, human capital, compensating differentials, discrimination, and so on.

2. *Human capital refers to the accumulation of investments in people*, for example, in the form of education, training, or health care.

3. *Compensating differential refers to a difference in wages that arises to offset the nonmonetary characteristics of different jobs.* Some jobs are more desirable than others; these typically need not pay as much as less attractive jobs in order to attract the same number of workers.

4. Sidney Crosby earned US$8.7 million in the 2007–2008 season, and he may be worth it. People often react in horror to high salaries by sports superstars. Upon learning that Crosby earned a salary of $8.7 million for playing hockey for the Pittsburgh Penguins, a common reaction is that he is overpaid, that "nobody deserves that much." Marginal productivity theory, however, tells another story: if Crosby is paid $8.7 million a year, it is because he is worth at least that much to the team. Suppose that he brings in US$18 million in additional ticket sales and advertising revenues to the Penguins during the contract year. Is he overpaid or underpaid? There is no easy answer, but remember that in this case he would be earning only about half of the value of his marginal product! Superstars can earn super salaries to a large extent because they can provide a service to many fans simultaneously through television. They earn a lot because we have made them valuable productive factors.

267

5.    *Different pay for different people does not necessarily mean that discrimination exists.* Different jobs and different people have different characteristics that affect the supply of and demand for labour. What seems to be a discriminatory wage differential may actually be a compensating differential that offsets a nonmonetary aspect of the job.

## II. Self-Testing Challenges

### A.  True/False Questions

_____1.    The rate of return to higher education in Canada has grown steadily in recent decades.

_____2.    Employer discrimination is hard to eliminate, because if one employer discriminates, competition forces others to follow suit.

_____3.    Efficiency wages theory holds that above-equilibrium wages arise because firms find it profitable to pay high wages in order to increase the profitability of their workers.

_____4.    The best evidence of continuing discrimination against women by employers is the wage gap in the market: women still earn roughly three-fourths of what men earn.

_____5.    The signalling theory helps to explain why wages have not risen over time in Canada as the average educational level has risen.

_____6.    The wage gap between men and women has actually increased in recent years, although this appears to be due mostly to changing job characteristics, rather than discrimination.

_____7.    Empirical and indirect evidence suggests that ability, effort and chance, although hard to measure, are likely to be significant contributors to wage differences.

_____8.    Profit-maximizing competitive firms cannot discriminate in the hiring of workers, unless consumers are willing to pay to maintain the discriminatory practice.

_____9.    The return to investments in human capital has increased over the past decade.

_____10.    Differences in earnings can be explained completely by differences in investment in human capital.

_____11.    International trade and technological change may bring about the growing wage inequality between skilled and unskilled labour.

_____12.    According to the human-capital view of education, increasing educational levels would not affect wages.

## B.  Multiple-Choice Questions

1.    If two jobs require the same amount of knowledge, skills, and experience, which one of the following is the likely description of the lower paying of the two jobs?
   a.  more pleasant
   b.  more unpleasant
   c.  more risky
   d.  more routine

2.    Which one of the following is an example of human capital?
   a.  basic population
   b.  on-the-job training
   c.  higher consumption

3.    Which one of the following would provide evidence favouring human-capital theory over the signalling theory regarding the effect of education on earnings?
   a.  High-school dropouts earn less than high-school graduates.
   b.  University graduates earn more than high-school graduates.
   c.  Earnings are higher for students who stayed in school longer because of compulsory attendance laws.
   d.  Technical school graduates earn more than workers who did not attend technical school.

4.    Which one of the following defines a labour union?
   a.  an association of workers working in the same industry, but in different jobs
   b.  an association of workers that bargains with employers over wages and working conditions for its members
   c.  an association of workers that tries to increase employment
   d.  an association of workers formed to restrain wage increases

5.    Which one of the following types of discrimination is the labour market **MOST** likely to cure?
   a.  employer discrimination
   b.  discrimination by customers
   c.  discrimination caused by government mandates
   d.  discrimination caused by racism

6.    Which one of the following is **NOT** a form of discrimination?
    a.  employers' preferences for employees with certain characteristics
    b.  customers who prefer to deal only with certain racial or ethnic groups
    c.  government mandates that some jobs are not available to people with certain characteristics
    d.  lower demand for the labour of certain groups with lower value of marginal product

The following graphs show the markets for autoworkers and steelworkers. Workers in the two markets have similar skills, so they can move freely between the two. In both markets the initial equilibrium is at the intersection of $S_1$ and $D_1$. Use the graphs to answer questions 7–10.

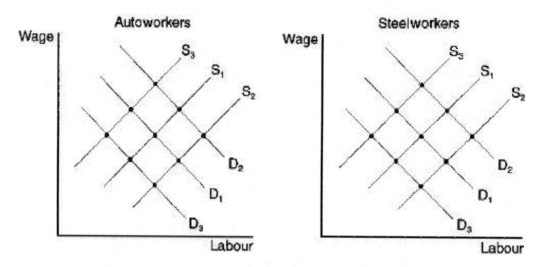

7.    A new study shows that steelworkers are much more at risk of injury on the job than was previously thought to be the case. Which one of the following is the likely result in the market for steelworkers?
    a.  Demand will increase and supply will fall, thus raising wages and employment.
    b.  Demand will increase, thus leading to higher wages and higher employment.
    c.  Supply will decrease, thus leading to higher wages and lower employment.
    d.  Supply will increase, thus leading to lower wages and higher employment.

8.    Referring back to the previous question, which one of the following describes what the change in the market for steelworkers will do to the market for autoworkers?
    a.  Demand will increase and supply will fall, thus increasing the wage rate and employment.
    b.  Demand will increase, thus increasing the wage rate and employment.

    c.  Supply will decrease, thus increasing the wage rate and reducing employment.

    d.  Supply will increase, thus decreasing the wage rate and increasing employment.

9.    Suppose that Canadian automakers hire American autoworkers who work in Canada but live (and spend their incomes) in the United States. Which one of the following describes what will happen to the markets for autoworkers in Canada?

    a.  Both the supply of and the demand for autoworkers will increase in the same proportion, thus leaving the wage rate unchanged.

    b.  The supply of autoworkers will rise, thus leading to higher employment but a lower wage rate; demand will not change.

    c.  The demand for autoworkers will decrease, thus driving down the wage rate and employment; supply will not change.

    d.  Both the supply of and the demand for autoworkers will decrease in the same proportion, thus leaving the wage rate unchanged.

10.    Assuming that workers can easily change jobs between the auto industry and the steel industry, what impact will the changes in the auto industry have (explained in the previous question) on the market for steelworkers in Canada?

    a.  The supply of steelworkers would increase to $S_2$, demand would not change, employment would rise, and the wage rate would fall.

    b.  The supply of steelworkers would decrease to $S_2$, demand would not change, and employment and the wage rate would decrease.

    c.  The demand for steelworkers will fall to $D_3$, and employment and the wage rate will fall.

    d.  The demand for steelworkers will rise to $D_2$, and employment and the wage rate will rise.

11.    Which one of the following will result in a wage differential between males and females?

    a.  discrimination against females by employers

    b.  differences in job choice by males only

    c.  differences in job choice by females only

    d.  clustering by workers into certain traditionally low-paying occupations

Use the following graphs to answer questions 12 and 13.

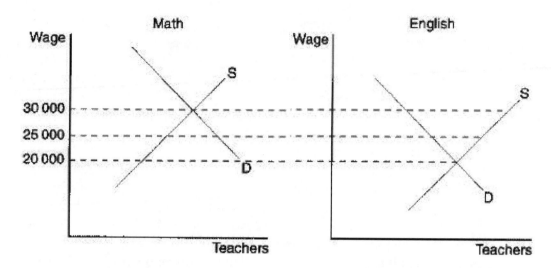

12.    If the government passes a law that all teachers with the same seniority must receive the same pay, and the salaries are set at $25 000 for both math and English teachers, which one of the following would be the result?
a.  a surplus of math teachers and a shortage of English teachers
b.  a shortage of math teachers and a surplus of English teachers
c.  just enough teachers, because on average the wage is at equilibrium
d.  an incentive for more teachers to become math teachers, because of the shortage

13.    Which one of the following would be the **MOST** likely outcome of equalizing salaries in the previous question?
a.  a reduction in the quality of teachers in both math and English
b.  an increase in the quality of teachers in both math and English
c.  the hiring of English teachers with better credentials than those hired in math
d.  the hiring of math teachers with better credentials than those hired in English

14.    Which one of the following is the immediate effect of immigration?
a.  an increase in the supply of labour
b.  a decrease in the supply of labour
c.  a decrease in the demand for labour
d.  an increase in the number of workers who cannot find jobs at any wage

15. Given the two characteristics of markets that give rise to superstars, the satellite broadcasting technology that allows millions of fans to enjoy the athletic skills of Jarome Iginla most likely _____ the cost of broadcasting Calgary Flames' hockey games to large audiences, _____ the income of Jarome Iginla, and _____ the incomes of average hockey players.
    a. increases, increases, increases
    b. decreases, increases, decreases
    c. increases, increases, decreases
    d. decreases, decreases, decreases.

16. Which one of the following terms refers to differences in wages that compensate for unpleasant working conditions, or riskiness of certain jobs?
    a. wage premiums
    b. employer discrimination
    c. compensating wage differentials
    d. signalling wage differentials

17. Which one of the following groups of workers is likely to receive the **HIGHEST** pay as a result of a compensating wage differential?
    a. garbage collectors
    b. waiters at ski resorts
    c. dish washers
    d. maids

18. Which one of the following defines the efficiency wage?
    a. It is higher than the market-clearing wage to reward workers for informing on others who shirk.
    b. It is lower than the market-clearing wage to allow managers the resources to monitor labour productivity.
    c. It is lower than the market-clearing wage because of workers who shirk.
    d. It is higher than the market-clearing wage to increase worker productivity.

19. Which one of the following refers to the natural antidote that many economists believe competitive market economies provide to employer discrimination?
    a. cost minimization
    b. revenue maximization
    c. profit motive
    d. wage differentials

20.    From the perspective of an economist, which one of the following is a type of potential discrimination in professional sports?
   a.   salary consistency
   b.   position fluctuation
   c.   hiring discrimination

## C.  Short-Answer Questions

1.   According to a letter to the *New York Times* several years ago, garbage collectors in New York City earned more than assistant professors at Yale University. The letter writer attributed this to powerful unions in New York City. Do you think that the letter writer was correct about the cause, or could there be other reasons for the garbage collectors to earn more?

   _____

   _____

   _____

   _____

2.   Debate continues over whether the free market can cure labour market discrimination without government intervention. What do you think? To what extent can the market solve problems of discrimination without government intervention? What problem areas are likely to remain without intervention?

   _____

   _____

   _____

   _____

## D.  Practice Problems

1.   A positive relationship exists between education (or training) and earnings. Workers with higher educational attainment earn more than those with lesser amounts of education or training. In fact, this wage gap has grown in recent years.

   a.   In economic terms, how do you explain the relationship between education and earnings? What are the two theories that might help to explain the relationship, and why is it difficult to determine which view is correct? Why is the wage gap growing between the educated and the less educated?

   _____

   _____

   _____

   _____

   _____

   _____

b.  Why is experience also correlated with earnings?

_____

_____

_____

_____

2.  A study by labour economists D. Hamermesh and J. Biddle (Source: *American Economic Review*, December 1994) found that people who are perceived as good-looking earn an average of 10 percent more than those who are perceived as homely, and 5 percent more than people of average looks.

a.  What do these findings indicate? _____

_____

_____

_____

_____

b.  Do these findings mean that there is a beauty premium or beauty discrimination?

_____

_____

_____

## E.  Advanced Critical Thinking

1.  According to a columnist for the *Edmonton Times*:

"Comparable worth legislation is long overdue. Women are paid less than 80% of the wages paid to men, and improvement is coming at a glacially slow pace. Until the law recognizes that women are equal to men and should receive equal pay for equal work, there will be no justice in the workplace. Female English teachers, for example, earn less than male economics teachers with the same training. A simple act of Parliament could solve this problem by requiring job evaluation and comparable pay for comparable occupations."

Write a letter to the editor critiquing this column, explaining why you agree or disagree. Whether you agree or disagree, acknowledge the arguments on both sides of the issue and then explain your position.

_____

_____

_____

_____

_____

_____

2.  Does attending school increase wages because it increases productivity, or does it appear to increase productivity because high-ability people are more likely to stay in school? Discuss.

_____

_____

_____

_____

_____

_____

## III.  Solutions

### A.  True/False Questions

1.  F; there has been no tendency for the wage premium to grow over time in Canada over the past decade.
2.  F; employer discrimination puts the employer at a competitive disadvantage, because other competitors who hire the best person for the job will have lower costs of production and be able to undercut the discriminator on price.
3.  T
4.  F; even though women still earn less than men, it is difficult to determine how much of the differential is due to discrimination.
5.  F; signalling theory works only to explain *relative* wages, because relatively more education by one person suggests relatively more ability or effort; if everyone has more education, then higher earnings must be due to increased productivity.
6.  F; the wage gap between men and women continues to narrow.
7.  T
8.  T
9.  T
10. F; not entirely: differences in earnings are also attributable to luck, ability, effort, and discrimination.
11. T
12. F; according to the human-capital view, education enhances productivity and thereby raises wages.

### B.  Multiple-Choice Questions

| | | | | |
|---|---|---|---|---|
| 1. a | 5. a | 9. b | 13. c | 17. a |
| 2. b | 6. d | 10. a | 14. a | 18. d |
| 3. c | 7. c | 11. a | 15. b | 19. c |
| 4. b | 8. d | 12. b | 16. c | 20. c |

## C.  Short-Answer Questions

1.  Although the unions could help to explain such a wage differential, it is more likely that New York garbage collectors receive a compensating wage differential that more than offsets the effect of their lower human capital. Even for a higher wage, it is doubtful that Yale's assistant professors would quit their jobs in order to collect garbage in New York City. In fact, a position at Yale is so desirable that lesser universities may even have to pay compensating wage differentials to compete with the nonmonetary aspects of a position at Yale.

2.  The labour market is likely to deal effectively with employer discrimination. Those employers with tastes for discrimination will be at a competitive disadvantage relative to employers who hire the best person for the job without regard for irrelevant personal characteristics. At least under competition, long-run profit is zero; there is no room for an employer to hire anyone other than the best person for the position without losing money. In the case of discrimination by customers, however, the employer may find it profitable to discriminate. If customers do not like to deal with certain ethnic groups, for example, a profit-maximizing employer will respond accordingly. Until attitudes change, the problem may well require government intervention to ban such discrimination, because the market will not take care of it.

## D.    Practice Problems

1.  a.    Education or training raises the value of the marginal product of the worker. It represents an increase in human capital that makes the worker more productive, just as a piece of physical capital increases workers' productivity. An alternative to the human capital theory is the signalling theory, which states that additional educational attainment tells the employer something about the ability and effort of the potential employee. Even if the education does not increase the value of the marginal product to the employer, it suggests that the employee is somehow superior to those who did not receive comparable education. This helps to explain why college graduates may find good-paying jobs outside of their areas of academic expertise: the degree itself signals something to potential employers. Both theories lead to similar conclusions, namely that better educated workers earn more. This makes it hard to

distinguish the signalling effect from the human capital effect. The education wage gap has grown as the demand for skilled workers has increased relative to the demand for unskilled workers in an increasingly technological society.

b. Experience is a form of human capital. Workers can gain skills through training or through on-the-job experience and training. Therefore, with experience, the value of the marginal product of the worker rises, at least up to a certain point. As a result, earnings tend to rise with age, and then peak and fall somewhat as the worker nears retirement, when productivity may be slowing down.

2.

a. These findings suggest that good-looking individuals are paid more. This may be interpreted that good looks are directly related to productivity and wages. Good looks are useful for workers who have to deal with customers, such as salespeople, and those who have to present themselves to the public, such as actors. In these cases, attractive workers are more valuable to firms and may command higher wages. These findings may also suggest that appearance correlates with higher self-esteem, which leads to higher productivity.

b. These findings do not necessarily mean that there is a beauty discrimination. However, further investigation might reveal evidence of discrimination such as customers' discriminatory preferences for good-looking salesclerks, actors, and waitstaff.

## E.    Advanced Critical Thinking

1. On the positive side, comparable worth is an attempt to deal with discrimination that the free market has been unable to eliminate. Competitive labour markets can stop employer discrimination, but not all labour markets behave competitively. Employers with preferences for discrimination may be able to indulge those tastes if they can afford somewhat higher costs. Comparable worth laws can stop such discrimination without waiting generations for attitudes to change.

Unfortunately, comparable worth laws often have unintended consequences. At first glance, it seems desirable: women are paid less than men when they cluster into occupations that pay less. However, those wage differentials reflect differences in relative supply and demand. Some occupations may seem more demanding, or less appealing in some other nonmonetary aspect. Without a financial incentive to go into that industry, not enough people will choose that occupation. As a result, there will be shortages. Also problematic is the loss of the incentives for little girls and little boys to reach for nonstereotypical jobs. Those pay differentials between traditionally male and traditionally female jobs have helped to break down the cultural barriers. More girls are growing up to become doctors, economists, and computer programmers today, rather than nurses, English teachers, and elementary school teachers, thanks in part to salaries that have encouraged them to take the chance. The irony of comparable worth legislation is that, however well-meaning it is, it would actually slow down this change and perpetuate the inefficiency of people clustering into occupations that may not be those most in demand by society.

2.  According to human-capital theory, education makes workers more productive. Increasing educational levels for all workers, therefore, would raise all workers' productivity and thus their wages. Signalling theory, on the other hand, holds that education is correlated with natural ability. Education does not necessarily make a worker more productive, but it signals the worker's high ability to prospective employers. Thus, raising all workers' educational levels would not affect wages.

    Both theories can explain why better-educated workers tend to earn more than less-educated ones. But the two views offer different predictions for the effects of education policies. The benefits to education are a combination of the productivity-enhancing effects of human capital and the productivity-revealing effects of signalling.

# CHAPTER 20 Income Inequality and Poverty

## I. Chapter Overview

### A. Context and Purpose

The previous chapter analyzed wage patterns in Canada, describing the factors that explain differences in wages. It extended the supply and demand analysis of Chapter 18 to investigate in more depth the factors that affect the labour market. Chapter 20 explores the resulting distribution of income in Canada and evaluates our efforts at curing poverty.

### A. Helpful Hints

1. *Equity and equality are not necessarily synonymous.* For some people, equity means moving toward greater equality of incomes. For others, equity may require only equal opportunity, even if the outcomes are dramatically unequal.

## II. Self-Testing Challenges

### A. True/False Questions

_____1. In 2007, the richest fifth of the Canadian population earned about 20 percent of the average family market income.

_____2. Roughly 25 percent of Canadian families lived below the low income cut-off (LICO) in 2004.

_____3. The problem with using the low income cutoff (LICO) as a measure of poverty is that it is a relative measure that is defined in relation to average income.

_____4. The high overall standard of living in Canada hides an income distribution that is among the most unequal in the world.

_____5. Under a negative income tax program, a family's income would not be allowed to fall below a specific guaranteed level.

_____6. Utilitarians tend to support only those income redistribution policies that increase work incentives.

_____7. In assessing income inequality, we have to be interested not only in the distribution of income, but also in the number of people who live in poverty.

_____8. Critics of the welfare program argue that it would generate very high effective marginal tax rates that may discourage poor families from finding low-paying or part-time work.

_____9. A negative income tax would eliminate all adverse effects of income redistribution on work incentives.

_____10. The Rawlsian maximin criterion justifies public policies aimed at equalizing the distribution of income by emphasizing the maximization of the sum of everyone's utility.

## B. Multiple-Choice Questions

1. Which one of the following statements is most accurate regarding the distribution of annual income?
   a. it overstates the degree of inequality because it overlooks the regular pattern of life cycle changes
   b. it understates the degree of inequality because it overlooks the regular pattern of life cycle changes
   c. it overstates the degree of inequality because it does not account for the distribution of human capital
   d. it understates the degree of inequality because it does not account for the distribution of human capital

2. Which one of the following philosophies is **MOST** closely tied to the notion of eliminating welfare in order to encourage people to become more self-reliant and ultimately more productive, thus increasing everyone's well-being?
   a. utilitarianism
   b. Rawlsian Theory of Justice
   c. democratic socialism
   d. libertarianism

3. Which one of the following views of inequality would conclude that "the equality of opportunities is more important than equality of incomes"?
   a. libertarian
   b. liberal
   c. utilitarian

4.  Which one of the following does "egalitarianism" refer to?
    a.  liberals' unwillingness to consider the incentive effects of redistribution policies
    b.  libertarians' unwillingness to consider the inequities generated by the unrestrained free market
    c.  government's inability to make decisions for people that maximize their utility
    d.  Rawls' view that justice requires we make the rules for the system before we know the part we will play in that system

5.  If the poverty level is $15 000, which of the following would be the effect of implementing a minimum-wage law high enough to generate income of $15 000 for a full-time worker?
    a.  It would eliminate poverty.
    b.  It would more than eliminate poverty because many families have two incomes.
    c.  It would make some workers better off and others worse off.
    d.  It would raise everyone's income, because even those above the minimum would have their wages pushed up by the higher minimums.

6.  Which one of the following is **NOT** an example of an in-kind transfer?
    a.  subsidized housing
    b.  provincial health insurance
    c.  old age security
    d.  free primary education

7.  Which one of the following explains why current welfare programs discourage work?
    a.  because they make people so comfortable that they have no incentive to work—welfare benefits are so high today that recipients earn more than most people in the middle class
    b.  because they provide benefits that are effectively taxed away at a high rate—often 100 percent or more—when recipients earn income
    c.  because they have no allowance for retraining in order to increase productivity and earnings
    d.  because they provide no in-kind support, such as benefits for day care and other vital goods and services that recipients need

8.  Which one of the following explains why the free market likely does not distribute income equitably?
    a.  because the free market is efficient
    b.  because the free market is not always perfectly competitive; some people can increase their income by exercising their market power
    c.  because even if the free market were perfectly competitive, it does not necessarily provide adequate necessities for the poor
    d.  both b and c

9. Which one of the following describes welfare programs designed to raise the living standards of the poor?
   a. They are government policies that supplement the incomes of the needy.
   b. They are government policies that collect revenue from high-income households and subsidize low-income families.
   c. They are government policies that provide in-kind transfers to the poor.

10. In which one of the following countries is family income more equally distributed than it is in Canada?
    a. Japan
    b. Mexico
    c. United Kingdom
    d. Brazil

11. Which one of the following is one of the most difficult problems that economists face?
    a. defining efficiency gain
    b. defining efficiency loss
    c. defining equality
    d. defining inequality

12. Which one of the following statements is true regarding the inequality of family incomes in Canada?
    a. Annual income is more unequal than is lifetime income.
    b. Income after taxes and transfers is more unequal than income is before taxes.
    c. Income, including in-kind payments, is more unequal than income without such payments.
    d. Since the 1970s, income inequality has been reduced.

Use the following information to answer questions 13–15.
Suppose that a small island with 100 residents has an income distribution such that 99 people have incomes of $25 000 and one person has no income.

13. Which one of the following is the utilitarian argument for redistributing income to the poor resident?
    a. It would be more efficient, because total consumption would rise, thus creating jobs and raising the standard of living.
    b. It would benefit the least advantaged member of society.
    c. It would increase the total well-being of the society as a whole.
    d. It would satisfy the criterion "from each according to his ability; to each according to his need."

14. Which one of the following arguments would John Rawls give for redistributing income to the poor resident?
    a. It would be more efficient, because total consumption would rise, creating jobs and raising the standard of living.
    b. It would benefit the least advantaged member of society.
    c. It would increase the total well-being of the society as a whole.
    d. It would satisfy the criterion "from each according to his ability; to each according to his need."

15. According to the libertarian view, which one of the following factors establishes whether the existing distribution of income is unfair?
    a. if the more affluent residents gained their position by cheating
    b. if the less affluent resident was a hard worker but simply unlucky
    c. if the initial distribution of income hurt the poor resident more than it benefited the others
    d. if the distribution of income fails to increase the well-being of society as a whole

16. Which one of the following is the major advantage of negative income tax over current welfare programs?
    a. It would cure poverty.
    b. It would reduce the work disincentives associated with existing programs.
    c. It would minimize the risk of welfare cheques being spent on alcohol or drugs.
    d. It would not cost the taxpayers anything.

17. Which one of the following is the **BEST** measure of a family's standard of living?
    a. annual income
    b. transitory income
    c. permanent income
    d. nonmonetary income

18. Which one of the following is considered an absolute measure of poverty?
    a. low income cutoff
    b. median after-tax income
    c. market basket measure

## C.  Short-Answer Questions

1.  The assumption of diminishing marginal utility and political philosophy of utilitarianism implies that the government should strive for a more equal distribution of income. Why? _____

    _____

    _____

    _____

    _____

2.  In 2001, the bottom fifth of all Canadian families received 5 percent of all after-tax income and the top fifth of all Canadian families received 43 percent. How do we decide if this is a desirable distribution of income? How would a utilitarian, a Rawlsian, and a libertarian respond? _____

    _____

    _____

    _____

    _____

    _____

    _____

3.  Should one define poverty absolutely or relatively? Explain your answer.

    _____

    _____

    _____

    _____

    _____

## D.  Practice Problems

1.  The negative income tax has been discussed for decades as an alternative to traditional welfare. The following table shows a hypothetical negative income tax for Canada.

2.

A Negative Income Tax Option:
Tax Paid = ⅓ of Income, less $15 000

| Earned income | Tax paid | Disposable (after-tax) income (= earned income less tax) |
|---|---|---|
| $0 | $_____ | $_____ |
| $15 000 | $_____ | $_____ |
| $30 000 | $_____ | $_____ |
| $45 000 | $_____ | $_____ |
| $60 000 | $_____ | $_____ |

a.  Fill in the table above.

b.  If the goal is to eliminate poverty in Canada without a major distortion of work incentives, why is it important to keep the tax formula as it is stated at the top of the table? Could we lower the $15 000 deductible and still cure poverty? What would happen if we change the fraction, currently ⅓, that is taxed away?

_____

_____

_____

_____

_____

_____

c.  What do you think the political repercussions would be from using the formula above, considering that most families in Canada would fall into the negative tax range? (Hint: what is the average family income in Canada, and at what income level does the negative tax switch over to a traditional positive income tax?) Would it help politically to raise the negative tax rate from ⅓ to ½? How would the critics respond? __

_____

_____

_____

_____

_____

_____

_____

_____

_____

## E.  Advanced Critical Thinking

1.  "To maximize total utility, the utilitarian government stops short of making society fully egalitarian." Discuss. _____

_____

_____

_____

_____

_____

2.  In a guest column recently in a weekly news magazine, an MLA argued for drastic welfare reform. According to the MLA,

> "Welfare is not working. When we give people cash, they blow it on frivolous expenditures, or even alcohol and drugs. We can eliminate this problem by giving them the basic commodities that they need to survive and cutting out all cash payments. Let's provide minimal food and housing and clothing, and nothing else. That will make the system a lot more efficient, cutting out the waste and fraud."

Write a response to this column, as you think an economist would have written it. To what extent is the MLA right? What is incorrect? You may want to present an alternative, if you believe that another policy would make more sense.

_____
_____
_____
_____
_____
_____
_____
_____
_____
_____
_____
_____
_____
_____

## III.  Solutions

### A.    True/False Questions

1.  F; the richest fifth of the Canadian population earned 51 percent of the average family market income.
2.  F; in 2004, 15.5 percent of Canadian families lived under the LICO.
3.  T
4.  F; Canada is about average in income inequality.
5.  T
6.  F; utilitarians tend to support income redistribution policies favouring the poor, because they value the additional dollars more than the rich do.
7.  T
8.  T
9.  F; a negative income tax would reduce but not eliminate the adverse effects on work incentives—the actual effect would depend on the rates chosen.
10. F; John Rawls' criterion would aim at maximizing the minimum utility; that is, it emphasizes the least fortunate person in society.

## B.    Multiple-Choice Questions

| | | | | |
|---|---|---|---|---|
| 1. a | 5. c | 9. a | 13. c | 17. c |
| 2. d | 6. c | 10. a | 14. b | 18. c |
| 3. a | 7. b | 11. c | 15. a | |
| 4. d | 8. d | 12. a | 16. b | |

## C.    Short-Answer Questions

1. The diminishing marginal utility assumption implies that an extra dollar of income is worth less to a rich person than to a poor person. That is, the poor person's marginal utility of income is higher than that of the rich person, because the poor person has less income. Utilitarians argue that the government should choose policies to maximize the sum of all individuals' utility, thereby maximizing society's overall well-being. A redistribution of income from the rich to the poor will, therefore, achieve this goal. Taking a dollar from the rich person to pay the poor person reduces the rich person's utility and raises the poor person's utility. Because of diminishing marginal utility, the decline in the rich person's utility is less than the rise in the poor person's utility; therefore, this redistribution of income raises the total utility of society, which is the utilitarian's objective.

2. These numbers provide a way of gauging only how Canada's total income is distributed. There is no "correct" or "best" distribution of income. Internationally, inequality may be measured, albeit imperfectly, by the ratio of the share of income earned by the lowest 10 percent to the income earned by the highest 10 percent of the population. According to this measure, Canada ends up near the top of the pack; it has substantially less inequality than China, the United States, Mexico, South Africa and Brazil. This, however, does not make the Canadian distribution of income desirable. There is a trade-off between equity and efficiency. We may believe that less inequality would be fairer, but that this inequality provides incentives that make people work harder and produce more. A utilitarian would look at the "greatest good for the greatest number," arguing that redistribution would shift the income to those for whom it has the highest value. A Rawlsian would agree up to a point, arguing that we should redistribute if we can make the least advantaged better off. A libertarian would argue that as long as everyone has a fair chance to compete in the marketplace, the equality of the outcome is irrelevant.

3. Both approaches can be defended. Poverty may be defined absolutely, because one of our concerns is that people have enough to eat, clothe, and shelter themselves. It can also be defined relatively, because another of our concerns is the distribution of income in society and the existence of the gap between the rich and the poor.

### D.    Practice Problems

1.  a.

### A Negative Income Tax Option:
#### Tax Paid = ⅓ of Income, less $15 000

| Earned income | Tax paid | Disposable (after-tax) Income (= earned income less tax) |
|---|---|---|
| 0 | ($15 000) | $15 000 |
| $15 000 | ($15 000) | $25 000 |
| $30 000 | ($5000) | $35 000 |
| $45 000 | $0 | $45 000 |
| $60 000 | $5000 | $55 000 |

b.  The formula balances the effective tax rate on earned income against the break-even point—the income at which a family neither receives nor owes money. If we increase to ½ the fraction that is taxed away, we reduce the "break-even" or zero-tax income level from $45 000 to $30 000, but we also discourage recipients from working. However, if we do not increase the fraction, then every family with an income less than $45 000 will receive a cheque from the government. If we lower the deductible to reduce this break-even income level, then the deductible will be below the poverty level of $15 000, and poverty will be reduced but not eliminated.

c.  As explained above, there is no practical way to use the negative income tax to eliminate poverty completely. With a fraction low enough to maintain decent work incentives, and with a deductible at the poverty line, the "break-even" level of income is $45 000, which is well above the 1993 Canadian average family after-tax income of just under $40 000. The result would be that most people would receive "welfare" payments from the government. The negative income tax certainly can reduce poverty, using less ambitious but more politically acceptable values for the deductible and the fraction to be taxed away.

### E.  Advanced Critical Thinking

1.  Utilitarians reject complete equalization of incomes because they accept the economic principle that "people respond to incentives." To achieve a more equal distribution of income, the government must pursue policies such as income tax and the welfare system. People with high incomes are taxed, and those tax revenues are then transferred to people with low incomes. Taxes, however, distort incentives and cause deadweight losses. If any additional earned income is taken away through taxation or reduction of transfers, there will be less incentive to work harder. Working less reduces society's income and its total utility. Accordingly, a utilitarian government has to balance the gains from greater equality against the losses from distorted incentives. That is, in order to maximize total utility, the government stops short of making society fully egalitarian.

2.  You are correct in pointing out that there are flaws in the current welfare system. In many ways welfare has distorted behaviour. It has penalized work by effectively taxing at a 100%+ rate welfare recipients who choose to work. It breaks up families by excluding families with both parents in the home, even when they cannot find work. However, in-kind transfers add additional problems. It is less efficient to provide goods and services, for several reasons. First, people know best what they want. If our goal is to maximize their utility for a given level of welfare spending, then, cash allows them to maximize utility at the least cost to the taxpayers. Giving them goods and services involves the same problem that we have with holiday gift exchanges with friends: we hope that we have picked the gifts that they really want, because otherwise we could have spent our money more productively. At least with family, we can rationalize a poor choice of gifts by arguing that "it's the thought that counts." Second, providing goods and services is more costly administratively than simply writing cheques. Third, the additional costs of in-kind transfers may be futile: if society provides certain basic commodities as in-kind support, it frees the recipients' own money for other uses, even those that society had hoped to prevent. Providing free food does not keep people from spending money on alcohol or drugs; in fact, it makes it easier. The most efficient approach to income redistribution would be cash grants without the extreme work disincentives that exist under traditional welfare.

# CHAPTER 21 The Theory of Consumer Choice

## I. Chapter Overview

### A. Context and Purpose

The previous chapters analyzed the supply of and demand for productive resources and explored the resulting distribution of income in Canada. The section concluded with a critique of Canadian antipoverty programs. This chapter returns to the earlier discussion of consumer choice, using indifference curve analysis to analyze consumer maximization of utility and its implications for demand.

### B. Helpful Hints

1. *Budget constraint shows the different combinations of goods and services that are affordable.* The opportunity cost of consuming more of one good is the reduced amount of the other good that can be purchased. The slope of budget constraint is equal to the relative price of the goods.

2. *The indifference curve is used to measure consumer's relative preference between two goods.* It shows the bundles of consumption that make a consumer equally happy.

3. *The marginal rate of substitution (MRS) is the rate at which the consumer is willing to substitute one good for another;* it is equal to the slope of the indifference curve.

4. *Optimization refers to the process of utility-maximizing consumers rearranging their consumption patterns until their marginal rate of substitution between the goods equals the relative price of the goods.* At this point, the slope of the indifference curve equals the slope of budget constraint.

5. *It is easy to get tripped up on the slopes of the curves.* The slope of the budget constraint is the $P_x/P_y$, where x is on the horizontal axis and y on the vertical. This may seem backwards, because slope is normally $\Delta y/\Delta x$. Remember, however, that the formula uses the *price* of x, not the quantity. The higher the price, the lower the quantity that can be purchased.

## II.  Self-Testing Challenges

### A.  True/False Questions

_____1.    For a demand curve to slope upward, the substitution effect must outweigh the income effect.

_____2.    The main problem with indifference curve analysis is that people do not actually calculate utility when making choices.

_____3.    The marginal rate of substitution (MRS) of good X for good Y is the relative price of good X versus good Y.

_____4.    A Giffen good must be an inferior good, but not all inferior goods are Giffen goods.

_____5.    For a normal good, the income effect of an increase in price leads to decreased consumption.

_____6.    The substitution effect of a price increase always leads to lower consumption.

_____7.    The indifference curve between Molson and Labatt beer is likely to be straighter than the indifference curve between Molson and Coca-Cola.

_____8.    It is not possible for every good to be an inferior good for a consumer.

_____9.    The substitution effect of a price change is the change in consumption that results from a change in the marginal rate of substitution.

_____10.   The income effect of a price change is the change in consumption that results from movement to a higher or lower indifference curve without any change in relative price.

### B.  Multiple-Choice Questions

1.    If a rational consumer likes cranberry juice twice as much as she likes orange juice, which one of the following would the consumer do?
      a.   buy only cranberry juice
      b.   buy cranberry juice until, at the margin, she is indifferent between the two juices
      c.   buy twice as much cranberry juice as orange juice
      d.   buy whichever juice gives her the most utility per dollar spent

2.    Which one of the following will be the shape of the indifference curves for two goods that are perfect substitutes?
   a.   straight lines
   b.   right angles
   c.   bowed inward
   d.   bowed outward

3.    Which one of the following will be the shape of the indifference curves for two goods that are perfect complements?
   a.   straight lines
   b.   right angles
   c.   bowed inward
   d.   bowed outward

4.    A consumer maximizes utility by choosing consumption bundles that have which one of the following characteristics?
   a.   maximize the marginal rate of substitution (MRS)
   b.   maximize the gap between the MRS and the relative price
   c.   set the MRS equal to the relative price
   d.   maximize consumption of the lower-priced good

5.    Suppose a consumer decreases her consumption of good X when the price of good Y rises. Which one of the following is the most likely explanation for this behaviour?
   a.   Good X is an inferior good.
   b.   Good Y is an inferior good.
   c.   The income effect dominates the substitution effect for good X.
   d.   The substitution effect dominates the income effect for good X.

6.    Which of the following would be the most likely reason for a backward-bending labour supply curve?
   a.   the income effect dominates the substitution effect
   b.   the substitution effect dominates the income effect
   c.   both income and substitution effects are quite weak

7.    Which of the following characterizes leisure?
   a.   it's a normal good
   b.   it's an inferior good
   c.   it's a Giffen good
   d.   it's not an economic good

8. Which one of the following is the reason for the bowed shape of the typical indifference curve?
   a. people typically preferring one good to another
   b. diminishing marginal utility
   c. increased average utility
   d. diminishing relative utility

9. Which one of the following would be suggested by the intersection of two indifference curves?
   a. consumers were inconsistent or irrational
   b. one of the goods must be inferior
   c. both goods must be inferior
   d. at least one of the goods must be normal

10. Which one of the following is indicated by the fact that winners of large lottery prizes often quit their jobs?
    a. irrational behaviour
    b. a strong income effect
    c. a strong substitution effect
    d. leisure as an inferior good

11. In the labour market, which one of the following occurs when wages increase?
    a. substitution effect encourages more work, but the income effect discourages work
    b. income and substitution effects both encourage more work
    c. income and substitution effects both discourage work
    d. income effect encourages more work, but the substitution effect discourages work

12. Suppose that Luigi prefers pizza to fried chicken 2:1. If pizza costs $9 and chicken costs $3, which one of the following should Luigi buy?
    a. More chicken and less pizza, until the prices are equal and the marginal utilities are equal.
    b. More pizza and less chicken, until the marginal utilities are equal to the relative price.
    c. More chicken and less pizza, until another pizza is worth three times as much as another order of chicken is worth to him.
    d. The same quantities of pizza and chicken as before.

Use the graph below to answer questions 13–17. The diagram shows the equilibrium for goods X and Y, starting at an equilibrium at point A. The consumer's income is $60.

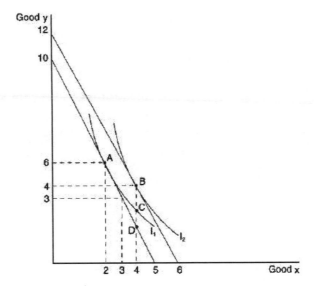

13.     What is the price of good X in the graph?
   a.  $2
   b.  $5
   c.  $12
   d.  $30

14.     Which one of the following statements is true?
   a.  Both X and Y are normal goods.
   b.  Both X and Y are inferior goods.
   c.  Good X is inferior and good Y is normal.
   d.  Good X is normal and good Y is inferior.

15.     What is the equilibrium MRS?
   a.  ½
   b.  2
   c.  3
   d.  ⅓

16.     Between which two points is the consumer indifferent?
   a.  A and B
   b.  A and C
   c.  A and D
   d.  C and D

17.    Which one of the following will occur if income is cut in half?
   a.    The marginal rate of substitution will be cut in half.
   b.    The indifference curve will shift down by half.
   c.    The budget constraint will shift down by half.
   d.    The indifference curve will increase by 50 percent.

## C.  Short-Answer Questions

1.    Joe has a marginal rate of substitution of beer for soda of 1/5. Beer costs $10 per case, and soda costs $5 per case. What should Joe do, and why? Can you tell how much beer Joe should buy? How much soda? What will his MRS be in equilibrium? Why?

_____

_____

_____

_____

_____

_____

2.    Explain what could make a labour supply curve backward-bending.

_____

_____

_____

_____

_____

_____

## D.  Practice Problems

1.    The indifference curve diagram below shows the tradeoff between ice cream and brownies for Ben.

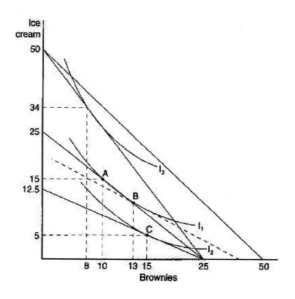

a. The prices of ice cream and brownies are initially $1 each, and Ben can buy 25 brownies if he spends his entire budget on brownies. How much ice cream and how many brownies will Ben buy? Explain. What will happen if the price of ice cream doubles? What is his new indifference curve? How much ice cream will Ben buy now? How many brownies will he buy? _____

_____

_____

_____

_____

_____

_____

b. Separate the effect of raising the price of ice cream into a substitution and an income effect. Illustrate on the diagram and explain in your own words.

_____

_____

_____

_____

_____

_____

c. Can you tell what Ben's income is? Show the effect of a 100 percent increase in income from the original budget constraint, due to a fabulous new job. Label the new curve(s) with ′. What will happen to his consumption of ice cream? Of brownies? Label the new equilibrium as E′. Can you tell from the diagram if brownies are a normal or an inferior good? How can you tell? _____

_____

_____

_____

_____

_____

## III. Solutions

### A. True/False Questions

1. F; for a demand curve to slope upward, the income effect must be dominant (and the good must be inferior).
2. F; people do not need to calculate utility in making choices for the model to predict behaviour and describe the outcome accurately.
3. F; the marginal rate of substitution (MRS) of good X for good Y is the rate at which the consumer is willing to trade X for y; only in equilibrium is it equal to the relative price.
4. T
5. T
6. T
7. T
8. T
9. T
10. T

### B. Multiple-Choice Questions

| | | | | |
|---|---|---|---|---|
| 1. d | 5. c | 9. a | 13. c | 17. c |
| 2. a | 6. a | 10. b | 14. d | |
| 3. b | 7. a | 11. a | 15. b | |
| 4. c | 8. b | 12. c | 16. b | |

### C. Short-Answer Questions

1. Buy more beer! Joe should cut back on soda and buy more beer, because beer is worth five times as much as soda to him, but it costs only twice as much. He can get more utility per dollar by buying more beer, until the marginal utility of beer falls and the marginal utility of soda rises enough to change the MRS of beer for soda to ½, which equals the relative price. We do not know, however, how much beer and soda he will actually purchase when he reaches that equilibrium, without knowing the exact shape of his indifference curve as well as his income.

2. As wages rise, the substitution effect encourages more work effort. At the same time, the higher wages make the worker feel richer, causing an income effect. Because people demand more leisure at higher incomes (leisure is a normal good), the income effect of a wage increase discourages work effort. If this effect is stronger than the substitution encouraging work, the net effect will be less labour supplied at higher wages: a backward-bending supply curve.

### D.   Practice Problems

1.   The indifference curve diagram below shows the trade-off between ice cream and brownies for Ben.

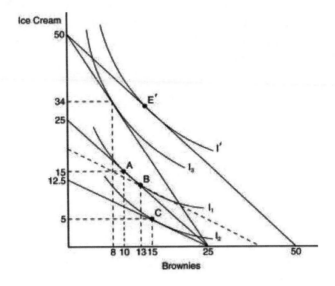

a.   Ben will buy 15 servings of ice cream and 10 brownies. This maximizes his utility at the current prices of $1 each. He must be on indifference curve $I_1$, because this is the only indifference curve that is tangent to a budget line with a relative price of one ice cream to one brownie. If the price of ice cream doubles, then the budget constraint will pivot around its intercept point with the brownie axis: maximum possible brownie consumption will not change, but potential ice cream consumption will be halved, from 25 to 12.5. At this new equilibrium on $I_2$, Ben will buy 15 brownies and only 5 ice creams.

b.   When the price of ice cream increases from $1 to $2, the budget constraint pivots from 25 to 12.5 ice creams. Ben cuts back on ice cream consumption for two reasons: first, brownies have become a better buy (the budget constraint slope has decreased), and, second, his income has fallen in real terms (he feels poorer because of the price hike). The first effect, the substitution effect, is the movement along $I_1$ from A to B, reflecting only a change in relative price. The second effect, the income effect, is the movement from B to C, which is a parallel shift in the budget constraint showing a drop in real income. The dashed line tangent to $I_1$ at point B is a hypothetical budget constraint reflecting the change in relative price while holding real income constant (utility has not changed from $I_1$). The combined effect is A to C.

c.  Ben's income must be $25, because his initial budget constraint allowed him to purchase either 25 ice creams or 25 brownies when the price was $1 for either. A 100 percent increase in income would double his budget constraint. The new equilibrium would be at E′, on indifference curve I′. If both ice cream and brownie consumption rise relative to his old equilibrium at point A (as shown on the graph at E′), this shows that both goods are normal goods (consumption rises as income rises).

# CHAPTER 22 Frontiers of Microeconomics

## I.    Chapter Overview

### A.    Context and Purpose

Chapter 22 is the last chapter in the microeconomics portion of the text. It is the second of two unrelated chapters that introduce some advanced topics in microeconomics. These two chapters are intended to whet the appetite for further study in economics.

The purpose of Chapter 22 is to provide a taste of three topics on the frontier of microeconomics research. The first topic is *asymmetric information*, a situation when one person in an economic relationship has more relevant knowledge than the other person. The second topic is *political economy*, the application of economic tools to the understanding of the functioning of government. The third topic we address is *behavioural economics*, the introduction of psychology into the study of economic issues.

### B.    Helpful Hints

1.  *The market for insurance demonstrates many of the problems and market solutions generated by asymmetric information.* For auto insurance, firms first screen prospective customers to reduce *adverse selection*—the problem of selling insurance to worse-than-average drivers. After the sale of the insurance, auto insurance companies require a deductible or co-payment on collision insurance. This reduces *moral hazard*—the problem of insured drivers driving more recklessly once they are insured.

2.  *No method of economic decision-making is always perfect.* Markets may not maximize total surplus due to externalities, public goods, imperfect competition, and asymmetric information. In addition, people and firms may not always rationally maximize their own well-being. But government may not be able to improve upon the situation because governments may not have any better information than markets; all voting schemes are imperfect, and politicians may choose to maximize their own well-being instead of the well-being of society.

## II.    Self-Testing Challenges

### A.    True/False Questions

_____1.    Asymmetric information is a problem that occurs when one person in a transaction knows more about what is going on than the other.

_____2.    In the principal–agent relationship, the principal performs a task on behalf of the agent.

_____3.    Signals to convey high quality are most effective when they are costless to all firms in the industry.

_____4.    The Condorcet paradox shows that majority-rule voting always reveals the outcome that society really wants.

_____5.    Arrow's Impossibility Theorem shows that no voting system can satisfy the properties required of a perfect voting system.

_____6.    According to the Median Voter Theorem, majority rule will produce the average preferred outcome.

_____7.    Politicians do not always choose the ideal economic policy because some politicians are corrupt and greedy, and others are willing to sacrifice the national interest for local popularity.

_____8.    In the real world, people always behave rationally when making economic decisions.

_____9.    Because people tend to care about fairness, firms may give bonuses during particularly profitable years to be fair and to avoid retaliation from the workers.

_____10.    People seem to naturally engage in delayed gratification, and they tend to follow through on plans made today to do something unpleasant in the future.

_____11.    To avoid the problem of adverse selection, health insurance companies screen their prospective customers to discover hidden health problems.

_____12.    The ultimate game demonstrates that people will always make choices according to their self-interest.

## B.    Multiple-Choice Questions

1.    John's car is in need of repair, therefore John decides to sell it to avoid the repair bill. Unaware of the problem, Susan buys the car. Which one of the following is this is an example of?
      a.    adverse selection
      b.    moral hazard
      c.    efficiency wages
      d.    hidden actions

2.    Judy wants to avoid buying a car that is a lemon. She takes a car she would like to buy to her mechanic to be inspected before she purchases it. Which one of the following is this is known as?
      a.    moral hazard
      b.    adverse selection
      c.    signaling
      d.    screening

3.    Chris is a travelling sales representative for an apparel company. Which one of the following is Chris's role in this employment relationship?
      a.    principal
      b.    agent
      c.    screener
      d.    monitor

4.    Which one of the following must be true about a signal that is used to reveal private information in order for the signal to be effective?
      a.    It must be free to the informed party.
      b.    It must be costly to the informed party but less costly to the party with the higher-quality product.
      c.    It must be applied to an expensive product.
      d.    It must be less beneficial to the party with the higher-quality product.

5.    Which one of the following is an example of a signal that is used to reveal private information?
      a.    Pierre randomly chooses a gift for Monique.
      b.    Lexus advertises its cars during the Grey Cup.
      c.    Consuela lived close to, so attended, the Richard Ivey School of Business.

6.    Which one of the following is **NOT** a method firms use to avoid the moral hazard problem in the employment relationship?
      a.    Pay above equilibrium wages.
      b.    Put hidden video cameras in the workplace.
      c.    Buy life insurance on their workers.
      d.    Pay employees with delayed compensation such as a year-end bonus.

7. Which one of the following **BEST** demonstrates the problem of moral hazard?
   a. Karen does not buy health insurance because it is too expensive and she is healthy.
   b. Kyoko chooses to attend a well-respected college.
   c. Namdar drives more recklessly after he buys auto insurance.
   d. A life insurance company forces Teemu to have a physical examination prior to selling insurance to him.

8. Under pairwise majority voting, if A is preferred to B, and B is preferred to C, then A should be preferred to C. Which one of the following is the name of this relationship?
   a. the property of unanimity
   b. the property of transitivity
   c. the property of independence
   d. the property of efficiency

9. Which one of the following is **NOT** a property required of a perfect voting system?
   a. the median voter always wins
   b. transitivity
   c. no dictators
   d. unanimity

10. Suppose that 40 percent of the voting population wish to spend $1000 for artwork in City Hall, 25 percent wish to spend $20 000, and 35 percent wish to spend $22 000. Which one of the following options contains the median preferred outcome, the average preferred outcome, and the modal preferred outcome?
    a. $1000, $14 333, $1000
    b. $20 000, $20 000, $22 000
    c. $20 000, $13 100, $1000
    d. $1000, $20 000, $22 000

11. Which one of the following is true under pairwise majority rule if people vote for the outcome closest to their **MOST** preferred outcome?
    a. The average preferred outcome wins.
    b. The outcome preferred by the median voter wins.
    c. The outcome preferred by the greatest number of voters wins.
    d. There is no clear winner due to Arrow's Impossibility Theorem.

12.  Which one of the following is **NOT** true about how people make decisions?
     a.  People are sometimes too sure of their own abilities.
     b.  People are reluctant to change their minds in the face of new information.
     c.  People give too much weight to a small number of vivid observations.
     d.  People are always rational maximizers.

13.  In the *ultimatum game*, which one of the following splits would be rational for both the person proposing the split and the person who must accept or reject the split?
     a.  99/1
     b.  75/25
     c.  50/50
     d.  1/99

14.  Which one of the following helps explain why firms pay bonuses to workers during particularly profitable years in order to prevent workers from becoming disgruntled?
     a.  People are rational maximizers.
     b.  People are inconsistent over time.
     c.  People care about fairness.
     d.  People are reluctant to change their minds.

15.  John's friend dies of a sudden heart attack. John rushes to his doctor for an expensive physical examination. Which one of the following is demonstrated by John's response?
     a.  People give too much weight to a small number of vivid observations.
     b.  People easily change their minds when confronted with new information.
     c.  People enjoy going to the doctor.
     d.  People lack confidence.

16.  Which one of the following is a response to people's inconsistent behaviour over time?
     a.  efficiency wages
     b.  year-end bonuses
     c.  forced contributions to a retirement plan

Use the following set of voter preferences to answer questions 17–20.

|  | Voter type | | |
|---|---|---|---|
|  | Type 1 | Type 2 | Type 3 |
| Percent of electorate | 35 | 25 | 40 |
| First choice | C | A | B |
| Second choice | A | B | C |
| Third choice | B | C | A |

17. When the choice is between A and B, which one of the following is the portion of the population that votes for A?
    a. 25 percent
    b. 35 percent
    c. 40 percent
    d. 60 percent

18. Under pairwise majority voting, which one of the following outcomes wins?
    a. A
    b. B
    c. C
    d. These preferences suffer from the Condorcet Paradox, so there is no clear winner.

19. If A is first compared to C, and then the winner is compared to B, which one of the following outcomes is the winner?
    a. A
    b. B
    c. C
    d. These preferences suffer from the Condorcet Paradox, so there is no clear winner.

20. If a Borda count is used, which one of the following outcomes is preferred?
    a. A
    b. B
    c. C
    d. These preferences do not exhibit transitivity, so there is no clear winner.

## C.    Short-Answer Questions

1.    Would the buyers of auto insurance be expected to have a higher or lower than average probability of having an auto accident? Why? How does the insurance company address the adverse selection in this market? How does it address the moral hazard in this market? _____

_____
_____
_____
_____

2.    To reduce adverse selection, firms signal high quality with expensive advertising. What are the necessary characteristics of an effective signal? Why do firms producing low-quality goods not use expensive advertising to falsely signal high quality?

_____
_____
_____
_____
_____

3.    Suppose that 30 percent of the voters want to spend $10 000 on a new park, 30 percent want to spend $11 000, and 40 percent wish to spend $25 000. How much does the average voter want to spend? How much does the median voter want to spend? If each voter chooses the point closest to his most preferred choice, what will be the final choice between these three choices of a majority rule? Does the Condorcet paradox arise? _____

_____
_____
_____
_____

4.    Do politicians always choose policies that maximize the well-being of society? Why or why not?_____

_____
_____
_____

5.    The most popular major on campus is economics. One student takes an introductory economics class and tells her friend that it was the worst class she has ever taken. The friend avoids taking any economics. Is this rational? Explain.

_____
_____
_____
_____

6.  Why does choosing a good gift qualify as a signal of love and concern to the recipient?

_____

_____

_____

## D.   Practice Problems

1.  For each of the following situations, identify the principal and the agent, describe the information asymmetry involved, and explain how moral hazard has been reduced.

   a.  Dental insurance companies offer free annual checkups. _____

   _____

   _____

   _____

   b.  Firms compensate travelling sales representatives with commissions (a percent of the value of the sales). _____

   _____

   _____

   _____

   c.  McDonald's pays twice the minimum wage to high school students.

   _____

   _____

   _____

   d.  Farmers in Ontario's Niagara Peninsula pay Mexican migrant workers bonuses if they pick fruit and vegetables for the entire summer rather than only part of the summer._____

   _____

   _____

   _____

2.  For each of the following statements, describe the information asymmetry involved, name the type of action that has been taken to reduce adverse selection (signalling or screening), and explain how adverse selection has been reduced.

   a.  McDonald's only hires high school students with good grades.

   _____

   _____

   _____

   _____

b. Hyundai provides a 100 000-km warranty on its new cars. _____

_____

_____

_____

c. A life insurance company requires prospective customers to take a physical examination. _____

_____

_____

_____

d. Labatt's sponsors the Grey Cup half-time show. _____

_____

_____

_____

3.   Answer the following questions regarding the Condorcet paradox for the two sets of voting preferences below.

**Case 1**

|  | Voter type | | |
|---|---|---|---|
|  | Type 1 | Type 2 | Type 3 |
| Percent of electorate | 15 | 40 | 45 |
| First choice | C | A | B |
| Second choice | A | B | C |
| Third choice | B | C | A |

a. If voters must choose between A and B, what are the percentages of votes that each outcome receives, and which outcome wins? _____

_____

_____

_____

b. If voters must choose between B and C, what are the percentages of votes that each outcome receives, and which outcome wins? _____

_____

_____

_____

c. If voters must choose between C and A, what are the percentages of votes that each outcome receives and which outcome wins? _____

_____

_____

_____

d.  Do these preferences exhibit transitivity? Explain.

_____

_____

_____

e.  If the voters choose between A and B and then compare with C, which outcome wins? _____

_____

_____

_____

f.  If the voters choose between B and C and then compare with A, which outcome wins? _____

_____

_____

_____

g.  If the voters choose between A and C and then compare with B, which outcome wins? _____

_____

_____

_____

h.  Does the order in which items are voted on matter in this case? Why or why not?

_____

_____

_____

**Case 2**

|  | Voter type | | |
| --- | --- | --- | --- |
|  | Type 1 | Type 2 | Type 3 |
| Percent of electorate | 30 | 15 | 55 |
| First choice | A | B | C |
| Second choice | B | C | A |
| Third choice | C | A | B |

a.  If voters must choose between A and B, what are the percentages of votes that each outcome receives, and which outcome wins? _____

_____

_____

_____

b. If voters must choose between B and C, what are the percentages of votes that each outcome receives, and which outcome wins? _____

_____

_____

_____

c. If voters must choose between C and A, what are the percentages of votes that each outcome receives, and which outcome wins? _____

_____

_____

_____

d. Do these preferences exhibit transitivity? Explain. _____

_____

_____

_____

e. If the voters choose between A and B and then compare with C, which outcome wins? _____

_____

_____

_____

f. If the voters choose between B and C and then compare with A, which outcome wins? _____

_____

_____

_____

g. If the voters choose between A and C and then compare with B, which outcome wins? _____

_____

_____

_____

h. Does the order in which items are voted on matter in this case? Why or why not?

_____

_____

_____

4.    a.    For Case 1 in problem 3 above, which outcome wins if a Borda count is used to determine the winner among outcomes A, B, and C, and what are the scores for each outcome? _____

_____

_____

_____

b.    For Case 1 in problem 3 above, eliminate outcome C and use a Borda count to find the winner from the remaining choices of A and B. What property required of a perfect voting system has been violated? Explain. _____

_____

_____

_____

c.    Compare the results of Case 1 in problem 3 under simple majority rule, a Borda count with three choices, and a Borda count with two choices. What conclusion can be drawn from these results? _____

_____

_____

_____

## E.    Advanced Critical Thinking

Pavel and Hamid are watching a television news story about lung cancer. Hamid says to Pavel, "I think it is terrible that people with cancer often can't buy supplemental health insurance. People who are ill are the ones who really need supplemental health insurance. Even worse, once someone gets supplemental health insurance, they often have to pay a deductible equal to 20 percent of the first $3000 of their medical bills each year. Only then does the insurance company cover the remainder of the medical bills."

1.  What problem caused by asymmetric information are insurance companies trying to avoid when they deny coverage to someone who may already be ill? What would happen if the insurance companies did not deny coverage to people who are already ill? _____

    _____

    _____

    _____

2.  What problem does charging a deductible help solve? What might happen if insurance companies did not require a deductible? _____

    _____

    _____

    _____

3.  How might public policy address the problems in the market for supplemental health insurance? What are some of the shortcomings of a public policy solution?

    _____

    _____

    _____

## III.    Solutions

### A.  True/False Questions

1.  T
2.  F; the agent performs a task on behalf of the principal.
3.  F; signals must be costly, yet less costly to the person with the higher-quality product.
4.  F; it shows that the order in which items are voted on can determine the outcome; therefore majority-rule voting does not always reveal what society wants.
5.  T
6.  F; it will produce the outcome preferred by the median voter.
7.  T
8.  F; there is evidence that people are only "near rational."
9.  T
10. F; people tend to seek instant gratification and fail to follow through on unpleasant tasks.
11. T.
12. F; conventional economic theory assumes that people are rational wealth-maximizers. However, people are also driven, in part, by some innate sense of fairness.

## B. Multiple-Choice Questions

| | | | | |
|---|---|---|---|---|
| 1. a | 5. c | 9. a | 13. a | 17. d |
| 2. d | 6. c | 10. c | 14. c | 18. d |
| 3. b | 7. c | 11. b | 15. a | 19. b |
| 4. b | 8. b | 12. d | 16. c | 20. c |

## C. Short-Answer Questions

1. Higher, because buyers of insurance know more about their probability of an accident, and those with a high probability of having accidents will need insurance. An insurance company checks a driver's driving history and offer policies that appeal differently to risky and safe drivers, and then it charges higher premiums to risky drivers. The insurance company requires a deductible to avoid moral hazard.

2. It must be costly, but less costly to the individual with the higher-quality product. Because low-quality firms will not generate repeat purchases from their advertising, it is not cost effective for them to engage in expensive advertising.

3. The average voter wants to spend $16 300 [0.3($10 000) + 0.3($11 000) + 0.4($25 000) = $16 300]. The median voter wants to spend $11 000. The final choice will be $11 000. No, the Condorcet paradox does not arise. For any pair, find the winner, and then compare it with the remaining choice— $11 000 always wins.

4. No. Some politicians may act out of greed and others may sacrifice the national interest to improve their local popularity.

5. No. People give too much weight to a small number of vivid observations. In this case, the friend's comment is just one additional observation out of thousands.

6. It takes time; that is, it is costly, to choose a good gift, and it also provides information that the gift giver is knowledgeable about the recipient.

## D. Practice Problems

1. a. The insurance company is the principal; the insured is the agent. Only the agent knows how well he takes care of his teeth. By checking the insured's teeth each year, the insurance company can better monitor the behaviour of the insured and reduce major future claims.

b. The firm is the principal; the sales representative is the agent. The firm does not know how hard the sales rep works. By paying the sales rep only a commission, the firm is able to better monitor the sales representative's work habits, and the worker is less likely to shirk.

c. McDonald's is the principal; the student is the agent. McDonald's does not know how hard the student works. By paying above-market wages, McDonald's increases the cost of shirking and the cost of being fired. The worker is less likely to shirk.

d. Niagara farmers are the principal; Mexican migrant workers are the agent. Farmers do not know how hard workers work. By paying them large bonuses for working an entire season, farmers raise the cost of shirking and the cost of being fired. The result is that workers are less likely to shirk.

2. a. McDonald's does not know the abilities of the potential workers as well as the workers do. McDonald's *screens* potential workers using past educational performance, and it is able to select high-ability workers.

b. Buyers do not know the quality of Hyundai cars because these cars are relatively new to the Canadian market. Hyundai *signals* high quality with a long warranty, and buyers are able to select high-quality cars.

c. The life insurance company does not know as much about the health of the insurance buyer as the buyer does. The insurance company *screens* prospective customers with a physical exam to find hidden health problems so its insurance pool is not sicker than average.

d. Beer buyers do not know the quality of Labatt's beer as well as the Labatt Brewing Company does. Labatt's *signals* high quality with expensive advertising because it could only afford to do so if it could generate repeat buyers. Customers are able to choose a high-quality beer.

3.   **Case 1**

   a.   A = 15 + 40 = 55, B = 45. A beats B.
   b.   B = 40 + 45 = 85, C = 15. B beats C.
   c.   C = 15 + 45 = 60, A = 40. C beats A.
   d.   No. A beats B and B beats C, so transitivity requires that A beats C but, in fact, C beats A.
   e.   A beats B, so compare A with C and C wins.
   f.   B beats C, so compare B with A and A wins.
   g.   C beats A, so compare C with B and B wins.
   h.   Yes, because these preferences do not exhibit transitivity.

   **Case 2**

   a.   A = 30 + 55 = 85, B = 15. A beats B.
   b.   B = 30 + 15 = 45, C = 55. C beats B.
   c.   A = 30, C = 15 + 55 = 70. C beats A.
   d.   Yes. C beats A and A beats B. Transitivity requires that C beats B and it does.
   e.   A beats B, so compare B with C and C wins.
   f.   C beats B, so compare C with A and C wins.
   g.   C beats A, so compare C with B and C wins.
   h.   No, because these preferences exhibit transitivity.

4.   a.   If choosing between A, B, and C, A = 30 + 120 + 45 = 195, B = 15 + 80 + 135 = 230, C = 45 + 40 + 90 = 175, and B wins.

   b.   If choosing between only A and B, A = 30 + 80 + 45 = 155, B = 15 + 40 + 90 = 145, and A wins. Independence of irrelevant alternatives: the rankings of A and B should not change when C is removed, but the ranking did change.

   c.   A wins, then B wins, then A wins. Thus, majority voting does not necessarily reveal what society wants, and deciding the order on which items are voted may affect the outcome.

**E.  Advanced Critical Thinking**

1.   Adverse selection. People who are already ill would seek to buy supplemental health insurance. Their medical bills would be far higher than average, causing premiums to rise. At the artificially high price for supplemental insurance, fewer healthy people would buy this insurance because the cost would exceed their expected bills. When healthy people drop out of the market, the price rises even further for the remaining participants, thus further reducing the size of the supplemental health insurance market.

2.    Moral hazard. Without a deductible, people might go to the doctor even if they do not really need medical attention. They also have little incentive to take care of themselves to avoid illness because they bear no cost of the illness. As above, this raises the cost of supplemental insurance above the expected bills of healthy people and many will fail to buy insurance.

3.    Some people advocate government-provided, supplemental health insurance where everyone, whether sick or healthy, would be forced to participate. Majority-rule democratic institutions may not generate the amount of supplemental health care that people want. Self-interested politicians may choose to provide an amount of supplemental health care that is different from what people actually want.